PuppyPerfect

The user-friendly guide to puppy parenting

BY SARAH HODGSON

Howell
Book House™

Library of Congress Cataloging-in-Publication Data:
Hodgson, Sarah.
PuppyPerfect : the user-friendly guide to puppy parenting / by Sarah Hodgson.
    p. cm.
ISBN-13: 978-0-7645-8797-9 (pbk.)
ISBN-10: 0-7645-8797-8
1. Puppies—Training. 2. Puppies—Behavior. 3. Puppies. I. Title.
SF431.H735 2005
636.7'07—dc22
2005017376
Printed in the United States of America

10 9 8 7 6 5

Book design by Marie Kristine Parial-Leonardo
Cover design by José Almaguer
Book production by Wiley Publishing, Inc. Composition Services

Table of Contents

Acknowledgments

Writing books for Howell Publishing always puts me in touch with so many cool people. I couldn't be more content with my team, from Kathy Nebenhaus, chief poo-bah; Pam Mourouzis, a terrific combination acquisition-editor-mediator; Lesa Grant and Lindsay McGregor, marketing and PR wizards; to my very hip editor Jenn Connolly, who gets an A+ in my book for constantly encouraging *way more* than she discourages. A big thank you!

On the home front, there are so many people who get my tail wagging and for whom I am eternally grateful; my life would be as boring as a dried bone without you. This is my first book since giving birth to a human "puppy," and I relied heavily on everyone to help take care of the day-to-day tasks: Mama Le'Rose, Sonya, Shelia, Aunt Carolyn, special friends and neighbors. You have a special place in our hearts. And I can't leave out the one who breathes life into my office day to day, Leah Bonfantini! I've watched you grow from a girl who quaked when the phone rang to someone who keeps me in check and can run the office blind-folded. You are more than an office assistant and a babysitter—you'd be my first pick as kid sister.

There is one person who deserves a twenty-one tail salute: my business partner, agent, task organizer, and friend, Nancy Shalek. You give me strength, faith, and endless encouragement. Kudos.

I hold my biggest snuggle for Lindsay and Whoopsie, my daughter and my dog. At the end of the day, you are still my favorites.

A Welcoming Wag

In the pages to follow, you'll learn about your puppy as an individual. How his personality, breed characteristics, and temperament all flow together to create a spirit that once understood is easier to direct, connect with, and train.

A helpful tool at the end of this book is my Doglish Glossary. Whenever you come across terms you are unfamiliar with, check out the glossary to see the definition, and be sure to also reference the index to find out all you can on the topic. The References shouldn't be skipped either—it's full of valuable resources to enhance your knowledge of puppies and training.

What you won't find within these pages are techniques that foster confusion. Rough handling and tough love frighten some puppies into submission, but they aren't effective, and they're just not fair.

You are sharing your life with your chosen puppy and are forever connected. Raising him well is a fabulous responsibility, and your puppy will reward you in ways immeasurable and unexpected. I am thrilled you have chosen me to help you in your journey.

So, off we go. I have lots to teach you, and I can't wait. Your efforts will be your own reward.

Introduction

When I first met Rocket, a 7-month-old Maltese, he bounded into my office, well, like a rocket. Trailing behind him was his mom, with a look of utter exasperation. Unleashed, he leapt into my lap and kissed my nose between bounces, and then raced across the room and peed on the couch. A whirlwind of positive energy with a dash of chaotic marking rolled in for good measure.

Okay, first things first. His mom made it immediately clear: he was one step away from adoption. "He's so willful." "He just won't calm down." "He knows he's wrong when he pees, but he just won't stop!" "He races away from me when I call and he eats his poop!" "You are my last hope!"

My initial read on this white fireball? His sweet, adoring, bright nature shone through the mania. He was enthusiastic, eager to please, and totally confused. So

why had things gotten so twisted around? Was his mom to blame?

No, Rocket's mom was experiencing what so many puppy owners feel: emotional exhaustion and mental strain. What started out as love at first sight had snowballed into a battle of wills. She suddenly had feelings of regret and desperation that she neither anticipated nor welcomed. She knew in her heart that this "monster" was the same sweet lovable puppy she'd adopted five months ago, but where had things gone wrong? And more importantly was she too late to help?

Fortunately I was spot-on in my assessment. Ninety minutes later, they left relieved, reconnected, and relaxed. As I explained Rocket's temperament and just how he'd become addicted to naughty behavior, his mother clearly started to understand just what it would take to reverse the trend. Here are just a handful of the things she learned that day:

- Rocket was simply repeating routines that got her attention: whether it was negative or positive attention didn't matter. Any reaction was considered interaction.

- One of his primary drives was to stay connected to her. To interface. To dialog. He was a people puppy.

- Frustrating the situation was the vicious cycle of isolation. Rocket had to be crated or gated in the kitchen to prevent accidents and mischief. Instead of educating him through organized exposure, his owners hoped he would "grow out" of certain behaviors. What happened instead is that new behaviors emerged, such as chronic barking, which brought about (can you guess) more attention.

First and foremost, the isolation had to end. Although I understood that he was isolated because he wasn't housetrained and raced around frantically when he escaped, the isolation was creating its own host of issues, from chronic barking to wall chewing. We agreed on a compromise: he was permitted in the house on a *teaching lead* (belted to her side) or he was securely stationed in rooms and taught to STAY on his mat. Companionship without chaos. A win-win all around.

We then established a host of displacement activities: from games to focus his enthusiasm and energy level, to lessons and housetraining routines. This gave Rocket some concrete rules to follow and this attention getter was more than happy to cooperate. His world had quickly gone from a cauldron of unexplained mayhem to life with a plan.

In the end, we decided that discipline was not an effective learning tool for Rocket: he had become immune to NO. It was more an invitation to play than an instruction. Secondly, he was so in tune with directions and patterns, I was sure he'd cooperate quickly. And you know what? He did.

So how exactly did I turn things around so quickly? Was I the "dog whisperer" as she claimed? Not necessarily. I just listened to both of them—to Rocket and his mom. By translating life from his paws, I helped her to understand his predicament. Once empathy emerges, the rest is simple modification. Together, we set out together to organize daily routines that would encourage the best in him and used calmer methods to extinguish his bad habits.

Chapter 1

Putting Yourself in Your Puppy's Paws

To say that I love puppies is quite the understatement. I can't keep my hands off them! Adorable, innocent, and interactive—like children and snowflakes, each one is unique. They are full of wonder and curiosity and need our direction, empathy, and companionship. Unconditional love must go both ways.

Although puppies share similarities, from sweet milky breath to tail wagging and nipping, the list of differences is a lot longer. Discovering your puppy's unique qualities and breed-specific traits will illuminate and calm the days in front of you. Getting to know your puppy's personality and likes and dislikes will also help you organize a life plan that will satisfy both of you. Knowing how to communicate your ideals and direct your puppy's impulses will calm her mental energy and ensure a greater trust between you.

If you're reading this book, you're either boning up to get a head start on lessons to avoid common pitfalls, or you're in the throes of frustration and hoping for a miracle cure. Although I can't guarantee an instantaneous fix, I will help you understand your puppy's behavior and shape a program to contain and redirect your puppy's mischief today. Whether you've got an 8-week-old puppy nibbling your shoelace, an 8-month-old puppy cruising your counters, or an 11-month-old puppy tearing through the living room with your favorite shoe, there is a well-timed developmental reason for her behavior. Simply stressing your disapproval won't be enough. In fact, as you'll learn shortly, your disapproval often gets misconstrued as confrontational play. There is a lot of activity going

I just love puppies!

Jodi Buren

Different Puppies, Different Needs

Here's an example of how two puppies of the same age can view and interact with their environment differently. Meet 12-week-old Zip and Dudley. Zip is a Cairn Terrier, whose ancestors were bred to listen for, hunt, and kill whatever crawled beneath the earth. Although these qualities are no longer required, you can't convince Zip. Dudley is a Labrador Retriever, whose ancestors were bred for companionship and trainability, as well as for retrieving water fowl on command. Aesthetics aside, their differences are poignant. Zip is sound-sensitive, instinctive, and intense. An independent hunter, he focuses on stimulation over direction. In his New York studio apartment, however, sound stimulation is constant, and the only thing beneath him is Mrs. Flowers, who doesn't appreciate his alert barks at three in the morning. Dudley, at home in the suburbs, is oral, interactive, and focused by nature. If left undirected or underexercised, however, he'll develop annoying, attention-getting habits that include stealing objects, behavior that I call *keep-away*, and destructive chewing.

To avoid these pitfalls, each puppy must have a custom-fit lesson plan that includes a list of displacement activities to satisfy their genetic impulses. To shape early cooperation, Dudley's list would include retrieving games and directional exercises. Zip, on the other hand, needs to play chasing games and do exercises that involve alerting to motion and sound, like *toy along, tag along*. (Games are further described in chapter 57.) Play training should be tailored to each puppy's genetic impulses.

on behind those beautiful eyes. From the moment your puppy is born, she begins to process information, and before long, she learns how to regulate and control both herself and her environment. This book will teach you how to influence her behavior positively by helping her feel safe and happy in your world.

GENETIC/HISTORIC IMPULSES

What lies behind my fascination with dogs? They accept our species as their own. Pretty profound. In fact, a trained dog will put her human's direction above her own impulses and will love unconditionally. Their evolution not only paralleled ours, it was directly influenced by our wants and desires. Some humans wanted a dog to pull a sleigh: they bred dogs that like that activity. They wanted a dog to retrieve a duck from a pond on a freezing November morning: they bred dogs silly enough to go for that idea. And so on. We didn't stop with instincts either; we also chose (through selective breeding) other traits such as coat type, size, and personality. Through a

process of organized tampering, we humans have shaped more than 400 hundred breeds, all bred for a specific purpose and look, worldwide.

The American Kennel Club recognizes 153 breeds, and 4 more are waiting in the wings in the AKC's runner-up "miscellaneous class." The AKC organizes the breeds into seven groups—Hound, Herding, Toy, Working, Terrier, Non-Sporting, and Sporting—and keeps records of every registered puppy. It's a serious business. I'm going to further divide the breeds into thirteen groups; the first twelve are organized according to specific predispositions, like hunting or herding. The thirteenth represents mixed breeds, inviting you to discover the blend of traits represented in your unique puppy. If you have a rare breed, discover which AKC-recognized breed shares your dog's ancestry and make comparisons.

> ### 🐾 Double Vision?
>
> Some breeds are listed in more than one category, as they were bred for various tasks. Highlight breeds you may be interested in, or circle your dog's breed or breeds, and use the table at the end of this chapter to discover her motivations and interest. You can further research each breed online or at your local bookstore or library.

All Together Now—Herding Breeds

Herding breeds have a zest for togetherness! Control-oriented, they prefer "their" sheep in a row and quickly determine within a family (even as young pups) who is a shepherding influence (shepherds give direction) versus who are sheep (sheep need to be directed). Undirected, their impulse for order can be misunderstood; insufficient exercise results in obsessive-compulsive behaviors such as pacing, relentless attention-getting, incessant barking or chasing, and lick granulomas (sores created by obsessive licking). On the other hand, a structured setting, family lessons, chasing games, and a task-oriented activity like catch or chase will help direct their impulses and bring out the best in their nature. Devoted to their family "flock," they're loyal, loving pups who enjoy togetherness, are home proud, and rarely wander.

- **Best quality:** They're very family-oriented, staying close to home and devoting themselves to all activities.
- **Chief frustration:** Barking and chasing.

Think Twice before Entering—Guarding Breeds

Guarding breeds, originally bred to guard either flocks or homes, are stoic and calm. This lot has a serious life focus. Although playfully accepting of strangers as young puppies, loyalty to their families can be seen early on. As maturity takes hold (between 6 and 10 months), these puppies become suspicious of unfamiliar people and places, and without proper socialization and direction, they perceive themselves as the protectors of home and hearth.

If you have or want a great guard dog, teach her to look to you for direction. If you're not around, she will protect naturally, but in your presence she'll defer to your judgment.

- **Best quality:** Solid devotion. They're patient with children when raised with them.
- **Chief frustration:** Powerful protection that can be hard to influence without consistent direction. These dogs can be dangerous if untrained.

Watchdog—Protective Breeds

A good protective dog is more bark than bite. Once this puppy hits puberty, there'll be no need for a doorbell! The goal is to develop an off switch. Left untrained, these puppies interpret lack of direction as lack of leadership, and they take the task of alerting the pack to every sound and stimulus quite seriously. Avoid this headache! If you're to share your life with a protector, teach your puppy to find you the moment she alerts to a stimulus and train her to watch for your direction. You'll have a trusted friend who will alert mindfully when you're home and will ward off intruders when you're gone.

- **Best quality:** Loyalty, to a fault.
- **Chief frustration:** Unchecked barking and aggression. Training this group is a must.

Play Ball—Sporting Breeds

Sporting breeds are a friendly lot, bred to work with people and retrieve objects. Well built, they're bright, loyal, and interactive. Happy souls, they take well to training and generally view all strangers as potential friends. A well-bred sporting dog shouldn't show aggressive tendencies. However, left alone, underexercised, or ignored, these dogs are prone to *hyper isolation anxiety*: destruction and hyperactivity borne of loneliness and separation. On the flip side, if exercised and given lessons and an outlet for their retrieving skills, a more cheerful companion would be hard to find.

 **Sidelining the Sporting Breed**

There are grades of protectiveness with some of the breeds in the sporting group, such as the Clumber Spaniel, Portuguese Water Dog, and Weimaraner. But any pronounced aggression is an aberration of the breeding standards and may be the result of *line breeding*, or questionable breeding conditions as with puppy mills.

- **Best quality:** Their cup is always half full: full of life enthusiasm and passion for people. They have few serious thoughts and are fun loving.
- **Chief frustration:** Their brain is in their stomach. They're prone to separation anxiety and can be very destructive. They'll show a thief their tennis ball collection as the thief robs you blind.

Sound the Alarm—Terriers

A spirited, fun-loving bunch, terriers aren't concerned with your opinion. Bred for serious missions, their ancestors hunted varmints beneath the earth. Active and agile, they generally prefer to do their busywork independently—after all, how many terriers can fit into a rabbit's hole? Although they enjoy family life, they need positive lessons and play training to spark their enthusiasm. If it's not fun and enticing, they'll tune it out. Untrained, they can be willful, single-minded, and destructive. Spatial aggression (guarding a prized object or a sleeping spot) is common and should be prevented before it arises. Read the section in chapter 6 called, "Spatial Aggression." Keep your training fun, simple, and prize-oriented. Involve the whole family, and your terrier will trip over you to be in on the action.

- **Best quality:** They're spirited, spunky, and fun.
- **Chief frustration:** They can be independent and prone to spatial aggression.

Self-Motivated (Dogs with Distinct Skills)

Some breeds have distinct bred instincts that are hard to categorize. The Dalmatian, for example, was bred to follow a horse-drawn wagon, lie under the wagon when it was vacated, and protect the space from intruders. That breed doesn't bode well for an impulsive environment with children, although many breeders are trying to breed the spatial reactiveness out of the Dalmatian. Listed in the following sections are breeds that fill a specific niche that is not represented in my grouping. In the AKC category, they'd be found under the Non-Sporting Group. Research each breed individually (see the reference section) to discover its historic roots and current lifestyle necessities.

- **Best quality:** A focused, quirky nature.
- **Chief frustration:** They're hard to redirect. Some breeds are prone to territorial and aggressive tendencies. Check each one out thoroughly.

Sweet Aroma—Scent Hounds

Oh, that nose! Bred to follow scent, these scent hounds are packaged to perform. If you've ever watched an 8-week-old pup as an aroma catches her attention, you'll know in an instant when it happens: the tail lifts high, and she puts her nose down as her head leads her body on an invisible pursuit. Sweet tempered and loving, they are amiable and easy to live with unless off-lead control is your goal. Lessons should match their attention span: short! Working harder for a satisfying treat, they will pay attention, provided there are no competing aromas. Left untrained, they can be bothersome, and the obsession for stimulation may lead them to bark continually and cruise the counters, the garbage, or worse. With a bit of structure and a few lessons, however, this group is easy to direct and can be fun to live with, as long as you don't mind coming in second in their roster of life's passions.

- **Best quality:** A goofy and amiable nature. They're fun to be around and have wonderful ears to pet.
- **Chief frustration:** They follow their noses, sometimes into troublesome situations.

Motion Detectors—Sight Hounds

Like scent hounds, these loving, stoic creatures have a life passion: chasing and bringing down big game. Although such talents are no longer necessary for our survival, you won't convince a sight hound. There may not be any boar in your backyard, but a gray squirrel will satisfy their urge. Graceful and agile, a sight hound in motion is a wonder to behold. Letting these dogs run requires a fenced environment. Left undirected or underexercised, puppies in this category will become frivolous in hyperactivity or dazed in a bored stupor. Although they appreciate the attention that goes into lessons, a few mutually recognized words and plenty of socialization create a satisfying existence for all involved. Serenely contained when their needs are met, these puppies mature into dogs that are lovely companions.

- **Best quality:** Regal, graceful nature and temperament. Beautiful runners.
- **Chief frustration:** They don't turn on a dime.

Mighty Hunters—Hunting Breeds

Brave and stoic, the hunting breeds are contained and mindful even as young puppies. As they mature, they're intensely insular with their families, desire little change in routine, and are most content in predictable homes. Constant socialization is a must to prevent territorial aggression. Courageous and strong, these dogs should be leashed or enclosed. Bred to make quick determination of a given situation, their behavior is often self-directed and intense—good for startling intruders but not ideal for friendly visits and roughhousing. Puppies in this group need a strong and constant training regime and constant socialization during their first year to ensure that their impulses are monitored and directed.

- **Best quality:** Puppies mature into stoic, cool companions.
- **Chief frustration:** They possess an instinctively intuitive nature, may wander, and are hard to direct when their hunting drive kicks in. Training is not an option.

Snuggle Puppies—Companion Breeds

Personally, I love miniaturized things: dollhouse furniture, little shoes, tiny dogs. . . . Who could resist a puppy that fits into the palm of your hand? Not all companion breeds think of themselves as small, however. Some have quite the identity crisis going. Call it what you will—Napoleonic Complex, Small Dog Syndrome—at the end of the day, these puppies have just as much pizzazz as their bigger brethren. Left undirected or, more commonly, overspoiled, these puppies develop habits that can be a real nuisance to live with. Housebreaking and incessant barking top the list. Nipping and outright aggression aren't far behind. Just as every child should not be left behind, so, too, all dogs need a directional foundation lest they get a swelled head.

- **Best quality:** You can hold them in your arms forever.
- **Chief frustration:** Unadulterated spoiling comes at a huge price. These puppies are not stuffed animals.

You Talking to *Me?* Fighting Breeds

Don't let this category startle you. Fighting dogs are no longer used to fight one another, livestock, or game (except in illegal circles). For decades, docility has been the chosen trait. Today, most are more interested in constant loving and sitting on your lap, rather than in fighting. When challenged, however, these breeds won't back down. Passive they're not! Left undirected and untrained, these powerful breeds are hard to control and can easily overpower. With a little effort, however, puppies from this group are responsive, cheerful, and loving to all, making them companionable family dogs. Early socialization (and lots of it) also guarantees a congenial attitude with people and other dogs.

If the dog is raised with a rough hand or beaten and encouraged to fight, the gene for aggression, which is usually inactive, can be stimulated. These dogs, and the people who own them, are dangerous. It is tremendously sad. If these puppies were raised in a different environment, they would know and return only love.

- **Best quality:** They're loyal to their families, sweet, and friendly.
- **Chief frustration:** They're stubborn, ignore direction, and jolly themselves out of reprimands.

Steam Engine—Draft and Sled Dogs

I grew up with two husky mixes: Shawbee and Kyia. They are, to this day, my best dog teachers. Strong-minded and instinctual, they listened only when I respected them and gave clear, sensible direction. This group is cheerful and energetic and has a strong sense of self. Heavy-handed approaches don't work, repetitive lessons bore them, and sweet talk will get you nowhere. Logic and patience are the only ingredients necessary. As puppies, these breeds have a tendency toward relentless chewing and outdoor destruction. Calm training routines repeated throughout the day have a greater impact. Sweet and loving, these puppies like involvement, appropriate displacement activities, and exercise, although their instinct to run requires a fenced area or a leash.

- **Best quality:** Their strong, spirited, interactive nature.
- **Chief frustration:** Pulling and jumping.

The "Pure" Mix Breed

In my opinion, there is really no such thing as a mixed breed: there is a "pure" mix of breeds. For example, poodle mixes are all the rage: Golden Doodle, Labradoodle, Schnoodles . . . the list goes on. Of course, these designer mixes, bred for a hypoallergenic trait, have a price tag. Yet not all mixes do—in fact, many cost very little and can be found at your local shelter or in private homes. With the same potential for love, a mixed breed spices up the fun you'll have trying to determine the breed combinations. If you know the breeds involved, refer to the breed descriptions of both. If not, ask a knowledgeable dog professional and make an educated guess. As your puppy matures, determine what's influencing your scent-sniffing, ball-chasing, protective puppy. Could it be a Basslabottiweiler? Labradoodle, step aside!

- **Best quality:** High-bred vigor! Two unrelated breeds bring an expansive gene pool to their offspring. The healthiest genes are often selected, making mixed breeds healthy and strong.
- **Chief frustration:** The unknown factor: Sometimes you get a breed instinct you may not have bargained for, such as protective barking or spatial aggression.

DISCOVER YOUR PUPPY'S PERSONALITY

When I meet a new dog, I immediately get a read on her personality. It is something I sense, an energy I feel. It takes less than five seconds. The puppy's disposition is as clear to me as the color of her coat. If I'm called in for a puppy consultation (between 8 and 12 weeks of age), the focus is on encouraging good

 **Identity Crisis**

My views on religion aside, I believe that many dogs have been reincarnated as another breed. Have you ever met a Great Dane who wants nothing more than to be a lap dog, or a Maltese who is bent on challenging the neighbor's Rottweiler? Although temperament, training, and handling have a lot to do with it, you can't convince me that greater forces aren't at work!

Jodi Buren

This puppy gladly would have come back as a teacup Yorkie!

behavior, shaping certain breed-specific tendencies, and developing a teaching program custom-fit for both the puppy and the people. If it's a training or behavior improvement session, I focus on what has frustrated this puppy to react in ways unmanageable. For example, a Sporty puppy with a spirited disposition who is not given outlets for her impulses or taught how to contain them may develop problems like grab-n-go and keep away. These sporty means of attention-getting are reactions to isolation and/or unjust regulations. Empathy is the first step in resolving these difficulties; when I give the puppy a voice and describe life from her paws, people enthusiastically modify their behavior, too.

The next step is determining appropriate displacement activities: appropriate outlets for energy—in this case, retrieving or playing with a toy. Then and only then can the corrections be issued and understood. And the corrections are dependent on the personality, the age, and the attention span of each individual puppy (see chapter 7, "Enjoying the First Year," for more on teaching techniques and corrective measures).

Personality Profile

Listed in the following sections are five personalities. Not one is ideal. Each holds traits that the others don't have. Your puppy may have qualities that belong to more than one group. Some qualities may be due to environmental influences, age, time of day, or handling. Or they may just simply be unique to your puppy—a charismatic blend. Once you've got an overview of the descriptions, use the personality quiz (see "A Personality Quiz" on page 12) to discover where your puppy fits in.

The Joy of Watching Them Grow

I am not writing this book alone. Vying for my attention are my 15-month-old dog, Whoopsie Daisy, and my 8-month-old daughter, Lindsay. Their presence is a lesson in individuality and dispositions. Their personalities were set in stone before I met either of them. We chose Whoopsie according to a predetermined personality test, and our daughter—well, she was a delightful surprise. Whoopsie earned her name at 9 weeks; she was (and still is) clumsy and very sweet. Lindsay, even in utero, was very alert to what was going on and within minutes of her initial cry was looking very intently around in deep thought. Happy and determined, interactive and sweet, both of our girls have stayed true to themselves. The joy for us has been seeing how each manages and copes with life's nuances. As parents, we measure our abilities by their confidence to express their true natures.

BOSSY

These puppies are serious, smart, and intense, even as youngsters. Lofty, task-oriented, and proud, they learn quickly and enjoy structure. In truth, many need to be encouraged to have fun. During early development, you may notice blocking behavior on stairs and walks, possessiveness during playing or eating, and stiffness when sleeping or being lifted off the ground. These puppies need a structured environment and strong, clear direction. If taught to respect everyone in the house, the puppies can develop into devoted, interactive family members. Left alone, these dogs can become bossy, defiant, or aggressive and dangerous to have around children or uninformed adults.

 Crossing the Line

It is not okay for a puppy to growl at people. Period. An intentional bite is a worrisome sign. If you experience either, speak to a professional behaviorist or trainer immediately.

COMIC

Active, clever, and often funny, these puppies want to be in on everything. Bursting into situations with a cheerfully energetic presence, they are hard to contain without serious protest, usually in the form of barking, pulling, or chewing. Eager to learn, especially if the lessons are entertaining, they need consistent structure and a team effort, or they'll learn to play each family member for his or her weaknesses. Ideal in busy households that encourage involvement or with single owners for whom they can be constant companions, these puppies are happiest when socializing. Their high energy level and constant demand for attention make them ideal for confident children over age 7. Untrained, these dogs are often viewed as hyper and can be destructive to home and yard.

EAGER

Although eagerness sounds like the perfect personality, eager puppies are vigilantly focused on your activities and will repeat a behavior that gets attention—any attention, even negative. If you're aware of this and you focus on good behavior, you'll have your puppy civilized in no time. If you're oblivious, your puppy may end up repeating behaviors that get you frustrated—not in an attempt to aggravate, but simply to stay connected. These puppies thrive in a home where directions are consistent; chaotic situations easily confuse them. In fact, many of these puppies are given up for adoption because the very quality that makes them endearing creates tension for the uninformed.

MELLOW

If these dogs could talk, their favorite word would be "chill"! Mellow and sweet, they are just as happy watching life go by as they are jumping into the mix. With an "Is this absolutely necessary?" attitude toward lessons, they often view this time as best for napping. Undirected, however, they can't be trusted off-leash, and they're hard to socialize. Although extensive training is not necessary, the basics are a must and, when introduced with spirit, can actually be viewed as fun. This is an ideal personality type for a chaotic household.

RESERVED

These puppies love to snuggle and check in with you. Sudden changes or too much energy (either in a situation or with another person or dog) can easily overwhelm them. Seemingly remorseful when heavily disciplined, these puppies are showing fear, not understanding. Training must come with patience and clarity. When these puppies are fearful of situations, their people must stand calmly as an example of strength; coddling is viewed as mutual concern. When fearful, these puppies should be directed with familiar word cues (like HEEL and STAY) to help them feel directed and safe. Best suited for homes where predictability reigns, these puppies often meld well with grown-up households or families where calmness is the norm. Socialization is necessary but must be done gradually.

 **Rating Your Family**

Rating doesn't have to stop with your puppy. You can rate everyone in your house, too! Our Whoopsie is relaxed. Lindsay, our daughter, is a mix of strong and spirited. My husband, Jim, is a mix of relaxed and strong . . . and me? Pure spirited. If I were a dog, I'd probably be a Border Collie!

TIMID

These puppies give the impression that they were abused. Skittish and nervous with anyone outside their immediate families, they need a lot of consistent direction to help them overcome their innate phobias. Their retention is short; they may not remember a person or a situation from day to day. As they age, many of these dogs develop fear aggression: an aggressive response to a perceived threat. Predictable households where one person gives constant direction is best; training is necessary to help them externalize their focus and to bring them out of their internalized world where danger lurks around every bend.

A Personality Quiz

Now that you've got a fix on the personalities that are out there, perhaps you're still confused as to where your puppy fits in. Here's a quiz to help you determine what your pup's little quirks mean in the broad spectrum. Just circle the number that best represents your puppy's reaction to each of the following situations.

Petting: Take your puppy aside when she's excited, and stroke her from her head to her back end. Speak in calming tones. Does she:

a) Turn to nip.	5
b) Playfully mouth or roll on her belly.	4
c) Relax.	3
d) Roll on her back submissively.	2
e) Tuck her tail or lower her body.	1

Lifting: When your puppy is active, lift her up 3 inches from the floor by her midsection. All four paws should dangle just above the ground. Does she:

a) Twist in frustration, attempt to nip, or blatantly growl.	5
b) Squirm playfully to be released.	4
c) Relax into it.	3
d) Lick anxiously.	2
e) Cringe in confusion.	1

🐾 Ideal Timing

If possible, give this test when the pup is between 12 and 14 weeks of age. Older puppies' reactions may be varied, due to genetic impulses or to social interaction within the home.

Knowing When to Get Help

If during these interactions your puppy growls defensively, stop. Call a behavior specialist for help. You've got a serious problem. If you have young children in the house, consider placing the dog in a more predictable environment and using my Puppy Assessment Form in the appendix to select a puppy with a more relaxed temperament.

Spatial Interaction: This is a three-part quiz.

Toy Interruption: Interrupt your puppy when she's chewing on a bone or a toy. What does she do?

a) Lay her head rigidly over the toy or growl defensively. 5

b) Playfully lick or paw your hand or interact with the object as you lift it up. 4

c) Pull her head back and watch you calmly. 3

d) Lick your hand submissively. 2

e) Pull away and roll back on her belly. 1

Sleep Interruption: Interrupt your puppy's sleep, and note her reaction. Does she:

a) Growl, accompanied by a stiffening body. 5

b) Rise quickly with spirit. 4

c) Barely awaken. 3

d) Lick your hand or face. 2

e) Startle suddenly with tail tucked; may be accompanied by a reactionary growl. 1

Food Interruption: Interrupt a meal, and note your puppy's reaction. Does she:

a) Lower her head rigidly over the bowl. 5

b) Stand still and playfully interact—paw, lick, or mouth. 4

c) Stop eating and step back calmly. 3

d) Lick nervously or lower her body in submission. 2

e) Lick, accompanied by a submissive posture, cower, or go rigid over the bowl. 1

Treating from a Box: Take a box of treats in your left hand. Kneel down next to your puppy, and dole out one treat at a time from your right hand. Does she:

a) Grab the treat quickly and then go to the box. 5

b) Take the treat enthusiastically, showing interest in the box. 4

c) Take it calmly, may show interest in the box. 3

d) Take it quickly and look for another. 2

e) Take it nervously; may look urgently in your hand or the box. 1

Hide-and-Seek: Use either a favorite toy or a treat. Show her the object, and get her excited with it. Next, hold her back and hide the toy or the treat under a piece of cardboard. Encourage her to find it. Does your puppy:

a) Find it immediately. 5

b) Run to you and playfully look around for it. 4

c) Go to you and act confused that the treat is not offered immediately. 3

d) Sit or move cautiously, in need of further direction. 2

e) Either not move or show interest in the object rapidly. 1

Training sequence: Use a toy or a treat to encourage your puppy to follow you. Walk around a familiar room, rewarding your puppy every five seconds. Crawl or lure your puppy under a table. Does she:

a) Confidently follow, urgently grabbing the reward. 5

b) Follow you to the table, hesitating at the table before moving or racing forward energetically. 4

c) Hesitate or lose interest; sit or move under the table casually. 3

d) Refuse or follow cautiously. 2

e) Refuse or run away. 1

Loud noise: Stand out of sight from your puppy. Very discreetly, drop a couple of metal pans to the floor. Watch her reaction. Does she:

a) Jump, bark, or run at the pans. 5

b) Startle, then move playfully toward the pans. 4

c) Stand alert, then resume activity. 3

d) Jump up, yip, freeze, or run to you for protection. 2

e) Run out of the room. 1

INTERPRETING THE RESULTS

Add up the numbers you circled to get your results, and use the following descriptions to assess your puppy's reactions. There are no right answers. Understanding your puppy's personality will enable you to provide a structured environment to bring out her best. For example, a timid puppy needs confidence-building and a soft touch, whereas a strong puppy needs structured guidance.

Timid Puppy (0–9): Sadly, this puppy is afraid of her own shadow. Although she may give the appearance of being abused, this level of caution is phobic and is either inborn or the result of early stress during the early stages of awareness (5 to 8 weeks). Professional behaviorists/trainers can help you better understand and manage your puppy, although her skittish, fearful nature will not diminish much.

The Reserved Pup (9–18): Unsure and reserved, this puppy prefers to observe life rather than jump into the mix. Sweet and submissive, she'll aim to please at whatever cost. A raised voice or an impatient correction may cause a withdrawn reaction, although it's a show of fear, not of understanding. Lessons must be centered around positive reinforcement: Encourage much more than you discourage! Your puppy will develop a positive self-image, leaving her feeling protected and safe.

Mellow Puppy (18–27): Easygoing and relaxed, this puppy is comfortable in most situations without feeling the need to control everything. Above all, she's comfortable with herself without needing to boss or humor anyone. Depending on the breed, she's calm socially. A centered disposition, albeit playful at times, is a noted personality trait.

Eager to Please (28–36): Intense eye contact, attachment, and unrelenting focus are the hallmark of this pup's personality. Her intense desire for direction, if overlooked, can quickly result in unwanted behaviors. If jumping gets attention (for example), this puppy will become addicted. The ensuing cycle of isolation and frustration can create mania in an otherwise responsive, adoring pet. A calm, positive approach to lessons is thoroughly rewarding to all. This puppy will do anything to please her people.

The Comedian (36–44): A true extrovert! This confident puppy plays off situations and people in her environment. Loving the spotlight, she is involved in every interaction and enjoys a challenge. Lessons must be clear and consistent—any slack on your part will be taken advantage of. With this puppy, you must lead, or you will be led.

A Bossy Pup (45): Your puppy has a strong sense of herself: she's driven and motivated to figure life's puzzles out and gain control. She'll need no reassurance—her confidence is instinctual. You've got quite a project on your hands; however, with assertive direction and a very structured program, she'll respect your direction. (If your puppy growled, and you're unsure how to handle the situation, call a professional to help you. Immediately!)

Scoring Skews

Breed traits often affect scores; for example, terriers, herding dogs, and guard breeds, selected for their acute hearing, will have a stronger reaction to the "startle" test.

UNDERSTANDING THE TEST

As you proceed through this book, empathy will serve you quite well. You'll have no trouble shaping lessons suited to your puppy's style of learning. Here's a solid overview of just what each test is determining:

- **Petting:** Impatient puppies have a strong sense of self and accept interaction on their terms. Smart and respectful of those who demand respect, they must be encouraged to cooperate. A puppy who relaxes when being petted is trusting and easygoing and can be soothed with a gentling caress. Fearful or cautious reactions signal insecurity with human handling. This puppy must be conditioned with patience and rewards to trust people.

- **Lifting:** Resistance to sudden interruption indicates a control-oriented puppy. The pup who relaxes is more laid-back and trusting. Immediate concern or fear reflects a puppy who prefers consistency and is resistant to change.

- **Interruption:** These tests focus on the social aspects of submission, trust, and sharing. Guarding or coveting is equated to independent, dominant, or challenging personalities. These puppies must be taught to share and to accept interruption by people. A puppy who is comfortable sharing when asked is relaxed. A fearful reaction signals a lack of trust and a fear of confrontation.

- **Receiving Treats from a Jar:** The ultimate IQ test for puppies. Does your puppy go to the source or cooperatively wait for you to dole out the reward? The puppy who goes for the box thinks quickly and independently. The puppy who waits patiently is generally a sweet-natured puppy who is dependent on human direction but over time will think on her own. A cautious puppy will wait for the environment to change to modify her behavior and will be content to eat treats from the offered hand without thinking further. Timid or fearful puppies may be equally smart but very untrusting of people in their environment: These puppies note the source but grab quickly in fear of confrontation.

- **Hide-n-Seek:** Another "smarts" test, this one focuses on your puppy's ability to use her memory and sense to manage a problem.

- **Training Sequence:** This also tests group cooperation, trust, and focus. There will be obstacles throughout your dog's life; will she trust in your direction, have her own internal confidence meter, or need coaxing to trust your guidance?
- **Loud Noises:** The startle reaction is universal, although what comes after that reaction varies from dog to dog. Self-directed alerting reactions are symbolic of a self-directed puppy; pausing or checking in registers a puppy who relies on group cohesiveness. A fearful reaction is usually a sign of an introverted puppy whose behavior, without guidance, would be shaped by reactions rather than by instructions.

OTHER CONSIDERATIONS

Here are four other defining characteristics. Consider how each relates to your individual puppy and how it will help you better understand her intentions.

- **Introvert or Extrovert?** Introverts keep emotions to themselves. They don't like to rock the boat. Behavior problems may set in when their sweet, contained nature is misunderstood. For example, many introverts are difficult to housetrain. Essentially, they don't like to interfere or make their needs known, so when their bladders demand, they slink off quietly. Extroverts, on the other hand, like to be in the midst of everything. They notice any change, enjoy taking part, demand attention when they're not getting enough, and are confident in new situations. Left undirected, they can become quite bothersome. Chronic attention getters, they'll resort to jumping, barking, and destruction, especially when left alone.
- **Spatial or Nonspatial?** I use these terms when referring to breed tendencies. As your puppy matures, she'll become either spatial or nonspatial. Spatial breeds, like my Labrador Retriever Whoopsie Daisy, love to be in everyone's space: physical enmeshment is best by far. Nonspatial breeds, like terriers and protection dogs, need their personal space. They have serious thoughts. Race up to one of these dogs, and you'll ruffle her feathers. They need to know you before they open up. Put a nonspatial breed with a spatial breed, and you're likely to hear some growling. Spatial dogs are just too cheery for the nonspatial lot.

Age and Socialization

Young puppies are usually very welcoming and submissive (spatial) when approached; however, as they approach puberty, certain breed characteristics, including nonspatial tendencies, come into play. Socialization can also influence a nonspatial breed's comfort zone when being approached by friendly dogs and people. I highly recommend it!

Jodi Buren

Is this puppy active or passive? Oh, so active!

- **Active or Passive?** This one is fairly obvious. Active puppies are alert, intense, and very involved. If you don't give them direction, you'll find yourself taking it! Their behaviors will direct just as surely as words could: "Open the door!" "Back massage now!" "Drop everything and chase me!" Passive puppies are either relaxed or timid. They need encouragement to get involved. Problem behaviors are generally self-inflicted: nervous chewing, lick granulomas (a sore created by obsessive licking), or chronic illness.

- **Cooperative or Challenging?** These words say it all. Cooperative dogs enjoy taking direction. Challenging characters must have proof of your intelligence and authority before they'll follow your lead.

NATURE VERSUS NURTURE

This is the big question. How much will your adult dog's personality be affected by her genetic blueprints versus the environment she grew up in? Can the breed tendencies that tell your puppy to herd, bark, dig, or swim be influenced at all? The answer is, of course, they can be influenced. But not erased. I, for example, could teach my Labrador to pull a sled, but at the end of the day she'll long for her tennis ball. If this were my desire, I can assure you that she would sulk whenever the harness was brought out. Her days would be long, tiresome, and depressing.

If you understand your puppy's nature and work with it, you'll give her a license to love the world she's in, and you'll ensure a more harmonious bond overall. I can teach you how to stop your herding breed from chasing the children, but we can't eliminate the impulse altogether. By assigning appropriate displacement activities, like chasing a toy on a rope or teaching her to trail your bicycle, her needs will be directed and respected, too. Then and only then will nature and nurture work together to create a balance for all.

Herding Breeds	Guarding Breeds	Protective Breeds	Sporting Breeds	Terriers	Dogs with Distinct Skills	Scent Hounds	Sight Hounds	Hunting Breeds	Companion Breeds	Fighting Breeds	Draft and Sled Dogs
Australian Cattle Dog	Akita	Belgian Malinois	Brittany	Airedale Terrier	American Eskimo Dog	American Foxhound	Afghan Hound	Akita	Affenpinscher	American Staffordshire Terrier	Alaskan Malamute
Australian Shepherd	Anatolian Shepherd	Belgian Sheepdog	Chesapeake Bay Retriever	Australian Terrier	Dalmatian	Basset Hound	Basenji	Chow Chow	Bichon Frise	Bull Terrier	Bernese Mountain Dog
Bearded Collie	Beauceron	Belgian Tervuren	Clumber Spaniel	Belington Terrier	Keeshond	Beagle	Borzoi	Norwegian Elkhound	Boston Terrier	Bulldog	Bouvier des Flandres
Belgian Malinois	Bouvier des Flandres	Black Russian Terrier	Cocker Spaniel	Border Terrier	Schipperke	Black and Tan Coonhound	Rhodesian Greyhound	Ridgeback	Brussels Griffon	Chinese Shar-Pei	Greater Swiss Mountain Dog
Belgian Sheepdog	Briard	Boxer	Curly-Coated Retriever	Cairn Terrier		Bloodhound	Ibizan Hound	Shar-Pei	Cavalier King Charles Spaniel	Chow Chow	Newfoundland
Belgian Tervuren	Bullmastiff	Doberman Pinscher	English Cocker Spaniel	Dandie Dinmont Terrier		Dachshund	Irish Wolfhound	Spinone Italiano	Chihuahua	Miniature Bull Terrier	Rottweiler
Border Collie	Canaan Dog	German Pinscher	English Setter	Fox Terrier (Smooth and Wirehaired)		English Foxhound	Pharaoh Hound		Chinese Crested	Staffordshire Bull Terrier	Saint Bernard
Cardigan Welsh Corgi	Great Dane	German Shepherd Dog	English Springer Spaniel	German Pinscher		Harrier	Saluki		English Toy Spaniel		Samoyed
Collie (Rough)	Great Pyrenees	Giant Schnauzer	Field Spaniel	Glen of Imal Terrier		Otterhound	Scottish Deerhound		Finnish Spitz		Siberian Husky
Komondor	Keeshond	Flat-Coated Retriever	Irish Terrier			Petit Basset Griffon Venden	Whippet		French Bulldog		

continued

continued

Herding Breeds	Guarding Breeds	Protective Breeds	Sporting Breeds	Terriers	Dogs with Distinct Skills	Scent Hounds	Sight Hounds	Hunting Breeds	Companion Breeds	Fighting Breeds	Draft and Sled Dogs
Giant Schnauzer	Kuvasz	Standard Schnauzer	German Shorthaired Pointer	Keeshond		Plott Hound			Havanese		
Mastiff	German Wirehaired Pointer	Kerry Blue Terrier				Red Bone Coonhound			Italian Greyhound		
Neapolitan Mastiff	Golden Retriever	Lakeland Terrier							Japanese Chin		
Rottweiler	Gordon Setter	Manchester Terrier							Lhasa Apso		
Saint Bernard	Irish Setter	Miniature Bull Terrier							Lowchen		
Shar-Pei	Irish Water Spaniel	Miniature Schnauzer							Maltese		
Tibetan Mastiff	Labrador Retriever	Norfolk Terrier							Miniature Bull Terrier		
	Newfoundland	Norwich Terrier							Miniature Pinscher		
	Nova Scotia Duck Toller	Papillon							Papillon		
	Portuguese Water Dog	Parson Russell Terrier							Pekingese		
	Pointer	Scottish Terrier							Pomeranian		

Poodle (Standard and Miniature)		
Pug		
Shiba Inu		
Shih Tzu		
Silky Terrier		
Tibetan Spaniel		
Toy Manchester Terrier		
Toy Poodle		
Yorkshire Terrier		

Spinone Italiano	Sealyham Terrier	
Sussex Spaniel	Skye Terrier	
Water Spaniel	Standard Schnauzer	
	Soft Coated Wheaten Terrier	
Weimaraner		
Welsh Springer Spaniel	Tibetan Terrier	
Wirehaired Pointing Griffon	Welsh Terrier	
	West Highland White Terrier	
Vizsla		

Chapter 2

A Welcome Home

Whether you've brought your puppy home or you're anticipating that day, this chapter covers all the preliminaries, from soup to dog bones. From that first mighty trip to the pet store to selecting dog food and doctors, this chapter will weigh in with facts and advice. And although giving your puppy a bona fide pedicure is an option, daily hygiene is not. A hit list of "must-dos" is arranged below. Ready, set . . . CHARGE IT!!!

SHOPPING FOR PUPPY SUPPLIES

Go to any pet store, and it's easy to feel overwhelmed! It's also hard to resist being impulsive. Each product touts great reasons you need to buy it . . . from promising to cure bad breath and doggy odor to preventing chewing, resolving house-training issues, and the list goes on. Before you whip out your credit card, let's walk through a hypothetical store, organize your layout, and target which products will really help!

- Crate
- Baby gates
- Puppy playpen
- Mat/bed
- Tag collar
- Identification tag
- Town license
- Three bowls (two for water, one for food)
- Puppy food

Jodi Buren

- Leash
- Play toys
- Chew toys/bones
- Clicker (optional)
- Target stick (optional)
- Daily hygiene tools
- Long line/expandable lead
- Snack pack

Your puppy's mat should have it all within reach.

Food and Bowls

You can get as fancy as you want, or you can use a dinner plate. As long as you're feeding puppy food, it really doesn't matter. Of course, stainless steel is easy to wash and is unbreakable. Plastic is not ideal. It can cause allergic reactions and makes a tempting chew. Get two or more bowls for water (more if you live in a hot climate or have a large home) and one for food. Keep the bowls in the same place: your puppy appreciates consistency!

Mats and Beds

You can go crazy here matching the décor in every room, or you can use old towels. The key is to give your puppy his own bedding and his own space. Throughout the book, I'll identify this material as a flat mat (my preference, as it's easy to transport and wash). Initially, place it in his main room, and use it for everything! Put his toys on the mat. Dole out treats and food on the mat. Store toys and bones on the mat. Have snuggle time on his mat. The goal is total mat bonding. Now, when you go into a new area, bring the mat, or have one like it waiting there. When you go for a car ride, bring the mat. Going on a trip? Think of his mat as a security blanket. In the waiting room or up on the examination table at your veterinarian's . . . you get the idea!

Buttering Up Your Puppy

Want to buy an hour of peace? Stuff a bone or a toy with trace amounts of peanut butter or cream cheese. Your puppy will work hard to get it out!

Bones

Puppies need to chew, especially when cutting their adult teeth between 4 and 11 months. Your quest will be finding a satisfying chew. Every biodegradable bone I've ever run into has pros and cons. White rawhide expands in the belly, which can cause room-clearing

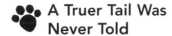

gas and a host of gastrointestinal complications (I don't generally recommend this one). Pressed rawhide is all right, although hunks can be swallowed, so if your puppy is a voracious chewer, keep your eyes on him. Plastic bones are ho-hum to most puppies; however, if yours is the exception, stock up. Corn starch/vegetable bones can be a favorite, but they break down quickly and create colorful stools.

> ### 🐾 A Truer Tail Was Never Told
>
> Your puppy will want whatever object you treasure most. He'll also want whatever you say he can't have. When you find a toy he loves, carry it and play with it. Covet it purposely, playing keep away, until it's the only thing he wants!

Although the penchant for hard bones is universal, beware—they can break off and cause havoc in the digestive tract. This happened with my Whoopsie (my Labrador Retriever)—a piece broke off and tore her stomach lining, causing bloody vomiting—quite a scare! Needless to say, I cleared the house of hard bones.

You're sure to run into chews created from animal parts (those parts not fit for human consumption): everything from the ears to the tail. Many puppies love these. If you can get beyond the concept and the smell (pee-ew!), go for it; just check to ensure that the parts have been processed in the States and don't contain any ink by-products (such as tattoos).

Get advice from other dog owners and speak to your breeder, your veterinarian, and pet store employees. Tell them about your puppy—his age, breed, temperament, and energy level. Try one bone at a time. When you find a few that satisfy, buy multiples. If one bone rises above the rest, set it aside for important times, such as dinner or when company visits.

Toys

Let's face it—puppies are funny. Of course, if yours is trailing a roll of toilet paper through the dining room for the tenth time, the humor may be wearing thin. To prevent problems before they arise, stock up on chews and toys that spark your puppy's enthusiasm.

It is truly mind-boggling! There are just so many toys available these days, with many making the jump straight from the shelves of Toys "R" Us. How will you know what to buy? Ask your puppy, of course. Call local pet shops and find one that will let you bring him along. There are toys that make noise, have holes, bounce, giggle,

Jodi Buren

Your puppy will want whatever object you treasure most.

> ### 🐾 To Treat or Not to Treat?
>
> Are you torn? I didn't start out as a treater, but when I saw how happy it made everybody and how quickly the puppies responded, it seemed right. The key is learning to phase off. If you don't, you run the risk of becoming treat-dependent, and then your puppy will listen only if you've got a treat in your hand. And that's no good. So in the end, you can choose; if you follow my method, you'll treat initially and then phase off as discussed in chapter 4, "Puppy Parenting Styles."

change color, and stow kibbles . . . you name it. Our Lab Whoopsie's favorite toy is a tennis ball; my Shayna (a Border Collie mix) lived for a Frisbee; and Hope, our terrier mix, didn't go anywhere without her Ducksworth—a stuffed yellow duck.

Once you've narrowed your search, buy several replicas for games like *two ball toss* and the *giving greeter* (for more on games, see chapters 5 and 7).

Treat Cups

A treat cup is a surefire favorite! Fill one-third of a plastic container with some kibbles, biscuits, and/or Cheerios. Take it a step further, and cut a hole in the lid just large enough for the treat to fit through. Now you and the kids can decorate the cup and make multiples to spread around your house. These come in handy for the *grab-n-show* and the *treat cup name game*.

Training Tools

Clickers are fun—not mandatory, but they are a positive, effective way to introduce new ideas and lessons. A handheld gizmo, the clicker makes a sharp, distinctive sound when pressed. I'll go into more detail about clicker training in chapter 4, "Puppy Parenting Styles." Can't find a clicker at your local pet store? Check out my website store!

Another fun technique that's rising in popularity is target training. There are two ways to target—with a target touch stick or with a pointer. If you're planning to venture forth into agility or competition obedience, you'll find these techniques quite helpful. I'll go into more detail in chapter 4. Can't find a target stick? You can improvise with a pen, a tent stake, or a kitchen utensil, or check out my website store.

For more advice on finding clickers, target sticks, and pointers, please refer to my website, www.dogperfect.com, or other resources listed in the reference section.

Enclosures

Letting your young puppy run free is a recipe for disaster. From his perspective, it's overwhelming. Indoors or outside, the transition from the whelping box to the real world must be gradual. Here are helpful tools.

CRATE

You don't have to get a crate. If the idea is loathsome to you, there are other options. But a crate, however confining, is not torturous. Most puppies love their crate, as it echoes back to their denning days: cozy and safe. It also conditions sleeping when you're out or busy, chewing as an appropriate displacement activity, and bladder control, as most puppies don't soil where they rest. For many households, it's a win-win.

There are always situations where a crate is not suitable. If you're a working puppy parent and your puppy will be spending more than six straight daytime hours alone on a regular basis, a playpen might be a better option. If you've adopted your puppy from a shelter or a pet store, your puppy may fear snug enclosures or may view the crate as a toileting area.

PLAYPEN

This foldout pen can be shaped to fit any open space and is an ideal option for long stretches alone or for semisupervised interaction. I love them! Large enough to allow movement, the space can be arranged for sleep, bathroom (if necessary), water, and toys. Ideal for long stints, they're a working puppy parent's best friend. Isolation longer than four to six hours mandates an enclosure that's larger than a crate.

GATES

Gates can be affixed to confine a certain area or erected in a doorway to provide in-room supervision. Avoid accordion-style gates, as they can trap small heads.

FENCES

The ideal enclosure is an aboveground fence that encompasses the home; it keeps your dog in and other dogs or animals out. Make sure that the fence is properly installed and that any openings or holes are secured. Pen enclosures away from the home often create hyperisolation anxiety. Your puppy won't be out practicing Pilates: he'll be pining for company and getting stressed out in the meantime.

Jodi Buren

Playpen—freedom within an enclosure.

If you're considering an underground fence, you have my blessing, but please don't activate the system until your puppy is 6 months old. That age was the accepted standard until the inventor lost the patent, creating market competition. In new companies' attempts to outbid each other, they insisted that they could train at 4 months. It's simply too young: the puppy's brain is barely developed. Wait until your puppy is 6 months old, please.

Collars, Leashes, Raincoats, Oh My!

Dressing your puppy up has never been so colorful or so confusing! There are so many collar choices out there that it's hard to know which one is best for your puppy and your situation. Use this section to check through your options.

First, let's start with a staple. You don't see many bare dogs around anymore. A proper American dog must have a collar with identification tags, a training collar, and at least one leash. Perhaps he'll have a coat, too—whether he needs it or not.

IDENTIFICATION COLLAR OR HARNESS

This is a plain collar or harness that you hang identification tags from and that you leave on your puppy whenever you take your puppy out. This collar should have

- **Identification tag:** "PLEASE HELP ME HOME 555-555-5555" is all it needs to say.
- **Rabies tag:** To validate vaccination.
- **Town License:** It is the law and should be worn if your puppy is loose.

IDENTIFICATION MICROCHIP

No puppy should leave home without a microchip: a small identification chip injected into the puppy's shoulder or neck. It requires your veterinarian's administration and a registration and will enable anyone processing the scanner to identify your puppy should he get lost or stolen. A bright yellow identification tag can be attached to your puppy's collar.

TRAINING COLLARS

All teaching collars must be used with supervision and used correctly. Without supervision, the collar could get tangled, twisted, or caught—a terrifying and potentially harmful scenario for your puppy. Summaries of each type of training collar follow; read each one and talk to other dog owners and professionals to determine which collar will work best for you and your puppy.

Head Collars

A head collar fits over your puppy's muzzle and snaps just behind his ears. Yes, it looks more like a muzzle than your traditional collar, but it's not. It has more in

The Teaching Lead Method

If your puppy is mischievous when unconfined or you just want to build some lesson time into your daily schedule, introduce him to the Teaching Lead (homemade or bought) in the house and out. It's a passive way of communicating your care and guidance throughout the day and when life is too hard to contain on his (or her) own! There are three applications:

- **Leading** is a form of passive control. You literally hold or wear your puppy's leash and lead her around with you. Inside and out, up and down . . . a couple of twenty-minute leading sessions in the early days will have a tremendous impact. Your puppy quickly learns to focus on you for direction.

- **Play stations** (also referred to in this book as **stationing**) are special areas custom designed for your puppy in the rooms you share. Provide an identifiable area with bedding and toys, and pre-secure a leash if she can't sit still.

- **Anchoring** involves sitting on the Teaching Lead when you're sitting still. It helps your puppy adjust to the rhythms of your day. Provide a toy/chew, giving her just enough slack to lay comfortably. If she needs to go out or play, she will find a clear way to let you know!

common with a horse's halter. The beauty of it? Where the head goes, the body will follow. Resistance doesn't come into play. It conditions good walking manners and can be used to calm behaviors such as nipping, jumping, barking, and chewing. Sound too good to be true? I'd have to agree, except head collars are my personal favorite. I walked my puppy on one until she was 18 months old, and it conditioned patient walking skills. Now she'll follow me with or without a lead. Here's how head collars work:

- Methodically holding a puppy on a head collar is equivalent to holding a child's hand versus dragging him around by his shirtsleeve. Your puppy will feel guided rather than choked during his walks.

- The pressure over the nose and behind the ears works on the "Mommy Principle": these two points remind him that someone else is in charge.

- Where the head goes, the body will follow. This is ideal for conditioning good walking manners and giving everyone the ability to handle your puppy.

- Head collars also help shape good habits. Left on indoors during chaotic times, the gentle pressure conveys a sense of calm. A slight tug of the lead will tuck your puppy's head into a submissive posture, helping to curb barking, nipping, jumping, and more.

Fitting the collar initially is a challenge, and it may take your puppy a few days to accept the strange feeling across his nose. Fitting is also subject to the type of head collar you choose. There are several on the market, but the top two include

- **Gentle Leader:** This patented design, by Premier, has my POA (Paw of Approval). Secured snugly around the neck (watchband tight), a single strap lays over the nose. To fit the nose strap, there is a clasp that opens and should be secured just behind the jowls. It comes in many colors and five sizes.
- **Halti Collar:** This one comes in six sizes and one color. The only adjustment is behind the ears, which should fit snugly.

The only drawback? The head collar conditions, it doesn't correct. If your puppy has been pulling you along for eight months, the head collar will eliminate his ability to pull; however, once it's removed, he may revert to old habits. If your goal is immediate, however, look no further. The head collar will control the pulling instantaneously. If your focus is to teach your puppy not to pull, and you're getting a late start on training lessons, you may need to find another option.

How often you use this collar depends on what you're using it for. If it's simply to condition cooperative walking skills, it should be used when walking your puppy on a leash. It is safe to use on a retractable leash and a long line as well. If you're using it to tame excitability around the home, leave it on when you can supervise household freedom. A drag lead should be attached for quick direction.

Traditional Slip Collars

Improperly referred to as a choke collar, the slip collar fits snugly over your puppy's head and rests just behind his ears. It is the sudden tug sensation and/or the sound, *not the restraint,* that gets his attention. *A puppy must be 4 months old to wear this collar, due to potential tracheal damage.* If you find yourself asphyxiating your puppy, choose a different collar. It can do more damage than good.

 Muzzling the Opposition

"Egad," some will say, "why is your puppy wearing a muzzle?" Don't be offended. Educate the uninformed: it's more similar to a horse halter. Your puppy still has the ability to eat, bark, and nip with it on. It is a simple system that guides your puppy's head rather than jerking his neck. Leash pulling is abolished. Nipping and jumping can be tamed humanely. The pressure over the muzzle and the nose harkens back to Mom, who would shake these areas to instill respect and calmness.

Martingale Collars/Check Chains

These collars have a flat, stiffer construction than traditional slip collars, limit the risk of head slipping and escape, and are ideal for long-necked breeds (such as Greyhounds) or puppies who are sensitive to the sound of a chain. These collars also prevent hair loss and matting and are a blessing for the dimensionally challenged: just slip it over your pup's head, and you're ready to go. There are two types:

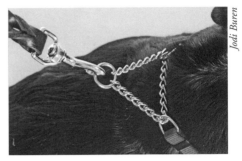

Check chains

- **Martingale:** All-cloth weave, these collars are three-fourths collar and one-fourth slip collar. A cross between a traditional tag collar and a correction collar, this is a safe and effective combination.

- **Check Chain:** These parli-chain collars are three-fourths material and one-fourth chain. As it's the sound of the collar, not the restraint, that hones your puppy's manners, these collars can be very effective if your puppy alerts to the sound. If not, he'll just keep on pulling, and you'll be caught in a neck-of-war battle for control.

Self-Correcting Collars

For puppies over 5 months only! There are two types of self-correcting collars on the market:

- **German Metal Prong Collar:** The original prong collar appears torturous, although it's not when used correctly. Shiny metal prongs latch together in a circle to create a collar that provides a continuous pinch whenever your puppy pulls or you tug on the leash. It comes in four sizes, from Lightweight to Extra Heavyweight links.

- **Good Dog Collar:** Constructed of blue plastic and manufactured by Triple Dog Academy in Texas, this collar is similar in cost and mechanics. It has my POA. It comes in two sizes, is less intense aesthetically, and issues a more blunt pinch than the metal collar. The only drawback I've found is in opening and closing the sections—I needed a voice lesson from the manufacturer initially.

Worn high on the puppy's neck, just behind the ears, these collars working on a "scruff shake" principle: self-correcting collars simulate a correction from a more dominant dog. Used to condition walking skills or to target inappropriate behaviors, they can be a real lifesaver.

> ### 🐾 Weaning Off
>
> The best way to wean your puppy off the self-correcting collar is to decide what collar you'd like to use instead and temporarily use both. For example, if weaning to a check chain, take two leashes or a teaching lead that has a clip on each end. Rely on the check chain as you handle your puppy, using the self-correcting collar only as a back-up or to issue a quick correction when things are getting out of hand.

If your puppy is a strong-necked breed who chokes himself on a chain collar, this may be an optimal choice for the initial months of training. Once the routine is established and your status as team captain is respected, you can wean him off its use gradually.

HARNESSES

There are many harnesses out there, but most of them condition puppies to pull like sled dogs. Instead of teaching cooperative following skills, they convey the opposite message: to run like a bullet when the pup is given any slack.

There are several "no-pull harnesses" that have my POA. These prevent pulling by limiting muscular flexibility.

LEASHES

Selecting a leash these days can get confusing. From the material and the pattern to the types, you'll have endless choices. To decide which leash or leashes will be right for you, consider how often you will walk with your puppy, where, and what activities you'll do together. Most people can get by with a six-foot leash (Teaching Lead or traditional), a seatbelt lead for car trips, a hand leash for house direction and a drag lead for outside control, but you be the judge. Read through your options to decide what will work best for you!

Teaching Lead

I patented this leash, so, of course, it's a favorite. Understand its uses, however, before you purchase it. The Teaching Lead enables

- **Hands-free walking control:** The transitional step to off-lead control.
- **Indoor conditioning:** Secured to your waist or tethered to an immovable object, it allows you to bring your puppy everywhere as you condition household manners—important in weaning off crate or gated isolation.

With clips on either end and holes in the middle, it can be used as a traditional leash or as a leash-belt combo. Fashionable, to say the least! The genius that went into creating both the Teaching Lead and the Teaching Lead method was originally made famous by the Monks of New Skete and by Carol Lea Benjamin, who called their technique "umbilical cording." Our proposed method encourages you to use the lead outside to condition following skills and inside to teach your puppy how to settle in each room and to contain inappropriate impulses.

Jodi Buren

The Handheld Leash

This traditional leash still dominates the market. Handheld, it comes in either leather or nylon. Although leather may seem stronger and more durable, nylon is just as powerful.

My patented Teaching Lead conditions cooperative learning skills.

Puppy Drag Lead

A short, lightweight nylon lead to be used during free play, allowing easy interference if needed.

Long Line Drag Lead

A twenty-five- or fifty-foot lightweight nylon lead is for use outside. If you're able to let your puppy run free in a yard, a park, or a field, I recommend this lead highly. By allowing his natural freedom to explore, you can influence his choice to stay with you by using the games and the exercises listed in chapter 7, "Enjoying the First Year," and in the games section of chapter 5. Whereas a short lead forces him to stay near you, this lead allows playtime while giving you the opportunity to reinforce his cooperation with treats, toys, and praise. Before he's cut his baby teeth, your puppy will be responding naturally to COME. In addition, the long line enables your calm interference from a distance should your puppy wander, get rough with the children, or explore your garden.

 Harness as Car Restraint

Here's where the harness shines. Clipped onto a seatbelt or a cargo lead, they provide a safe restraint while you're driving.

> ### 🐾 Rope Burn
>
> Both the flexi-lead and the long line can inflict painful rope burns. I can attest to the fact! Be careful when using either around children. If your puppy is very active, avoid the flexi-lead altogether, and practice jumping rope to keep ahead of your long line.

Hand Lead

At a length of eight to twelve inches, this lead can be attached for easy handling or can be left on when the puppy is supervised, as a physical reminder and for quick control. Older children can easily use it to guide the puppy around the house.

Finger Lead

A short finger-size lead can be left on a tag or a head collar for quick control.

Seatbelt/Cargo Lead

Either lead can be used to secure your puppy in the car. The seatbelt lead slides through the seatbelt; the cargo lead secures onto a clip. Both should be attached to a harness.

Flexi-Lead

These retractable leashes seem so ideal. Your puppy can zip back and forth. No tangles, no fuss. There can be serious consequences, however. Foremost, while the brake is on they can "pop," causing the line to release and your puppy to zip out. For this reason alone, do not use them near a street. I've had three clients witness their dogs' deaths—tragic beyond words. Next, be careful using them around other dogs. They're hard to manage and can lead to a serious fight if the dog being greeted is not welcoming. They work best in open fields or on beaches.

FEEDING TIME

Whole books have been written on this topic. I'll give you a quick overview. Of course, if you have a puppy from a self-spoken breeder, you've probably already been educated on nutrition. If you're in the dark, never fear.

Human Food

Until the 1950s, dogs ate our leftovers. During World War II, however, nutritionists devised a feeding system for dogs, and since then it has become nothing short of a science. The nutritional requirements for your puppy's age, size, and breed are well documented. Leftovers are discouraged, as they don't provide the balanced diet your puppy needs. If you want to cook for your puppy, that's a whole different story! But before you start, buy a couple of books or surf the Net to make sure that you're up to the task.

Canned Food

The majority of canned foods are 75 percent water, diluting their nutritional value considerably. Given no choice, your puppy will thrive on a high-quality dry food, but no one could argue against the fact that canned food *looks* more palatable and *seems* more appetizing. If you're sold, buy only high-end brands whose meat by-products are fit for human consumption.

> **Water**
>
> Here's a nugget: your puppy can live for weeks without food but will die within days without water. How much water he'll need depends on his activity and the climate. Panting is like sweating—it calls for a drink! Has your puppy discovered the toilet bowl? To offset this habit, place a water dish next to each one.

Dry Kibbles

Dry kibbles are the mainstay of most diets. Go to any supermarket or pet store, however, and it's easy to become overwhelmed. You'll have more choices than you would at your local Starbucks: nugget size, shape, growth formula, lamb and rice, fish and potato, a vegetable blend . . . what's what? To help you decipher the labels, I've broken dry food into individual components. Listed next to each of the following sources is an ideal dietary percentage. The term *human grade* refers to ingredients fit for a human diet. If reading labels scares you, surf the Web or go into a respectable pet shop and ask lots of questions. It's your puppy, it's your pocketbook, it's your life—and it's your right to know!

PROTEIN (21 TO 26 PERCENT)

Identifying the source of the protein will help you determine the quality of the food. The highest-quality proteins are the meat proteins that consist of organ or muscle meat. Down a notch are proteins listed as "animal proteins," consisting of

> **The Four Ds**
>
> The Four Ds refer to meat sources that are dying, decayed, diseased, or deceased. It is a reality that many commercial canned dog food manufacturers acquire their meat from sources no longer fit for human consumption. Spruced up with dyes and odor additives, they may look like filet, but filet they're not.

Poop Patrol

The end product of a balanced diet should be two to four compact, low-odor stools a day.

any animal part (hooves, eyelids, hair, etc.). At the bottom of the list are vegetable or grain proteins sourced from plant products. Too much vegetable matter can lead to a host of problems, from nutritional deficiencies and indigestion to bloat and allergies. Your puppy needs animal protein. When reading the label, find a food that lists two sources of animal protein. Although high-quality protein costs more, it has considerably better health benefits.

The lower the quality of protein, the more your puppy will have to eat to meet his daily requirements. And we know what more food means . . . more poop. Many puppies develop allergies to vegetable proteins—after all, dogs have not descended from farmers. This can lead to an irritable bowel and a host of skin allergies. Here are my final protein tips:

- Protein needs change throughout your puppy's life. Broken-down protein equals energy, so any time there is a demand for more energy (strenuous activity, fever, or certain illnesses), your puppy needs more protein. This is why more protein is needed during their growing phases.

- That said, more protein is not better. Super-high-protein diets are used for athletic dogs; if you've got your puppy on a normal routine, stick to the recommended daily allowance.

- Ever wonder what the difference is between active, low active, lite, puppy, and performance foods? You guessed it—the percentage of protein!

Bloat

A dark and horrifying word, bloat causes the stomach of its victim to twist, which causes shock due to decreased blood pressure and other life-threatening conditions. If not addressed immediately, it will cause death. Symptoms include abdominal distention, salivating, and retching. If you have a breed that's susceptible to bloat (commonly, large deep-chested breeds, including Akitas, German Shepherds, Great Danes, Bloodhounds, Sight Hounds, Weimaraners, Setters, and like breeds), elevate your dog's eating and drinking stations, feed/offer water in smaller quantities, and avoid extreme exercise for thirty minutes after each meal. For more on bloat (find out all you can), please refer to my reference section and ask your veterinarian. (Note: If your puppy inhales his food, scatter the food on a pan, strategically placing several large rocks to slow his consumption.)

Carbohydrates (42 Percent)

Here's where the bulk weight comes into play. It is common for carbohydrates to come from vegetables; however, not all veggies are created equal! Oats, barley, and bran are carbs with a punch; in addition to aiding in proper digestion and stool formation, they pack some vitamins and minerals along, too. Corn, a less-expensive carbohydrate, is used frequently; however, it is a common cause of food allergies, so make sure you read labels and watch your puppy for his reaction. Keep carbohydrates balanced but not excessive. A diet high in grains has its drawbacks—namely, smelly stools, gas, bad breath, and tartar.

> ### 🐾 Fruits and Veggies
>
> Supplementing your puppy's food with fruits and veggies or using carrot or apple bits as treats is a great idea. Sometimes we give our Whoopsie a broccoli stalk or an apple core to chew on. As with humans, though, too much fiber may cause diarrhea.

Fats and Preservatives (15 to 20 Percent)

These necessary ingredients are what drive up the cost of the food. It's the quality that demands your attention. Good fats include chicken, fish fats, sunflower or canola oil, flaxseed oil, and fish oil—they're all good! Tallow fat—now that's bad. It's an unusable fat that is also used in the production of candles.

Vitamins (1 Percent)

Vitamins unlock nutrients from food and provide energy. There are two types to look for:

- Fat soluble (A, D, E, and K)
- Water soluble (B and C)

Depending on your puppy's lifestyle, his need for vitamins will vary. If you are concerned that your puppy may not be meeting his daily requirement, ask your veterinarian about a possible supplement.

> ### Different Strokes
>
> Certain puppies call for special diets. Fast-growing, large-boned breeds like retrievers and shepherds that are prone to joint malformation (commonly, hip and elbow dysplasia) are often placed on a low-protein diet or adult food to slow growth. Other puppies may need prescription diets for conditions ranging from irritable bowel syndrome to allergies. Speak to your veterinarian or a pet store professional when considering your puppy's food.

> ### 🐾 Mealtime Manners
>
> Puppies like consistency; predictability is comforting. Feed your puppy at set times and at an established feeding station. Wait until he's calm and sitting before you lower the bowl, even if it takes ten minutes. Civility over chaos gets my Paw of Approval.

MINERALS (1 PERCENT)

Minerals help with circulation and energy production. Although mineral deficiencies are more common than vitamin deficiencies are, do not supplement your puppy's diet without your veterinarian's written permission. An imbalance can be harmful.

HEALTHFUL HABITS, HAPPY HOME

Of course, material objects and lessons aren't all that your puppy will need to feel chipper and alert—just as important are good nutrition and healthful hygiene, the building blocks of positive mental energy and the daily requirements for a long and happy life with you. In this section, I'll cover everything from what brush to use to diet and how to select the best veterinarian.

Is There a Dog Doctor in the House?

Find a veterinarian whom both you and your puppy like—a lot! You'll be spending many years working together. It's important to establish a positive rapport.

The saying "different strokes for different folks" could not apply more. Although you can get recommendations from a friend, you alone will be the judge. Speak to each potential doctor about what matters the most to you: diet, holistic alternatives, exercise regimes, inoculations, where they went to college, who covers for them when they are not in the office—whatever you want to know.

Talk with your veterinarian about his vaccine schedule and his recommendations on prevaccine socialization. Many of the potential diseases are airborne. For this reason alone I suggest keeping a puppy home or in a known indoor setting until he has received his third set of shots.

Everyday Hygiene

Your puppy's vanity kit usually won't extend far beyond a few good brushes, a nail clipper, shampoo, drops for the eyes and the ears, and a toothbrush. Yes, a toothbrush!

Homeopathic and Natural Healing Remedies

Some experts claim these are quackery, and others swear by certain healing remedies. I'm of the opinion that the body (dog or human) is capable of immense healing powers if you stock it with the right nutrients. Disease is a body out of balance or a body infected by foreign bacteria too powerful for the body to fight on its own. I always try a homeopathic remedy when symptoms *aren't extreme*. However, if your puppy's health is faltering, please take him to his doctor immediately.

Mindful grooming ensures a healthy outlook, and your participation will alert you to ailments before they get serious. Here are some things to keep in mind:

- **Brushing:** Make this task enjoyable for both of you. Introduce it at restful times and distract your puppy by spreading peanut butter or yogurt on a vertical surface or in his bowl.

- **Bathing:** The same rule applies: make it enjoyable with a lickable spread, and you'll avoid the infamous soap-suds-shaking-escape routine. If you're bathing in a tub, place a mat on the bottom for secure footing.

- **Clipping nails:** If you're going to clip your puppy's nails, invest in a high-quality clipper and buy some styptic powder to stop bleeding. If I'm scaring you, it's with good cause. Clipping into your dog's nail bed is like tipping off the end of your finger. Not only does it bleed, it hurts! Take a lesson in clipping from a groomer or your veterinarian before you try it on your own.

- **Cleaning ears:** Dogs' ears are constructed differently from our own. A vertical canal creates a greater risk for infection, especially if the ears are folded (as in retrievers and hounds). To prevent infection, wipe each ear out regularly with an antiseptic such as witch hazel or a store-bought version, noting wax build-up or odor (more common during hotter months). An infection causes extreme discomfort, causes itching, and in later stages will affect balance.

- **Cleaning eyes:** Your puppy possesses a third eyelid, know as the nictitating membrane. This inner eyelid works like a windshield wiper to keep your puppy's eye free of dust, but it can get infected, causing a condition similar to conjunctivitis, a highly contagious ailment. It can also be malformed at birth or during development, causing conditions that affect tear production—these congenital defects can be cured surgically. Locate this lid by pulling the lower lid gently forward. If tear production increases or you see wincing or redness, note any change and speak with your veterinarian immediately.

Hygiene Habits

Sunday is Whoopsie Day in our house! In her drawer, she has a "beauty bag" with all her hygiene essentials.

- **Ear swabs:** First, I wipe down her ears. Especially in hot weather, I watch for signs of infection. If excessive brown wax builds up or there's a funky smell, it signals the onset of an infection. I watch closely and notify her doctor before it causes itching or affects her balance.

- **Eye wipes:** Eyes need attention, too. The third eyelid, known as the nicitating membrane, can get scratched or infected, causing wincing and excessive discharge. To locate this membrane and watch for irritation, simply pull the lower lid out gently. Do you see it?

- **Nail clipper:** I tip her nails once a month. Also on hand is styptic powder to stop bleeding in case I accidentally tip her nail bed.

- **Toothbrush:** Next, out comes the toothbrush. It's quite entertaining reaching for the back molars. Fortunately, she adores her special chicken-flavored doggie toothpaste.

- **Shed blade:** During shedding season, I use a shed blade up to three times a week. A must-have for all short-haired breeds, the shed blade rakes dead hair to the surface, which you can then bag or let it fall free. The neighborhood birds will thank you—it's wonderful nesting material!

- **Bath time:** Once a month, it's bath time for Whoopsie. When she was a puppy, I'd rub the sides of the tub with peanut butter; now it's hard to keep her out—even when I'm showering!

Prevention Beats a Cure, Hands Down!

As the old adage goes, an ounce of prevention . . . and it's true. Here are some tips from my home to yours!

- Always scout out the location of a possible play date. Just as you wouldn't send a child to a home where guns were left out in the open, puppies should not be allowed to play where poisons are left out.

- Keep the poison control hotline number by your phone. Ask your veterinarian or local animal shelter for the best phone number to call in an emergency.

- Go with your gut, and trust yourself with the safety of your dog. If you think your puppy is getting inadequate care and attention at the vet or at an animal hospital, speak up and make demands—your puppy's life may depend on it.

🐾 Condition Now!

The time to introduce a toothbrush or a dematting comb is now! An 8-week-old puppy can be positively conditioned to her adult grooming tools by rubbing peanut butter or yogurt onto a upright surface (such as the side of the refrigerator) as you gently go over her coat.

Jodi Buren

- Go though your home, and look at everything from your puppy's eye level. All puppies are impulsive and quick! If you have a puppy who learns to open cabinets, secure them well. If you have a puppy who's tall enough to reach the countertops, keep them clear of dangerous objects and toxic products. In other words, puppy-proof your home because, soon enough, your puppy will mature and learn better manners, but for now, life is one big, exciting playground, and he can hurt himself in an instant.

Thanks to some peanut butter, Tucker lets anyone clip his nails!

- Make sure no, make double sure—that you proof the homes and the yards he'll visit.

Chapter 3

Doglish 101

Imagine being flown to Romania to live with a family. Everyone is friendly and welcoming as they show you around, explaining their activities and customs. You want to understand each other, you want to feel connected, but you don't. Why? Because you don't speak the same language. How would you feel if they started getting angry at you for not responding appropriately?

Now imagine the same situation with a translator. You'd feel a lot better with everyone.

Well, your puppy's in the same pickle—she doesn't understand English. Fortunately, I can help translate your thoughts and can teach you to speak to your puppy in her language: Doglish. Without this mutual communication, learning is difficult, cooperation is often misunderstood, and despair can set in quickly. Yell at your puppy, and she'll think you're barking. Your fast flailing motions are seen as confrontational play. Hitting is seen as an aggressive display that causes your pup to get depressed or to retaliate. On the flip side, if you take the time to learn and understand Doglish, the picture will get a lot rosier!

Now imagine your puppy's energy and behavior on a scale from 1 to 10: 1 is sleep; 10 is wildly out of control. Let's set level 8 as the dividing line between polite and uncivil interactions.

All puppies are capable of this range, and the goal is to keep your daily interactions between 1 and 8 and to teach your puppy how to contain or displace her 8- to 10-zone impulses. Don't worry—it's easier than it sounds. Keep reading for your crash course in Doglish!

AHEM!—GETTING YOUR ATTENTION

Your attention—positive or negative—influences your puppy's behavior above all else. And if you really come to understand this concept, you'll be way ahead of the pack. Your puppy craves your attention—she savors and emotionally longs for it when you're busy or out. And she can't distinguish the attention as negative or positive.

Think of the feeling of interacting with you as, metaphorically, a plug and a socket. When the plug and the socket are one, everything works. There is a solid feeling of connectedness. When the two are separated, there's a disconnect. To your puppy, interacting with you gives her developing ego a sense of security. Getting your attention, negative or positive, becomes her early life's focus.

Your puppy will repeat behaviors based on their attention-getting potential. Remember, she won't care if the attention is negative or positive. If jumping, stealing stuffed toys, barking, or nipping gets a rise out of you, your puppy will repeat these behaviors over and over. If sitting still, chewing a bone, giving sweet kisses, or retrieving toys are the ticket, you'll be guaranteed a repeat performance.

You give your puppy attention in three ways—through eye contact, body language, and your tone of voice. The following sections give you some pointers on how to use these attention givers in a positive way for your puppy.

Eye Contact

Remember that whatever you focus on, you reinforce. Just looking at your puppy is giving her attention. The goal is to look at your puppy when she's in the 1- to 8-zone and not when she's in the 8- to 10-zone. Now I can hear some of you exclaiming, "Are you saying that I'm supposed to ignore her wild side?" Not necessarily. Throughout the book, I'll walk you through the handling of every situation. However, when you are dealing with the 8- to 10-zone behaviors, please don't glare at your puppy! Eye contact, even a glimpse, is attention. Instead, look at your puppy—a lot—when she's being good.

Body Language

Think of a time when you were playing on a team. Did you want a captain who slumped, shuffled his feet, or looked unsure? Probably not. How would you have wanted him to interact with you if you got confused or scared or felt out of control—frantic and angry or calm and empathetic?

Remember that example when dealing with your puppy. The calmer you are, the more confident you appear. Your puppy needs a role model. So, if your puppy is losing her composure, stay calm and remain upright. If her behavior heads south, don't pack your bags and go with her. Negative actions, such as flailing arms, bent postures, and shoving, signal escalating chaos and confrontational play to your puppy. Set an example of composure and confidence. Send her to a quiet area, or call her to your side.

Who's Your Team Captain?

Have you heard of the pack theory? Alpha role, etc. . . .? It was the theory I was taught, yet it was hard for me to relate to, having never been in a pack. I came up with the *team metaphor* instead. There are a few givens that apply to team play:

1. You need a captain, someone to organize the space and the activities of everyone on the team. (Hint: You can have co-captains as long as they agree!)

2. You need structure within the team: a hierarchy, where seniority is a factor.

3. New players will automatically look to others to fit in and for direction. If no one communicates with them, their behavior will likely be unpredictable and confused.

Think of yourself as your puppy's captain. If you have many people in your home, develop a hierarchy so that your puppy learns from and can trust everyone to be consistent.

Be a team captain you'd respect.

Jodi Swem

Tone

Your puppy recognizes three tones:

- **Directional:** Right now, out loud, say, "Pass the ketchup," as if you were gathered at a table. Next, say, "Out the door and to the left," as if you were giving someone directions. Now, in the very same tone, say, SIT, BONE, MAT, NOPE . . . you get the idea. When you're teaching your puppy to follow your direction, use this tone: clear and confident—directional.

- **Praise:** There are no rules here. Find your natural praise tone. Some puppies aren't able to contain their enthusiasm: they lose focus and become hyperactive. If this sounds like your puppy, tone it down a bit.

- **Shame:** Puppies don't like being shamed any more than children do. Used sparingly and timed well, your disappointment will have a tremendous impact.

FIRST WORDS

Once again, let's think of you, your family if you have one, and your puppy as playing on the same team. You're the captain—you organize her space and activities. If there are other players (who have seniority), they should help your puppy along, too. Your puppy will feel most relaxed in a home where everyone follows the same program down to the words and the routines she'll need to know.

Whether you're starting this book with an 8-week-old or an 11-month-old puppy, your first words should mirror her basic needs. Like a human baby, your puppy has five basic needs: to eat, drink, sleep, go to the bathroom, and exercise.

When a human baby is confused by one of these needs, he or she cries. A caregiver then determines what to do. No one would yell at a baby who cries from hunger or exhaustion.

A puppy, just like a baby, feels restless when her body is having a need sensation. Instead of crying, however, puppies get very nippy, oral, and/or fidgety. The goal of this behavior is exactly the same as a baby's cries: to release tension and get help. The opportunity for bonding with your puppy, just as with your baby, is tremendous: whoever helps is revered.

 Regular Routines

Help your puppy feel totally plugged in! Assign a word to each routine you repeat on a daily basis, such as INSIDE, CAR, and UPSTAIRS. You'll see her enthusiasm sparkle. It's like being a foreigner in a distant land and hearing one word you recognize. To foster family bonding, identify each family member by name: "Where's Lindsay?" "Let's go find Daddy!"

And the long-term goal is also the same: babies learn to use words to communicate, and puppies use the words you speak to them to learn to instigate routines, such as going to the door or fetching a toy. But in the beginning, needs are really confusing, and the time you spend helping your puppy organize herself will win you big dog bones in the end.

Remember, nipping is often misconstrued as "naughty" when it's actually a very normal way of communicating confusion about her needs. To help your puppy learn a more civilized way to communicate her needs, make a Needs Chart (see the example on this page) and show it to everyone so that all of you work together as a team—using the same words and routines—when interacting with your puppy. This consistency and repetition encourage cooperation and understanding.

When making your needs chart, label each need in the first column, using, for example, HUNGRY for eating, OUTSIDE/PAPERS and GET BUSY for housetraining, and BONE or TOY for play. Choose any word; just be consistent. Overemphasize your words, and encourage everyone to do the same.

In the next column, assign a specific routine, such as a place for the food bowl and a required SIT before meals, one door to one spot for housetraining, and similar bones for chewing and toys for play.

NEEDS CHART

Need	Word	Routine
Eating	HUNGRY	Schedule feeding times. Place the bowl in the same spot, and encourage SIT before feeding.
Drinking	WATER	Keep the bowl in the same spot. Encourage SIT.
Bathroom	OUTSIDE/PAPERS and GET BUSY	Follow the same route, to the same spot. Use a bell to encourage a signal. Restrict attention until the pup eliminates.
Rest	ON YOUR MAT or TIME FOR BED	Designate an area in each shared room. Provide a mat and toys; secure a leash if necessary.
Play	BONE, BALL, or TOY and GO PLAY!	Establish a play area inside and out; make sure all four paws are on the floor before you toss a toy or give a bone.

THE CIVILIZED PUPPY

A lot of time, thoughtfulness, and structuring goes into civilizing a puppy. Just think how many years it takes to civilize a human child. This may disappoint some of you, but civilizing does require effort. Metaphorically, civilizing a puppy

The Infamous Tether

It's a sad and all too familiar sight: a dog tied out in the yard on a tether. Isolated and alone, this dog is often driven to barking or aggression out of sheer anxiety, fear, or frustration. When these behaviors are successful at driving passers-by away (from the dog's viewpoint), the ego boost is intoxicating.

is a lot like teaching children to look both ways before they cross a street. When babies are young and learning to walk, you must watch them near the road, but eventually those children will learn to check before crossing. The same goes for your puppy. Initially, she'll need constant monitoring. Inevitably, she will mature and encode all the civilized skills you've been teaching her. Having a beloved dog live into her teens isn't such a bad thing after all.

Where you live affects your daily plan to a great extent. Here are some thoughts on three living locales:

- **Country dogs:** Dogs in the country have a lot less to think about—free space abounds, and people are more relaxed about property lines. The direction HEEL isn't a top priority. Left completely untrained, however, the country puppy often feels displaced and can become destructive and annoying. After all, a puppy is still a puppy is still a puppy—structure and direction give her a sense of belonging. Teaching the basic skills that are explained in the following chapters helps the country dog know that her world is protected and that staying close to home is the safest place to be.

- **Suburban Dogs:** The best thing that happened for the suburban dog was the leash law. Of course, one needs to know how to use a leash to make a positive transition. If the leash were to slip from your hand or your puppy were to escape, disaster could occur within minutes. Let's not let this happen. In the following chapters, you'll learn leash skills and see the lesson applied everywhere.

 **Curbing**

Teaching your puppy to eliminate at the curb requires consistency and repetition. That's it. If you've started with a pad or papers, bring a soiled pad outside. Each time you bring your puppy out, direct her, using the command CURB. Then stand calmly until she eliminates. If she's confused, offer some water and/or hold or isolate her for several minutes. Try again. If all else fails, try the matchstick trick described in chapter 6. Reward any cooperation with your attention, play, and a walk. Say TO THE CURB as you escort your puppy out each time she needs to eliminate.

- **City dogs:** Some people think it's cruel to keep a dog in the city. I don't. Some of my most responsible dog owners live in Manhattan and the other boroughs. Devoted to their responsibility, they make up in effort what they lack in space. They get up early, join play groups, send their puppies to doggie daycare, and hire dog walkers to come in when they can't be home. And to top that off, city streets are very stimulating! Wonderful smells and lots of socialization, which also means tons of attention. It's really not a bad life, no matter what your size!

  Of course, there are special considerations to be had in the city, too. First and foremost, you'll want to socialize the buttons off your puppy to ensure that she grows up dog- and people-friendly, regardless of her breed's inclinations. The directions WAIT and HEEL to navigate the streets, elevators, and alleyways, and UNDER and CORNER take top priority. And then there are the joys of curbing!

Chapter 4

Puppy Parenting Styles

I recently became a mother—of a human child. Many moments have marked this the year of wonder, but as my husband and I scanned all the parenting books on the shelf, I was constantly amazed at how many opinions exist on everything from sleeping patterns to feeding, bathing, and socializing. We could have spent months trying to decide which of these approaches work best, and it did take us months to develop confidence with our own approach.

Raising a puppy is a very similar experience. In this chapter, I'll expose you to various philosophies and help you establish routines that make sense and feel comfortable.

WHAT FEELS RIGHT

There isn't one right way to parent your puppy. Like clouds and paw prints, everybody's experience will be unique. You'll have days when you feel exalted and others when you feel like throwing in the towel. There will be times you question everything you're doing and others when you'll want to write your own book. Such is life. To give you a little forward direction, I'll describe the following three approaches to raising your puppy and explain just how each one affects his developing mind:

- Attachment puppy parenting
- A more separate approach
- Outdoor living

Attachment Puppy Parenting

The central tenet of Attachment Puppy Parenting is that your puppy stays with you nearly all the time and you teach as you go. Although crating or isolation is used sparingly, it's still advisable to confine your puppy when you're busy or out. At night, your puppy is crated or stationed in your bedroom. During the day, the

🐾 Crates: My Opinion

Crates aren't horrible dungeons if they are used in moderation (three hours for 8- to 12-week puppies, four hours for 12- to 18-week-olds, and six hours for older pups/dogs). In fact, most puppies are so in love with their crates that they'll go there undirected. Think of a crate as being like a mini-room. You like having your own room, don't you? And when you go to bed, you like to snuggle up in bed, right? Well, a blanket in a crate is like a bed in a room. Closing the door of the crate when you leave isn't cruel, either; it simply teaches your puppy to rest when you're not around. A valuable lesson—the sooner it's learned, the better!

crate is positioned in a communal room such as the kitchen or the family room. As soon as your puppy is leash-trained, he should be led or stationed.

Emotionally, this approach gives your puppy a strong sense of security within the group. Sharing nighttime creates calmness throughout the day. Puppies who are attachment parented tend to mature and learn faster, as they're directed all day long. If you ascribe to this approach, be mindful not to overbond with your puppy. Yes, bringing him into bed with you is reassuring and calming in the short term, but long term you'll pay the price: equality in young puppies may not lend itself to cooperative behavior. Level training (where you sit/sleep a level higher) begets respect. One other caution! Teach your puppy early on to tolerate short separations. If your puppy fusses, ignore him (provided you're sure of his safety). Go to him when he's calm or busying himself with his toys. For more on this issue, refer to "Separation Anxiety" in chapter 6.

A More Separate Approach

If you're going with a more separate approach, choose a select time for leash training, ideally guiding him through the house for twenty minutes while you tidy up. Use your foundation words, covered on page 214, to give your puppy a full sense of inclusion.

Next, decide what areas you will share with your puppy. Some of my clients limit their puppy to the kitchen and the family room. If you're still concerned that your puppy will misbehave, bring him into the areas on a leash (lead/station him if he's 12 weeks old), and give your puppy some chews to entertain himself. By eliminating the option to misbehave, you're conditioning a more contained experience. Housebreaking, chewing, and general mania are prevented.

Consider the sleeping arrangements. Puppies love company, so he'd opt for a spot next to your bed. If this isn't an option, he'll adapt. Just be sure to select an area most conducive to sleep: a darkened, quiet room with classical music playing to drown outside noise. Puppies, like babies, sleep best when stimulation is low.

Entertained in Your Absence

It may take a week or two for your puppy to adjust to periods of isolation, but he will learn how to entertain himself in your absence. Here are my suggestions:

1. Pick a quiet area for your puppy to stay in when you're busy or out. Select a small, gated room or use a puppy playpen to fold out on the floor. (If your puppy scales the gates, erect two: one on top of the other.) You can use a crate for up to four hours.
2. Program a classical music station to play within earshot.
3. Proof the area from cords, chemicals, and crevices. Paws can get stuck easily.
4. Decorate the area with bowls, toys, beds, and pads for housetraining if your puppy is not capable of holding his bladder. Leave satisfying chews to help him displace his anxiety.
5. Run through your Needs Chart (page 47) before leaving him alone, to ensure that all his needs have been met.

Outdoor Living

A loving family, two square meals a day, and satisfying attention counts for a lot in this world. Many humans would be happy with as much. If you're someone who either can't or doesn't want to welcome your puppy into your living space, stay mindful of your puppy's needs by following these tips:

- Young puppies get nervous being alone, especially at night. If left to their own devices, the results can vary from chronic barking to overt fearfulness that extends throughout the day, to mania. So, give your puppy an enclosure or a crate in either the garage or the basement that is decorated with a snug bed and toys. Music soothes isolation; classical music is best.

- If you have a large yard, you'd probably appreciate a specific bathroom area. Outdoor freedom holds no guarantees, but it's worth a shot. Each time you're getting your puppy from his confinement or think he might need to go, say GO POTTY and run him to your choice location. As he goes, say GET BUSY. If he stops to make when you're outside playing, say GO POTTY and run to his area . . . GET BUSY. Keep your fingers crossed.

- When reuniting with your puppy, ignore hyperactivity. It is the result of isolation anxiety, and attention guarantees a repeat performance with you and anyone else who approaches. Wait until your puppy is calm to reconnect.

- Provide lots of stimulating toys and games. Bones, toys, and ropes tied to a pole or a tree for tugging, as well as plastic bottles or large balls hung from a tree branch, will provide entertainment when you can't be there.

- Water, water, water. Freshen it daily and make it available at all times. Food should be left out for fifteen minutes and then removed. Left out longer, it may attract other animals or bacteria. Yuck!

- Lessons are so important. Constant direction helps him feel connected to you when he's alone.

SWEET DREAMS

Nighttime is still quality learning time. Decide where you want your puppy to sleep, and create an environment that is conducive to a solid rest.

Rooming In

Sleeping near you at night (crated or stationed), your puppy will look to you when he feels restless or unsafe. It's eight hours of bonus learning time that passively says you're the leader and the protector. The mere act of looking up to you is a lesson in itself. The biggest attraction here, however, is that your puppy will sleep thirty minutes to two hours longer, waking up in a restful state. It's not that your puppy can't acclimate to sleeping alone; he's simply programmed to sleep in a pack.

Solitary Sleepers

Solo sleepers develop more independent attitudes or (the reverse) are needy and demanding. It's nothing personal. Eight to ten hours of isolation and darkness

Jodi Buren

A bedside sleeping station is best.

don't bode well for a dog who is a social groupie by nature. If circumstance demands, however, create a cozy nook, dimly lit, and leave classical music playing.

Two Heads on One Pillow

Although you can (as I do) sleep or rest with an older puppy (8 or more months), I don't recommend that you start earlier than that. Here's why: co-sleeping conveys equality. For your puppy to feel safe and secure within himself, he needs you to assume the leadership role. One of the more passive ways you have of doing that is to level train: sit and sleep a level above him.

MYSTICAL TRINKETS AND TEACHING TECHNIQUES

Whether your aspiration is ribbons and prizes or simply to get your puppy to stop jumping up, here are a few modern methods that inspire learning. Although they're optional, they put a fun spin on the process and are more effective than many old-school techniques.

Clicker-Happy Learning

The clicker, a toylike, handheld gizmo, is an innovative and effective way to teach puppies. It makes a sharp, distinctive sound when pressed.

Think of a camera. You know the sound. You're trained, in fact, to smile when you hear it. The clicker also creates a quick alerting response, and when used to target cooperative moments, it will help your puppy develop behavior memory.

So, how does it work? Well, at first you make an association between the sound and getting a reward. One click, one treat. After ten to twenty click-treat repetitions, your puppy will alert to the sound and will expect his treat. Don't fail: for every click, you must offer a treat.

Once the association is made, use the clicker to reinforce cooperative behaviors, like going to the bathroom in the right place or sitting for attention. Click to reinforce the moment, and then treat—one click, one treat. There are some who insist that you should have a clicker with you 100 percent of the time. Hats off to them. Personally, I can't find my dog's leash half the time, but if you're that organized, by all means keep it with you. Otherwise, you can follow my example. I

Was That a Grumble?

If your puppy growls at you when interrupted on the bed or on the couch, you're interrupting his space. To reclaim your home, call a professional. This is serious stuff. Meanwhile, attach a *drag lead* to your puppy's collar, using it to pull your puppy off the couch when he jumps up. Refer to "Tough Puppy" and "Aggression 101" in chapter 6.

🐾 Other Sound Markers

The clicker is a distinct sound that alerts your puppy's attention. If your puppy is afraid of the sound or you'd like a more homespun version, try clicking with your mouth or simply use a sharp word like YES or GOOD!

chose specific behaviors that I wanted to reinforce, like housetraining, chewing, or a direction like DOWN. I kept many clickers in treat cups around the house. As often as possible, I used the click-treat combo to reinforce good behavior or Whoopsie's response to direction. Then, once I was convinced that she understood, I continued to use it for a week or so before phasing off. Phasing off involves unscheduled reinforcement: I started clicking every other time, every third time, and so on. Click or not, I always applauded Whoopsie's cooperation!

Here are five skills that can be reinforced with the clicker:

- *Sit*: Hold a toy or a treat over your puppy's head. The instant he sits down, click and treat. Keep offering him the reward until he sits automatically.

- *Come*: Initially, teach this word to reinforce your togetherness. Click and say, COME, whenever your puppy chooses to be near you.

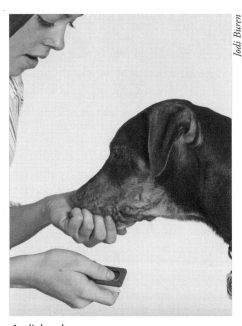

Jodi Buren

- *Housetraining*: Click and reward as your puppy finishes going to the bathroom in the right place.

- *Chewing*: Any time your puppy is chewing on an appropriate object, click, treat, and praise warmly.

- *Jumping*: *Close shop* when your puppy jumps. Fold your arms over your face, and ignore him until he's calm. Click and treat!

A clicker-happy puppy.

Targeting

Here's another fun technique that's rising in popularity. There are two ways to target—with a target *touch stick* or a targeting *step disc*. If you're planning to venture forth into agility or competition obedience, it's invaluable. If having a cooperative family member is your goal, it's a fun way for the puppy to make sense of many of your directions.

TARGET TOUCH STICK

Training your puppy to the touch stick is similar to point training. You can get a professional touch stick or can use something more homespun like a pen, a pointer, or a tent pole. Your extended point can be used to direct your puppy to his bed and is a real asset in more advanced adventures like agility and pet therapy. I use the touch stick to socialize insecure puppies and to direct the more assertive ones. (Follow the point-training steps described in this chapter.)

STEP DISC

This involves getting your puppy to step on (target) a flat disc. Once your puppy grasps the concept, the disc can be placed to help him understand a particular direction, including ON YOUR MAT, GO OUT, and OUT OF THE KITCHEN.

The disc can be bought or can be made from a coffee can lid, a book of matches, an index card, or a paper plate. We'll use a coffee can lid for our example. Gather some favorite goodies, and practice before a meal! Here's the progression:

1. Place the lid on the ground, and wait for your puppy to sniff it or step on it.

2. Mark the moment your puppy touches the lid, using a sound marker (YES or click), and instantly give him a snack. Continue with as many repetitions as your puppy will repeat enthusiastically. End on a high note.

3. As he catches on to your game, gradually move the lid away from you. Continue to work with food, rewarding each successful contact.

4. When you're sure that your puppy understands this direction, put a word to the behavior. I say, TARGET. For two weeks, say it the moment your puppy steps on the lid. Then try to prompt him to go to disc by saying, TARGET.

Want to get really fancy? Start linking your directions and pairing your trinkets. Your clicker can be used to encourage focused targeting, and as your dog learns other words like DOWN, and even some tricks, you can mix them into this exercise. Tell your dog TARGET—WAIT, TARGET—DOWN, and TARGET—ROLL OVER. Soon you'll be able to direct your puppy from across the room.

You may also use your target to help your dog with his lessons. For example, in chapter 7 you'll learn how to send your dog to a predesignated area when you're eating or watching a movie. Targeting can speed up the process. And don't forget that your target can travel. It can be used to ease stressful situations, like visiting the veterinarian, and can be used for other advanced activities, like agility and pet therapy.

For more advice on training your puppy to targets, please refer to my website or other resources listed on the reference page.

Point Training

Here we will teach your puppy to follow the point of your finger and will teach you to use it to direct him during lessons, around your home, or out and about. By giving visual cues, you're teaching your puppy to be focused and to watch you for direction. Your index finger can make all the difference between your puppy feeling confused and undirected to suddenly feeling like he's part of your team.

The end goal is to be able to direct your puppy with a point of your index finger, without using a food incentive. The first two steps however, involve treating, so have plenty on hand. A small, soft snack is best. Start with a sharp vertical point, curling your other fingers back for clarity.

1. **Treat immediately.** Hold the treat in your hand, and extend your index finger in a point, no more than six inches from your puppy's nose. When he hits your finger with his nose, mark the moment (YES or click) and give him the treat. Continue to practice this, pointing within close range until you see that your puppy is catching on. Begin slowly to move your hand farther distances away. Eventually, left, right, up, down, behind, or in front, he should follow that finger everywhere! And when he hits the point, treat him immediately.

2. **Delay treating.** Place your goodies in a snack pack, in a pocket, or on a counter top. Point at close range. When your puppy goes to your finger, say YES or click. Bring the treat from its location. You're still treating for every accomplishment, but now the treating is delayed. Vary the points as described in step 1.

3. **Phase off treating.** Gradually, phase off treating your dog for every successful point. Always mark the moment with an enthusiastic "YES! Good pup!"

Point training is a must.

4. **Vary the reinforcement.** As your puppy "gets the point," vary the reinforcement to pique his continued interest! Have him touch two points before you click or treat. Move your hand slightly to encourage him to follow.

Now you can point your dog into his bed, up the stairs, to your side, or off the couch. The directions you can give are unlimited—be creative!

OUTSIDE HELP

Having a puppy and a baby at the same time was a challenge. It was well worth it, but it took some finagling. Somehow we all survived, and I attribute this in large part to the help I received from friends and other dog-care professionals. If you're feeling overwhelmed day to day or need someone to watch your dog when you travel, consider these options. Just be sure, no matter which option you choose, that you also write out an emergency sheet with all pertinent information. See the sample Puppy Information Sheet on this page. We filled in our information, laminated the page, and posted our filled-in copy by the phone. Feel free to copy it!

PUPPY INFORMATION SHEET

Dog's Name:

Address:

Phone Number:

Breed:

Current Age:

Weight:

Immunizations:

Medical Problems:

Unusual Fears:

Allergies:

Sheet last updated:

Contact	Phone	Name/Address
Mom's Cell:		
Dad's Cell:		
Mom's Work:		
Dad's Work:		
Neighbor:		
Animal Hospital:		
Emergency Animal Hospital:		
Fire Department:		
Poison Control Center:		
Police Department:		
Electric Company:		
Gas Company:		

Dog Walker/Pet Sitter

If your life is spinning out of control for whatever reason—you're overworked, overtired, sick, pregnant, whatever—hire a dog walker or ask a friend to pitch in so that your puppy's needs don't quadruple your stress. Although you may have to pay a fee, it will be small compared to the damage a restless puppy can wreak or a potential accident that you might have because you're so frazzled. Here's a quick checklist for your potential candidate:

- There is now an association of pet sitters (please refer to my website www.dogperfect.com for a cross link). Although I wouldn't rule out an excellent referral, do ask for references and/or membership in dog-related associations. And check the references! This is your precious puppy; make sure he's left in good hands.

- Talk to potential pet sitters about your puppy-raising philosophies. Share the words he knows, his schedule, and his habits. Do they take interest? That's a good sign.

- Ask them to come by and meet your puppy. Do they connect? This criterion was at the top of my list!

- Have your sitter leave a daily note detailing his or her arrival and what happened. I used to ask Sally whether Whoopsie pooped. This was somewhat graphic, but telling all the same. I also asked her to let me know when she got to the house and how long she stayed.

Doggie Daycare

A well-run doggie daycare is a real asset. If this is an option, check out how the facility is run. How do they take reservations? Do you sign up per day or for certain set days? Where are the dogs kept when they're together or separated? Is play supervised? How is the staff trained to handle fights that may break out? How do they determine which dogs will play together? Do they offer auxiliary services such as grooming, pick-up/drop-off, or overnight kenneling? How do they handle medical emergencies?

The concept of doggie daycare seems flawless, but there are drawbacks and other issues to consider. After attending doggie daycare, some dogs become assertive at home, more physical, less focused on their lessons, and doubly revved up on their off days. Other clients complain that their puppies come home exhausted and just want to sleep. In the end, you must determine what's right for you and your puppy.

Kennel

There is a "no worry" factor when kenneling your puppy, which is awfully attractive. After all, not much can happen in lockdown. When my Whoopsie was 5 months old, I had to leave her for a week around the holidays. Though there were many volunteers, at that time I wouldn't have left her with my worst enemy. She had just discovered the countertops and was shredding everything she could get her mouth around. Not a bad puppy—quite normal, in fact—she just needed lots of supervision to prevent incidents and injury. We kenneled her, and she made lots of friends. She ended up sleeping all the way home and was rather bored the first few days after getting back. If your puppy has had his inoculations, he may be left at a kennel. Here's a list of particulars to go over when making your reservation:

> ### When Housetraining Goes Awry
>
> After a stint at the kennel, it's common for a puppy to have an accident or two. Don't freak out. Go back to square one for three to five days, using your crate and stations and supervising the pup's house freedom diligently. At this point, don't correct your puppy; he needs a few days to realign himself. For reminder tips, refer to "House-breaking 101" in chapter 6.

- Drop off and pick up arrangements? (Some kennels have escorts.)
- Cancellation policy?
- What cleaning products are used? Your puppy will be stepping on these and may lick his paws: avoid heavy toxins.
- Feeding schedules? Will they dispense your puppy's food (and are there additional charges)?
- If there's medication to administer, go over this ahead of time. Usually, there is an additional fee.
- How do they handle medical emergencies?
- Free playtime. Many kennels offer play periods where they will take your puppy out and interact with him. There is generally a charge.
- Can you bring your puppy's toys or mat? Label all objects with your name ahead of time.

Limit the drama at the door. Treat it like a fun experience, and your puppy will trail off with his tail wagging!

Chapter 5

Fun, Structure, and Communication for All

Who's being trained? The answer to that question, if you hadn't already guessed, is . . . drum roll, please . . . you! You are being trained to structure and interact with your puppy so that she understands what you'd like her to do. And while you're learning to control yourself and your reactions, your puppy is learning how to operate in your world.

From your puppy's perspective, it's all pretty new. Her habits are shaped by your example and your interaction, and she will repeat whatever you pay attention to. If you shout "No!" at every infraction and react to every transgression, the constant stress will guarantee a frazzled pup, addicted to reactionary behavior. If you can, however, contain your impulses and train yourself and those around you to use better communication skills, you'll have a well-mannered puppy in no time.

> *In any relationship, it only takes one person to change*
> *for the whole dynamic to shift. Let it be you.*

The effect of your behavior and your reactions on your puppy's self-esteem and developing ego are powerful. In the next sections, we'll explore how one simple change in your behavior can influence the way your puppy responds, and how your reactions should vary according to the age-appropriate discipline for your dog. And to ensure that you don't spend all your time just correcting your puppy, you'll find plenty of games you can play—tricks, too—specified for different breed categories. Have fun!

Jodi Buren

Who is the teacher—can you tell?

> ### 🐾 What's Really Important
>
> The most important thing in your relationship with your puppy is the relationship itself. It's not your shoes, carpet, bagel, napkin, or anything else your puppy may have destroyed. Those things can be replaced or, even better, be put out of reach to avoid confrontation altogether. Your relationship with your puppy will grow for more than a decade, infiltrating many aspects of your home life. It should be one of your highest priorities.

A LOOK AT YOURSELF

Put yourself under the microscope. Take a truthful look at just who sits behind your steering wheel. Are you passive? Controlling? Assertive? Serious? Playful? Involve the family. Know your shortcomings as well as your strengths. Here are some situational questions to get you started:

When you see something spilled on the floor, you
a)	Clean it up right away.	4
b)	Clean it up as soon as is practical.	3
c)	Delay indefinitely, hoping someone else will clean it up.	2
d)	Blame it on someone else, and wait for them to clean it up.	1

If you drop a cookie on the floor, you
a)	Throw it out.	4
b)	Brush it off and then eat it.	3
c)	Pick it up and continue munching.	2
d)	Leave it on the floor.	1

If your puppy runs away, you
a)	Get furious and discipline her when reunited.	4
b)	Call the police and enlist the help of neighbors, family, and friends.	3
c)	Walk the neighborhood calling to your puppy.	2
d)	Go inside and wait for her to come home.	1

If a 6-month-old child pulls your hair, you
a)	You'd never hold a 6-month-old child.	4
b)	Yell out in pain.	3
c)	Pry your hair loose calmly.	2
d)	Wait until the child releases your hair.	1

If you lend a tool to a friend and they don't bring it back, you

   a) Get frustrated, call them immediately, and insist they return it now.   4

   b) Go over to their house to pick it up.   3

   c) Call and ask them to bring it back when it's convenient, if they're finished using it.   2

   d) Wait until the next time you see them to bring it up.   1

If a friend is late to meet you, you

   a) Fuss and fume.   4

   b) Call their cell phone.   3

   c) Converse with people around you or read a book.   2

   d) Worry.   1

Your answers are very telling: none are wrong or inappropriate. What they reveal will help you enormously in your effort to understand how you and your puppy are likely to relate. Here's a quick synopsis:

20–24: You're the intense lot; not that there is anything wrong with that! Your drive is what makes you unique. You're a leader with a win-win mentality. Your self-respect shows. On the flip side, you may need to develop patience and empathy—necessary ingredients for raising a well-adjusted puppy.

15–19: You're fond of being in control, and you frustrate easily if things do not go your way. Organized and bright, you're quick to summarize a situation and voice a plan that suits most everyone. Empathy and patience are not beyond your reach, although you'd rather not have to exercise them. Raising a puppy is exhilarating until things don't go according to the plan. Learning to roll with life's follies is your challenge.

10–14: You're easygoing yet like to be actively involved in what's happening around you. Nurturing and patience come naturally. You have an affinity for your puppy's needs, and, as a result, she feels safe with you. It is more difficult for you to be controlling when your puppy's active side emerges or to be strong when she's bossy.

🐾 Human Stress

Stress is a big component of our lives these days. As our stress levels rise, our patience fades. Too bad you can't explain that to your puppy. Ask for help or contain your puppy on days when you have a short fuse. A stress-relieving outburst can really damage the trust you've built with her. Remember, your puppy doesn't have a clue.

6–9: Your relaxed attitude is both a charm and a frustration. Your comfortable nature reflects contentment. Control is not your game. For a puppy to feel safe, however, she needs someone to take charge. She needs you to organize her space and activities. Without that structure, a puppy feels lost and confused. Maturity may spell aggression as hierarchical impulses develop. Rise to the occasion, if only by faking your leadership qualities.

Now list three adjectives that would best describe your personality—better yet, ask someone close to you to list those adjectives. . . . Let's just say they may see things you don't. Are you demanding, sweet, forgiving, or intense? Compare notes with your puppy profile (the results from your puppy's personality quiz from chapter 1), and see how they mesh. If you're a sweet, gentle soul and your puppy is bossy, one of you will have to change. Since your puppy is like a child and you're the parent, there's little room for debate: you must grow and develop a new side to your personality. If you're passive, preferring solitary activities to outdoor excursions, and you've selected an athletic breed, you'll need to develop an exercise regime.

The ideal scenario is that your puppy would act like, oh, say, a 5-year-old dog. Here are some more ideals to put to rest:

- **Whatever it is, she'll grow out of it.** Maybe in four years, when she's thirty pounds overweight, but why wait?

- **She knows what I'm talking about!** Remember, she's a puppy, not a grown-up human being. Anyway, why would your puppy misbehave if she knew it bummed you out? Her body language spells fear and confusion, not remorse.

- **Physical reprimands are effective.** Physical reprimands communicate fear or play. The result? More stimulation at best, aggressive retaliation at worst.

- **Yelling is effective.** Although it might stop a behavior temporarily, yelling is barking. You're not only guaranteed a repeat performance, you're setting an example.

🐾 When Anger Boils

Everyone feels angry at their puppy sometimes. I do; I get frustrated when Whoopsie pulls to get to another dog or jumps on the counter. Try to channel your anger into an effective response rather than blowing your top. Your puppy is acting quite normally. Puppies do nip, chew, jump, bite their leashes, and piddle where they're not supposed to. These are frustrations every puppy owner shares. Learn how to transform your frustration into interactions that influence your puppy, not overwhelm her. Lessons on that are straight ahead.

CHOOSE YOUR BATTLES

Could your puppy be confusing NO with part of her name: "Rosy-NO, Daisy-NO, Tucker-NO"? It's used so commonly, I once shouted, "No!" at a dog park in NYC, and a pack of dogs came running—with their tails wagging!

Refrain from saying NO too often. Your puppy will perceive it as everyday chitchat. It will often invite more play, more resistance. The concept of "you are wrong" should be taught as an instructional warning and used sparingly to highlight its importance.

Choose your battles!

If your puppy is not retaining your corrections, she's not understanding them.

Your puppy is not going to suddenly wake up tomorrow thinking, "Oh! Now I get it! When they are all shouting NO, they want me to stop." It's not going to happen. If your puppy is not retaining your corrections, she's not understanding them. My recommendation? Ease off on your corrections, teach age-appropriate lessons, and target one problem behavior at a time. Pick your battles, and outline them one at a time.

AGE-APPROPRIATE DISCIPLINE

Before you get started on discipline, be sure you understand the following concepts:

Displacement activity: To redirect your puppy, choose activities that are aligned with your puppy's interest and breed-specific tendencies. Check out the sections "Game Gallery" on page 72, as well as "Breed and Personality Tricks and Games" on page 79, for some ideas.

Intensity: Intensity refers to
- the collar you choose to use,
- the level of your tug, and
- the ferocity of your frustration when you yell at inanimate objects such as garbage cans, stuffed toys, or paper products.

    Yes, you read that right: "when you yell at objects." As you'll learn in chapter 6, yelling at your puppy instills fear, not understanding. Yelling at objects instills respect for your authority and caution to not go near the objects corrected.

Young Puppies (7–18 weeks)

Life is unfolding. Imagine it . . . imagine never having seen a lamppost or a pillow or a table leg before. Imagine hearing a vacuum or a child laughing or a train whistle blowing for the first time. Bring yourself to your puppy's level, and think of it from her vantage point. Get down on all fours if you must.

Depending on your puppy's personality, her reaction to new experiences will vary. Some pups will look and ponder; others will stiffen and get ready to pounce; still others will run and hide. None of these are right, none are wrong. They are just signals to help you understand exactly who your puppy is.

The only corrections I condone at this age are warnings, ideally reinforced with a light tug of a *drag lead*: the puppy version of a leadership tap on the shoulder. Use a clear guttural sound like EP, EP to discourage forays into forbidden areas such as garbage, gardens, and tabletops or to head off impulsive behavior such as rowdy jumping, chewing, chasing, or nipping. For more detailed explanations, refer to chapter 6.

Developing Adolescence (4½–9 months)

The age of reason and bonding. By 4½ months, puppies are very aware. These puppies know you better than you know them. Their minds are free of stress, and they live to learn. They're as absorbent as sponges. You and your family are their first models, their template for all things human.

> *Your goal here is to learn your puppy's reactions*
> *as well as she's learned yours.*

Corrections need to be defined, and impulses need to be redirected. You need to be able to identify the gleam in her eye that warns of mischief, notice the look that says, "My bladder is full," or understand the frenzied look of an overstimulated pup.

To discourage your puppy properly, your interference must come as a warning, similar to shouting out as a child reaches for a hot stove. The stove is hot; the child is not bad. For your puppy to learn this, you must focus on timing and must respect your puppy's limited sense of reason. For example, if you shout after your puppy has eaten a muffin or even as she's swallowing it, your presence is an intrusion—all you're communicating is prize envy (that you value what she's got). To teach your puppy NO, you must catch her while thoughts of thievery, jumping, barking, nipping, and so on, are still forming in her head. Interfere *before* she's fulfilled her mission. (In chapter 6, I discuss ways to discourage specific issues.) Be aware that your puppy is processing everything and is mindfully in tune with your reactions. Boisterous threats will limit your authority. You'll be viewed as a playmate and nothing more.

Redirection is an essential element to teaching NO. It says, "Stop that and look to me for direction." The usual reaction is to dead-end with a NO—but then where does that leave your puppy? NO must be taught just as surely as any direction, such as SIT or COME. But your puppy's breed tendencies and personality affect the displacement activities (fun games, pastimes, and tricks that can be found at the end of this chapter) you choose and the intensity of your reactions.

Puberty (9–18 months)

The age of consciousness. I hope it lands in your favor! Your puppy has a dog's mind now but is still straddling her puppy impulses and hormonal surges. It's not a fun time for your puppy. She is mindfully aware of what behaviors affect her environment: what gets attention, praise, frustration, or fear from those around her. Puppies who bark protectively note reactions—even when the reactions are predetermined—such as when your postman moves on. Guarding breeds are cued into every body posture and they sense tension (fear as threatening). Terriers feel the surge of a potential catch, draft or sledding breeds pull, herding breeds choose a focus (children, bikes, cars, or squirrels), retrievers latch on to their instincts, and so on. At this age, we learned that our puppy Whoopsie's ball addiction was here to stay, although her digging and frenzied racing eventually subsided.

As your puppy's true genetic blueprint takes hold, you'll find yourself at a crossroads with one question on your puppy's mind: Will you lead our team, or shall I? Should I develop my own sense of awareness, or can I look to you to define what's right from wrong?

> *Your puppy wants to know:*
> *Do my impulses define me or do you define me?*

My effort at this stage is to help my clients, and you, to develop your puppy's consciousness, which is more about praising cooperation than about focusing on defiance/slow response. Anyone raising a pubescent dog will get the equivalent of a teenage eye roll from time to time, but it's your ability to stay calm and be directive that will gain the puppy's respect and influence her adult behavior.

Discipline at this age should be pitched as "wrong," not bad. As if you could say, "You silly pup, you know that's not what we do here!" Scream and yell and you'll only draw more attention to the bad behavior and draw yourself into a confrontational battle that's sure to frustrate you and drain you of energy. We'll go over just how to teach the direction NO as wrong in more detail in chapter 6, but for now, follow this routine:

- Remember, pubescent puppies still need a lot of direction. When they're restless, a DOWN-STAY will calm their nerves; when they're cavorting after the neighbor's cat, instead of yelling, direct them to WAIT or COME.

- Get in the habit of saying, YES, or GOOD PUPPY (using the clicker if that's your habit) more frequently than you say NO.

- Pitch your NO communication as though I'd just handed you a fork when you asked for a spoon. You wouldn't have to jab me to make your point, or even yell. When communicating to your puppy, enforce NO with a leash or a collar tug. Some of my clients tap their foot on the floor.

- Avoid the gigantic pitfall of repeating your directions. If your puppy doesn't respond, simply tug the leash, say, NO, and position her.

- Catch the thought process. Whenever you see your puppy *about* to do something errant, catch her, issue a quick, NO (attach a drag/hand lead to tug if you need a physical reminder), and just as quickly direct her to a spot or an activity, such as, "Go to your MAT," or "Get your BALL!"

MODIFY YOU, MODIFY PUPPY

Your puppy is learning constantly. Whether she is 10 weeks or 10 months old, the first year is all about developing lifelong interaction skills. Her chosen behaviors are based in large part on your interactions. Yes, you have that much influence—a fact that should be enlightening. Why? Because to change a behavior, only one of you will have to change your routine, and that one is you.

Take a minute, and split a sheet of paper into two columns. Head the first column "His/her frustrating behavior" and the second "My reaction," and list those behaviors and your reactions to them. Keep this list handy as I give you strategies in chapter 7 to help change these behaviors.

What motivates your puppy's behavior is the simple equation of cause and effect. Go over your list and consider whether, in your puppy's eyes, the effect of her behavior—your reaction—is reinforcing her behavior.

Here are some examples of how your typical reactions get misconstrued by your puppy:

- *Grab-n-Go:* When your puppy grabs a dinner napkin, everyone gets up from the table and runs in hot pursuit. Cause and effect? Grabbing a napkin makes everyone participate in a fun and friendly game of chase.

- **Pulling Away:** Your puppy nips, and you jerk your hand away and shout, "NO." Cause and effect? Nipping makes you do fun things like jump and bark.

- **Yelling:** Your puppy barks, and you yell at her to quiet down. Cause and effect? A self-activated bark-fest!

- **Shoving:** When your puppy jumps on you, your immediate reaction is to step back and push her away. Cause and effect? Jumping is worth repeating: it's a surefire reaction getter and leads to confrontation play. Double fun!

In addition, there are some puppies who are less concerned with attention than with the satisfaction of the prize. That prize may be edible or of obvious value.

Cause and Effect

If the effect of any given behavior is that it gets more attention, you know what? Your puppy is going to repeat it. Negative or positive doesn't factor in. The more riled the attention, the higher the play factor: confrontational play, that is!

How can your puppy tell that an object is of value? Well, she doesn't determine it monetarily. She judges the amount of time you spend with an object and how fiercely you guard it. Here are three examples:

- **Counters:** You spend your entire kitchen time focused on counters; food is prepared there and objects are placed on them.
- **The remote:** Now, here's a prized possession permeated with our scent. We look at it, hold it, fight over it. Your puppy takes note. What you love *must* be divine.
- **Stuffed animals:** The children are your puppy's most trusted confidants and competitors: littermates in human guise. Their stuffed animals are their special treasures. These toys have value, highlighted by the screeches that children emit when your puppy snatches one.

The best way to combat situations like snatching prized possessions when your back is turned, barking, jumping, and so on (just look at your list again!), is to stage setups. Stage no more than two a day to ensure that your attention is focused and the timing is spot on. (For details on setups for these situations and others, refer to chapter 7 and the Doglish Glossary.)

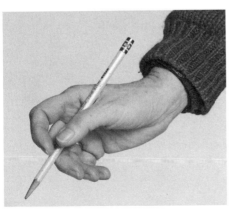

Jodi Buren

People hold it, puppy holds it, too.

> ### 🐾 Bells, Whistles, and Mirrors
>
> When staging your setups, pull all the magic tricks from your sleeves. I've used bells tied to socks, mirrors angled toward counters, and penny cans tied to garbage cans to blow a puppy's cover. If your puppy is smart enough to wait for you to leave, you must outsmart her!

THE GAME GALLERY
Positive Play Training

Many great lessons in life are learned through games. Play training is, in fact, my favorite way to teach nearly every skill, from the natural COME to all the basics from following to containment. With just a little bit of ingenuity, each direction can be shaped into an exciting game. It stimulates learning and is a great way to end each lesson. Your puppy's enthusiasm will rise, her attention will improve, and the instinct to be near you will solidify.

Does the idea of being silly with your puppy make you nervous? Have you tried only to find that it ends in rough confrontational play? We need to restructure your relationship slowly and ease into games specially chosen for your individual puppy's breed and temperament.

In the following sections, I've listed a bunch of fun games and tricks to try out with your puppy. Each one has a theme and uses familiar words or behaviors to jazz your puppy to all your interactions. I've separated them into three categories:

Civility and Manners: Manners don't have to be boring! Use this list to teach your puppy everything from how to say please to coming when you call.

Breed- and Personality-Specific: Sporting breeds love to retrieve, terriers love to dig, and Nordic breeds love to pull, although there are exceptions to the rule (and I urge you find them!). Use my guidelines to start with the activities best suited to your puppy's genes.

Temperament-Specific: These games specify the temperament they're best suited for. For example, *tug with me* is a perfect confidence builder for reserved and timid temperaments. I don't recommend it for temperaments that are confident by nature, as it can easily translate into hierarchical confusion.

Some of the games require prior word association, which I address in chapter 7. Read the games over, highlighting what you like, and come back to them as soon as you've got the basics down.

Down on the Floor

I know there are people who feel that getting down on the floor is a no-no, but I couldn't disagree more! That's taking the leadership thing too far—after all, leaders like to play and be affectionate, too. I love to snuggle my Whoopsie—and every other puppy I meet—at her level. First, however, I gauge her energy level. Go back and refer to my 1 to 10 zone on page 43. Get down and snuggle when your puppy is at an energy level of 3 or less. If she gets riled, it may not be the best time—get up and try again later.

CIVILITY AND MANNERS

Clicker Advance

Goal: Comfortable sharing and social skills
Props: A favorite bone or food dish, a treat cup, and a clicker if you're using one
Players: 1
How to Play: Approach your puppy when she's eating or chewing on a bone. Click or exclaim YES as you're nearing her, and treat immediately.

Elevator Up and Elevator Down

Goal: To teach your puppy to sit for toys and food, and to contain the impulse to jump and grab
Props: Food or a toy to lure
Players: 1 at a time
How to Play: Hold a lure above your puppy's head. If she jumps, raise the lure up above your head. Bring it above her head again. If she jumps up, bring it up; if she sits down, drop it quickly below her chin and say, YES, or click and reward.

Follow the Leader—Off-Leash

Goal: A fun way to encourage natural following skills
Props: A long line if you're practicing outside (a drag lead if you're indoors), a treat cup, and a clicker if you're using one.
Players: 1 at a time
How to Play: Shake your treat cup as you say, LET'S GO! Run twenty steps in one direction, stop suddenly for emphasis, (click) and reward.

Follow the Leader—On-Leash

Goal: That your puppy pay more attention to you than to her surroundings
Props: An appropriate teaching collar (chapter 2) and a leash
Players: 1
How to Play: Secure the leash around your waist or hold half the slack in your hands as you clip your thumbs to your waistband. Call out your puppy's name and walk forward. The moment she moves away, call to her as you pivot and rush in the opposite direction. Cheer her when she focuses on you! Click and/or treat, too, if you're super-coordinated. Keep changing direction when she focuses more on the environment than on you. Try not to get dizzy!

Grab-n-Show

Goal: To have your puppy show you everything she picks up
Props: A treat cup, a drag lead, and a clicker if you're using one
Players: 1
How to Play: When your puppy grabs something you consider inappropriate, don't yell. Find a treat cup, kneel down, and call to her in a positive tone: WHAT DID YOU FIND? If she's leery, attach a drag lead and step on it first. Shake the cup and exchange a treat for the object: THANK YOU FOR SHARING.

Hidden Treasure

Goal: Gentle treat taking
Props: Snacks and a stick of butter or peanut butter
Players: 1 or more
How to Play: Let your puppy watch as you fold a treat under your fingers. Spread some peanut butter over your knuckles and then extend your hand and say, KISSES. The moment your puppy licks, pop your hand open and say, YES! Soon you won't need the peanut butter at all.

Jodi Buren

What's inside?

The Anthropomorphic Myth

I've read it over and over: Do not anthropomorphize your puppy's feelings. *Anthropomorphize* is just a fancy way of saying attribute human emotions to your puppy's behavior. Well, I do, just a little. After all, there are certain parts of the brain that we share; we are animals, too. Besides, it helps me to imagine how I might feel if I were a puppy and whatever was happening to her were happening to me. Of course, puppies can't reason, so, for example, if a puppy is destructive when her people leave her alone, I would deal with that at face value. A puppy doesn't understand the concept of retaliation or revenge. We know, however, that she's a social groupie and that the isolation can make her anxious. For a puppy, a sweet, smell-like-you sock fits the bill.

Paw and High Five

Goal: To teach your puppy a positive greeting skill
Props: Treats if you like and a clicker if you're using one.
Players: 1 at a time
How to Play: Tell her to SIT. Extend one hand in front of your dog's paw. With your other hand, press her shoulder muscle gently until her paw releases. Catch it, saying, PAW, the moment her foot pads touch your hand. Highlight the moment with a YES/click and reward.
High Five: Once your puppy catches on to PAW, slowly rotate your hand 180 degrees. Say, PAW—HIGH FIVE, simultaneously. Your puppy will figure it out in no time!
Recommendation: Put off teaching this trick until your puppy is 8 months old, especially if she's paw-expressive. Otherwise, you'll wind up with a puppy who'll paw you for everything!

Puppy Push-Up

Goal: A fun way to reinforce SIT and DOWN
Props: Treats and a clicker if you're using one
Players: 1 to 2
How to Play: If you've got two people, assign one direction to each. One person can play easily. Hold the treat to your puppy's nose. Bring it up and over her ears, instructing, SIT. From here, bring the treat down to the floor directly in front of her toes. Instruct, DOWN, as she lowers her body. As she catches on, vary the reward: a treat for a full push-up only (SIT-DOWN-SIT) and then for two or three in a row!

Getting the Kids Involved

Kids need a good example to follow. A lot of children get overwhelmed by a puppy's energy, especially with nippy or jumpy puppies. Constant orders or threats don't endear them to one another, either. Have you heard yourself repeating phrases like . . .

- "Don't let her jump!"
- "Stop getting her so riled up!"
- "If you don't help, we're going to give her back."

You're making matters worse. Instead, map out five or six games that the kids can play with the puppy. Remind them of these activities when you're trying to redirect chaotic energy. Refer to the appendix for more techniques.

Run-Away-Come Game

Goal: To teach your puppy the natural come
Props: A long line, a treat cup, and a clicker if you're using one
Players: 1 to 2
How to Play: Put your puppy on her long line outside. Shake the treat cup as you race away, calling her name. Turn to face her and stop. As you're giving her the treat, say, COME. COME will mean closeness, not frustrated separation.

Say Please

Goal: SIT as a Say Please equivalent
Props: Anything your puppy wants, from food and toys to your attention
Players: NA
How to Play: Each time you'd remind a child to say please, instruct your puppy to SIT—for treats, for pats and greetings, to toss a toy, and so on.

Clicker Tag

Goal: To develop the natural come
Props: A snack pack, a clicker, and treats
Players: 1 or more
How to Play: Pack your snack pack or load your pocket with treats/a clicker. Go outside with your puppy. Each time she checks in with you, click or say, YES, and treat. Ignore her if she lingers, waiting at least a minute between each reinforcement. If your puppy show no interest in you, be clever. Think of ways you can get

her attention without having to beg for it. Squeak a toy, pretend to find something in the grass, tap some sticks together. Reinforce your togetherness the instant she comes near.

Treat Cup Name Game

Goal: To teach your puppy the name of everyone in your home
Props: Multiple treat cups
Players: 2 to 5
How to Play: Initially, equip everyone with a treat cup. Instruct your puppy to go to one of you by saying, MOMMY. When Mommy hears her name, she should shake the cup, and call out to the puppy. If the puppy races to anyone else, that person should *close shop*. Once Mom treats, she selects the next person to send the puppy to. *Special Rule:* Your puppy must follow the Four-Paw Rule at all times: all four paws on the floor!

Two Ball Toss

Goal: Retrieving skills, cooperative sharing, containment, and respect
Props: Two or more favorite toys
Players: 1 at a time
How to Play: Take out one toy, and bait your puppy with it. When she's excited, shake it above her head, say, SIT, and then toss it! Praise her enthusiasm. However, once she grabs it, bring out the second, identical object and start playing with that. Totally ignore what she's doing. Stay focused on your toy—you're encouraging her to see you as the one to watch. Play keep away to encourage her interest and respect. Instruct, SIT, and toss that one. Now pick up the first, and start from the top. This is a great one for kids, too!

 Positive or Negative Reinforcement?

I can hear some of you asking, "Won't treating my puppy when she grabs things teach her to grab everything?" Well, yes and no. When puppies are young, they grab everything anyway. And honestly, your puppy doesn't know one object from another. As she matures, you can use the techniques described in the chewing section of chapter 6 to teach your puppy appropriate chews, but there will still be times when you're not looking that she'll find something new. Wouldn't you rather have her *grab-n-show* than *grab-n-go*? It makes for a more comfortable cooperative relationship all around.

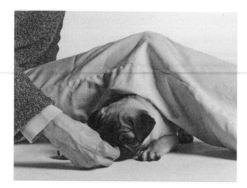 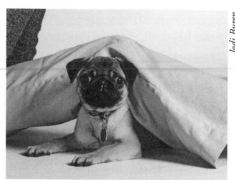

Practice the tunnel down under your leg or a chair.

Tunnel Down

Goal: To teach your puppy to lie under your feet or a chair or a table, not on top of them

Props: Treats or a toy

Players: 1 at a time

How to Play: Initially, make this lots of fun before using it in real-world situations. Practice around your home, luring your puppy under chairs and tables, as well as under your legs. Once your puppy gets it, use it whenever it's appropriate—when visiting, at the café, when you have company. When your puppy crawls under your legs she knows that you're the protector and she can just relax. If you're going to be a while, give her a displacement activity. Everything is safe.

Wiggle-Giggle-Freeze

Goal: To teach your puppy how to contain a sudden burst of excitement and how to calm down and take direction quickly

Props: Treats and/or a clicker if you're using one

Wiggle, giggle, FREEZE!

Players: The more the merrier

How to Play: Put on some cool tunes. You'll have two modes: the wiggle-giggle, a free-for-all where everybody bounces and zooms around and gets silly; and stop, when everyone freezes. At this point, the person closest to the puppy gives a chosen direction, like SIT or DOWN, and gives her a treat. Then you start over from the top!

Wipe Your Paws

Goal: To get your puppy to wipe her paws

Props: A large floor mat and some treats (a clicker is always optional)

Players: 1

How to Play: Practice this first when your puppy's in a calm mood. Bring her to the mat with food or a toy to lure her around. Lure your puppy to her tail very slowly. Praise partial turns initially, gradually asking for more and more of a circle. Then two circles, then four . . .

> ### 🐾 In Depth
>
> You can always get more involved in each activity. In the following sections, you'll find an overview of just some of the neat things you and your puppy can do together. To find out more on individual activities, log on to my website, www.dogperfect.com, or refer to the reference section at the back of the book.

Your eventual signal and direction will be to rotate your index finger above her nose as you say, WIPE YOUR FEET. For now, keep the lure level with her spine.

BREED AND PERSONALITY TRICKS AND GAMES

Once again, there are exceptions to every rule. Don't let my suggestions of breeds and personality types dissuade you! If you think your puppy will love a game, test it out. All personality types can engage in these. The outgoing ones are going to readily gravitate toward what they love to do. The more passive types should be encouraged to "perform," as it gives self-confidence.

Bait & Toss

Ideal for: Terriers (all), hounds, sporting, Nordic, and herding—all puppies who love to chase!

Impulse: To chase and catch

Age: Any

How to: Take an empty juice bottle, a milk jug, or a heavy plastic toy. Slather a creamy substance (peanut butter, cream cheese, or yogurt) on the inside of the container. Tie it onto a long string, ten to twenty feet, and fling it around. Sweep it low to the ground in a circle, toss it into brush or leaves, enticing your puppy to use both sight and scent to track it down. Let your puppy "catch" it often enough . . . the spread should encourage licking instead of tugging. If a tug-fest starts, tie your end of the rope onto a tree, and wait it out.

Break Dance

Ideal for: Companion dogs and puppies who enjoy spending time on their backs

Impulse: Movement and play

> ### 🐾 The Healing Power of Play
>
> Play enhances the emotional and mental growth of every puppy, but puppies who have been traumatized or abused are in special need. If you've adopted one of them, you can see firsthand how their trust in people has been shaken: Perhaps they shy away from a hand or a shoe. Loud voices or noises might cause them to tremble. It is so, so sad. You have done a wonderful thing in bringing them into your home and into your heart. Although it may take weeks for them to interact playfully, use the lists here and your own creativity to find silly ways to teach new words and concepts.

Age: Any

How to: When your puppy is high-spirited and playing on her back, you may find that she gets nippy. A fun alternative is to teach her to BREAK DANCE: tickle her belly and cheer her on by saying BREAK DANCE as she wriggles on her back. At first, she won't know what is making you so happy, but she'll figure it out soon enough. It's just one more outlet for all her enthusiasm, no matter what her position!

Combat Crawl

Ideal for: Companion breeds, terriers, play ball, Nordic, self-motivated, hounds—puppies who show a natural propensity to stretch out and crawl

Impulse: Comfort and crawling

Age: Any

How to: When your puppy stretches out, say, CRAWL, praising even the slightest motion forward. A couple of times a day, take treats, encourage her to lie down, and then lure her forward by kneeling next to her and slowly stretching the treat just an inch in front of her nose. Don't bring it up—she'll stand up. Instead, keep it level to the floor. If you notice that she wants to rise, keep your free hand two inches above her back. Press gently if she attempts to stand. Say, CRAWL as she moves forward. Gradually increase the length of the crawl.

Disco Doggin' It

Ideal for: Companion breeds, self-motivated, some herding, and agile puppies who balance well standing on their hind legs

Impulse: Attention and limelight

Age: 12 weeks

How to: Practice in a quiet room when your puppy is spry and full of energy. Bring a treat back from her nose to above her ears. The instant she jumps up, say, DANCE, (or click) and reward her! Gradually encourage longer dances, putting a spin on it by slowly twirling your hand around or inching your hand forward: WALK LIKE A LADY. Now you can show off, suggesting a dance for every greeting. You'll have your very own showgirl in no time!

Note: Is your puppy a dancing fool? Teach her FOUR PAWS. Cheer her on for ten seconds of dancing, then stand tall and say, FOUR PAWS, and look away until she's grounded.

Four-Footed Fax

Ideal for: Retrieving, guard, protection—all puppies who enjoy carrying things in their mouths

Impulse: To retrieve and carry

Age: 5 months

How to: Once your puppy has mastered the retrieving skills outlined in the following games and can identify household members by name (see the *treat cup name game*), teach her to ferry objects from person to person and from room to room. In our house, I often request Whoopsie to deliver a diaper or a pacifier. I hand it to her and say, BRING IT TO DADDY, or GO FIND LINDSAY!

Frisbee Flying

Ideal for: Sporting, herding, protective, terriers (all), self-motivated, motion detectors (sight hounds)—all puppies who are agile and like to chase and catch toys

Impulse: Chasing, retrieving

Age: Any

How to: You can't start this game early enough! Here are a few early ways to encourage your puppy's enthusiasm:

- Roll the Frisbee on its side along the ground to encourage your puppy's interest. Do this often, shouting, FRISBEE! as your puppy chases after it.
- Place treats in the disc, and have your puppy follow you for them.
- Use it to give your puppy water and food.
- Carry it with you—let its presence be known!
- Bring several out when you play, and roll one after the other.

Wait until your puppy is older than 6 months to introduce the toss. Initially, hold it slightly above her head and move it slowly through the air as if it were flying in slow motion. When your puppy jumps for it, cheer her and let her have it. Introduce a second and a third disc. Gradually pick up the pace, encouraging her to grab it before it moves away. To encourage a strong hold, tug on it slightly, then teach the release by saying, GIVE IT, as you pop a goodie in her mouth. Next, start light tosses repetitively. As your puppy's coordination improves, teach her to WAIT as you back up and toss it to her. Gradually increase the distance. Then teach her to go out from your side, using the same step-by-step progression. Refer to the reference section or to my website for an excellent referral on Frisbee training by Peter Bloeme—it helped me turn our Whoopsie into a star Frisbee player!

Buried Treasure

Ideal for: Terriers, sporting dogs, herding—any puppy who enjoys digging
Impulse: Predatory, comfort, fun
Age: Any
How to: Pick a special digging area, either in your yard or in a discreet corner of a field or a park. Bring your gloves, a small shovel, and some treasures to bury (treats and some bones). Say, GO DIG, as you dig with your puppy, burying goodies for her to unearth! Continue to dig with her, as long as she's participating, repeating GO DIG as you do. Other family member can join in the fun too! Eventually, you'll be able to remind your puppy to go on her own!
Note: If your puppy begins to dig everywhere, put red pepper and some of her stool in the hole and cover it up. And remember, no gardening in front of your puppy: puppy see, puppy do!

Jump Over/Leapin' Lassie

Ideal for: Any puppy who loves to jump, from teacup size on up!
Caution: Keep all jumps below your puppy's hock (her elbow) until she turns 1 year old. Developing tissues can be easily ruptured.
Impulse: Movement, freedom
Age: 4 months
How to: Start with a broomstick (or similar pole) balanced on two objects of equal height—cans, boxes, toilet paper rolls, etc. Remember to keep it very low to start and always below the level of your puppy's elbow. Leave at least five paces for a running start, and use a treat cup to excite your puppy's interest. Say, OVER, as you run forward and jump over the broom. If she follows, cheer! If she'd rather watch, let her. Toss and chase a toy over the obstacle, too. She won't be able to resist for long.

Gradually eliminate yourself as an escort until you're able to say, OVER, and she takes it solo, perhaps while you prompt her with a toy. Now you can get fancy.

- Create a course in the kitchen or out in the yard.
- Raise the height (below the elbow for the first year).
- Add props like a hula hoop or your arms circled.
- Have one of your children lie under the broom, encourage, OVER, and let the silliness begin!

Eventually, you'll be able to eliminate the broom altogether!

Heave-Ho

Ideal for: Nordic, guarding, fighting breeds—any puppy who clearly needs an outlet to pull
Impulse: Pulling and strength
Age: 5 months
Caution: You must use a balance harness for this activity. A neck collar is not appropriate; it will cause damaging strain.
How to: If you can find a harness, get one. There are drafting harnesses for stocky, compact breeds and racing harnesses for lithe, agile breeds. I had a racing harness for my husky mix Kyia and a drafting harness for our lab Whoopsie.

Introduce the harness as you did the leash: leave it on for twenty minutes a couple of times each day until your puppy is comfortable. Next, get a helper to hold a treat cup and coach your puppy forward. Secure a leash to the back of harness, and apply light pressure as your puppy pulls you toward your helper. She may twist around initially: release all pressure, look up, not at your puppy, and stay calm. Gradually increase the pressure and say something snazzy like HIKE! Here you can keep it simple, using this skill to improve your running times or help you up a hill (your puppy must always be on a balance harness to pull you), or you can get fancy and buy a professional sled. Refer to my website or the reference section for catalogs and books on this sport.

Ricochet Rover

Ideal for: Sporting, some terriers, companion breeds—any puppy who carries or retrieves toys
Impulse: Retrieving, mouthing objects
Age: 3½ months
How to: Teach the three parts of this skill separately, and then bring them all together.

1. GIVE: Use a treat cup or a clicker and approach your puppy cheerfully when she's got something in her mouth. Say, GIVE, and pop a treat, or click and treat, to reinforce sharing. Praise her; if it's her toy, simply walk away. If it is your object, exchange it with something else. You can practice this skill at her food dish as well; interrupt no more than one meal in four.

2. THE CHASE: Toss toys to your puppy. Cheer her on when she's chasing them. Go ballistic when she grasps the toy. YES—GOOD GIRL! End there. If she runs back to you, hug her. Do not take the toy from her mouth—let her keep it!

3. BRING: Using your enthusiasm or food (if she'll keep hold of her toy), say, BRING, as you run away from her. Hug her into your body. Toss the toy and hide as she chases it. Say, BRING, when you know she's going to follow through.

If at any point your puppy won't cooperate, don't discourage her. It takes some time for the steps in this game to come together, and even then, it can be touch and go through the first year. When you're first bringing these three sections together, practice in a small room or a hallway with few distractions. Make it fun, and for the first few weeks run away from your puppy as you encourage, BRING. If you stare at her, she may stop and stare back at you, slightly confused.

Roll Over

Ideal for: Agile breeds of all shapes and sizes—they must feel comfortable on their back
Impulse: Comfort and play
Age: Over 3 months
How to: Each time your puppy is naturally on her belly, say, ROLL, as you tickle her over by scratching her belly. To build her enthusiasm for this trick and build her success rate, break the trick into four sections, using treats or a favorite toy as a lure:

1. **Roll to Your Side:** From a down position, bring the treat around your puppy's nose, under her chin to her ear. As she lies on her side, say, ROLL. Treat, praise, and repeat until your expectations are well understood.

2. **Belly Up:** Now take the goodie and bring it out to the side of her ear. If she's confused, gently rock her foreleg into a belly-up position. Say, ROLL, as you give her the treat. Repeat until this is natural.

3. **Flip Over:** Now bring the treat down to the floor, once again right next to her ear, guiding her foreleg as needed. Say, ROLL, as you give her the goodie.

4. **Full Roll and Stand:** To bring her into a full upright position, say, ROLL—UP UP, as you stand quickly and clap. Now you can put it all together. Your eventual signal will be a circular rotation of your right forearm. Yippee!

If you want to get really fancy, you can teach repetitive rolls or ROLL OVER, ROLL BACK. Everything starts with the food lure, step-by-step breakdown.

Volume Control and the Mathematical Puppy

Ideal for: Noisy breeds of every shape and size
Impulse: Alert, guarding, the desire to be heard
Age: 4 months
How to: Our catchwords here are SPEAK and QUIET. Only interested in the off switch? Unfortunately, it doesn't work that way. You must have a discourage

(SPEAK) in order to have an encourage (QUIET); plus, if she's a barker, she'll need an outlet or she'll burst. First, teach her a cue for barking:

- **Caught in the Act:** If you catch your puppy barking, say, SPEAK, and praise her. She'll be shocked! Shake a treat cup, or clap and run away from her, and say, COME TO ME. Reward her with praise, a toy, or food (a clicker works here, too).

- **Spurred On:** If your puppy's mute when you're around, bait her into barking. Ring bells, stand out of reach, and wave cheese in her face; rough, tumble, and bark in order to get her to open up. When she barks, say, SPEAK, with a snazzy hand signal, cheer her on, and reward her.

- **The Off Switch:** You may notice that when you reward her, she settles down. As soon as she catches on to SPEAK, start saying, QUIET, as you praise her. Gradually lessen the time between the two directions. Use hand signals for both, and when she is a master, ask questions like, "How old are you?" "How many treats are behind my back?" "How many paws do you have?" Signal her to bark, then signal her to stop. Presto—the counting companion!—you get the idea.

Swing & Tug

Ideal for: Herding, terriers (all)
Impulse: Predatory, capturing
Age: 5 months
How to: Tie a plastic toy (a bottle or a ball with a handle) onto a rope. Secure the rope onto a high tree branch so that the toy hangs above the ground, an inch or two above the puppy's nose level. Let it swing! This is a self-activated activity.

Treasure Hunt

Ideal for: Scent hounds especially, although it's fun for all puppies who enjoy using their noses
Impulse: Scent tracking
Age: 3 months
How to: Start this game with treats. Once your puppy has mastered the SIT-STAY, have her SIT and SNIFF a treat: Hold it in your fingers, right to her nose. Instruct, STAY, and toss the treat out in front of you. Brace her until she holds still, then release her with GO FIND. Practice alone or with a partner until you're able to leave her side and hide the treat around a corner. If she looks confused, get down on the floor and show her how to use her nose. Next, introduce other items, like a glove. With each new object go back to the beginning, toss it in front, say,

GO FIND, and treat (or click and treat) the instant she touches the object. Progress until you can hide objects in obscure places. Toss in the remote control and the keys while you're at it. Put that nose to work.

Note: This is a great game to play while you're getting dinner on the table. Take some treats or some raw veggies, tell your puppy to STAY, and hide them in the next room. She'll have a fun time while you're busy!

TEMPERAMENT-SPECIFIC GAMES

In the following paragraphs, you'll find a series of games; some (like tugging or *toy along, tag along*) I suggest only for certain temperaments. Remember, you don't have to master them all—just pick a few you like and stick to those!

Peek-a-Boo Puppy

Ideal temperament(s): All
Props: Treat cups
Players: 1 or more
How to Play: If your puppy knows STAY, use it to get a jump-start on finding a choice hiding spot. When you're ready, use your puppy's name to call out: PEEK-A-BOO, WHOOPSIE!

Soda Bottle Soccer

Ideal temperament(s): Bossy, comic, eager, mellow, some reserved
Props: Empty plastic bottles
Players: Multiple
How to Play: Take out at least one more plastic container than there are people and puppies. Simply kick one that the puppy is not playing with. (You want her to look to you and avoid injury.)

 Self-Expression

Think of all the games you loved as a child. My favorite board games were Kerplunk, cards, backgammon, and Monopoly; outside, I loved running games and hide-and-seek. Your puppy will have list of favorites, too, which may or may not coincide with your idea of fun. List your puppy's top three games, and see if you notice a theme. Are they chasing games, retrieval, shaking, digging, or finding games? This is yet another clue into the mind of your puppy.

> ### 🐾 Lofty Aspirations
>
> If you've got your sights on even higher goals, I commend you. Your puppy loves involvement, and more structured activities such as Agility, Flyball, and Pet Therapy are wonderful outlets for her enthusiasm. Please refer to the reference section or to www.dogperfect.com for more information.

Toy Along, Tag Along

Ideal temperament(s): Reserved, eager, timid
Props: Rope or a leash, a toy or a bone
Players: 1
How to Play: Tie one end of a four-foot leash or string to a toy and the other end to your foot. Just walk around doing whatever you've got to do. Let the fun begin!

If your puppy starts losing control, slip your foot out and tie the end onto an immovable object.

Tug with Me

Ideal temperament(s): Reserved, timid
Props: Rope and a stuffed toy, treats, and a clicker if you're using one
Players: 1
How to Play: Razz your puppy up with the toy. When she grabs hold, jiggle it softly, saying, TUG. Be gentle—her mouth and neck are delicate. After a few seconds, say, GIVE, and pop a treat in her mouth. Work at this over time so that your puppy learns the difference between a gentle game and a quick release.
Special Consideration: If your puppy gets mouthy or physically aggressive, stop. Tie the toy onto a tree as described in the following game. This game is an ideal confidence builder for internalized puppies.

Tug-o-Tree

Ideal temperament(s): All
Props: A tug toy tied to a tree
Players: 1 or more
How to Play: Get a rope toy and show by example how much fun it is to swing around. If your puppy mimics, you can take it (or another like it) and tie it onto a tree. Encourage tugging: it's a natural behavior, a wonderful stress release, and, as long as you pick a strong tree, your puppy can have a real tug-fest.

Push Away Come Game

Ideal temperament(s): Reserved, eager, comic—not too mouthy
Props: None
Players: 1
How to Play: Sit on a slippery floor, legs outstretched in a V. Hug your puppy to you, then gently push her out in front. Most puppies think this is fun, and they scramble back into your arms. If yours does, she's ripe for this charade. Say, COME, as she reaches you!

Push Away Come Game!

Jodi Buren

Chapter 6

The Not-So-Perfect Puppy

Okay, by now you might be ready to admit that nobody's perfect: not you, not your kids, not your significant other—not even your puppy. Imperfections are, in fact, the spice of life, and many are good signs that your puppy is developing normally. Take, for example, the puppy who steals the remote control: a classic sign of monkey see, monkey do. The remote control is an object of your fascination and constant use. Love me, love my remote. Your puppy's expressions are oral and interactive but no less a sign of observation. The same holds true for food on the countertops and stuffed animals.

Fortunately, there are ways to shape puppies' behavior. You won't have to clear the countertops and hide the remote forever. However, the first step in resolution is respecting your puppy's spunk and creative interest. I find the puppy who can orchestrate a family chase simply by stealing a napkin to be quite clever. This puppy doesn't know he's bad: he's having a great time. Even his cooperative cower at the end of the game doesn't erase the fun of the chase. So step one in problem resolution is to rethink the problem from your puppy's perspective, and step two is to reshape your approach, knowing that blaming your puppy and confrontational corrections will get you nowhere.

Remember the behavior scale from page 43? A quick review will remind you that your attention reinforces your puppy's behavior. And the puppy doesn't care whether the attention is negative or positive. If you pay attention to the puppy, you're guaranteeing a repeat performance. The more assertive you are, the more assertive he'll be: these are the ground rules for confrontational play. As you read through this chapter or the sections that apply to you directly, stay very calm. Be the authority. Metaphorically, it's like being a team captain with a new player who doesn't know the rules. If you scream at your new player, you'll overwhelm him. If you keep it up, he'll quit or get defensive or frightened. Repetition is always kind and helpful, so come up with a plan and be patient.

This table will give you an overview of age-appropriate interference: the timing, meaning, and when it's use is appropriate.

CORRECTION SOUNDS

Sound	Age	Sound	Meaning	Behavior
Ep-ep	Under 3½ months	Light and peppy	A gentle discouragement	All
Shhtt	Older than 7 months	Sharp and fierce	A sound to indicate strong disapproval	Barking, nipping
Nope	5 months and up	Short, quick bark	A clear direction to discourage a specified impulse	All
Shame on you	5 months and up	Very disappointed	Indicates your disappointment	House soiling, destruction
That's unacceptable	Older than 7 months	Strong, dominant	Absolutely forbidden	Mounting, aggression, rough play

UNDERSTANDING THEIR IMPULSES

Most of your puppy's behavior is motivated by five basic needs: to eat, drink, sleep, play, and eliminate. Unlike babies who cry when a need's not being met, your puppy will get nippy, distracted, and impulsive. Underscore nippy. Ninety-nine percent of early nipping is simply the result of a puppy who is confused by his own body's impulses. Metaphorically, have you ever tried to think about something serious when, let's say, you really had to go to the bathroom? I mean, really had to go? Or when you were hungry? Really hungry?

Puppies, especially young ones, are like infants—when they need something, they don't understand "five minutes." Mentally, they can't grasp time. Don't take it personally if your puppy piddles as you're putting on your coat or nips you really hard when you're playing past his meal time. My husband, a grown man, gets very testy when he's tired and hungry. I don't banish him for that—I feed him!

Nobody, not a dog or a puppy, an adult or a child, likes to be told that they're bad at something. Would you like it? You're a bad spouse. You stink! I can't stand your work. Bad employee.

 Social Creatures Like Us

Puppies, like young children, need a lot of direction and ideas. Imagine spending time with a 3-year-old. Would you quietly putter around the house ignoring the child unless she did something wrong, or would you play with her and give her fun toys to interact with when you were busy? Think of your puppy in those same terms, remembering that your puppy thinks of you as a big dog—a big, lovely Mama or Papa dog.

How would hearing something like that make you feel? Before harassing your puppy, who really just wants to play and get his needs met, ask yourself what you're trying to accomplish. Next, ask not what your puppy is doing wrong, but what you're not doing right. Reference the specific section of the book, borrow my insights, and with a few minor adjustments in your delivery everyone will fell better.

> *Ask not what your puppy is doing wrong,*
> *but what you're not doing right.*

Creative Connections

Think of your puppy's attempts to get your attention as being like a plug in a socket. Your puppy wants to stay plugged into your thoughts. When puppies are very young, they need constant reflection. By this, I don't mean that they need time alone to reflect on the meaning of life. Quite the opposite. They need to continually see themselves reflected in your eyes, in order to gauge their own progress and status in the pack by whether or not their behavior meets with your approval. As they mature, your lessons will teach them that you're with them even when you can't be watching or physically present. But what about the young puppy who never got enough reflecting time when he was small? Either circumstances demanded isolation, or his parents were just unaware of his needs. This youngster will grow into a needy adolescent with a laundry list of annoying behaviors: jumping, barking, chewing, and *grab-n-go*. And what do these behaviors have in common? They're efforts to get more attention. Yes, even negative attention beats none at all. This puppy isn't bad: he simply needs reassurance that his parents understand his needs, and his parents need to learn better communication skills. Even naughty puppies are healthy puppies. They're letting you know that staying connected and being a part of your world is their top priority.

> *Puppies use their mouths to grasp things: our hands are a mouth*
> *equivalent. What we pick up, they'll want to pick up, too!*

Is It Fear or Understanding?

Some of you are convinced that your puppy knows he's been bad. He cringes when you shout, grovels when you storm at him. I do understand your argument. On face value, many would agree. I, however, would describe the reaction in terms of fear, not understanding. Imagine just for a moment that you're in my classroom. I'm a cheerful teacher most of the time. Suddenly, in the midst of the lesson, I notice that you are doing something wrong, but instead of pointing it out and showing you, I go ballistic—running at you and screaming. How would you react?

CC

CC's mom couldn't love her dogs more. Having worked with four generations of her Labradors, I met CC when she was just a wee pup: 8 weeks old. At that time, I structured plenty of Mommy and Me time as I explained that CC was a soft, sweet puppy who needed plenty of proactive direction to help her feel important and safe. She was not the sort of puppy who'd respond to corrections: even a raised voice would scare her to the core.

The next time I saw CC, her mom claimed she was a 9-month-old "brat! She was grabbing everyone's arm, jumping on everybody, and constantly underfoot and stealing!" What happened? Even CC's mom knew she was a sweetheart underneath it all. Well, a quick observation told me this: CC was trapped in hierarchical confusion. A follower by nature, she was desperate for someone to give her direction. Desperate being an understatement! Her mom, on the other hand, had a serious adoration problem when CC was young. A recent empty nester, she fawned over CC a little bit too much. She looked at CC constantly with soft, weepy eyes and patted her for hours when on the phone or watching TV. CC's interpretation? That her mom was even more submissive and needed her direction. Since CC wasn't born with leadership skills, she compensated the best she could; however, instead of a confident attitude she emanated insecurity. It was her best attempt to keep the relationship structured. Her minute-to minute-nose nudge and pawing were the human phrase equivalent of "Do you love me now? It's been five seconds: do you still love me?"

The truth is that assertive corrections actually create *more* mischief. Yes, more. It's nerve-racking to be disciplined by someone—especially throughout the day. A puppy can't develop normally in this environment. On the other hand, if good behavior is highlighted and encouraged, and mischief is downplayed and redirected, the world will be a safe place to grow up in.

If you've got a family, gather everyone around the table and use the metaphor of a team dynamic to pitch your plan. Most issues can be resolved by all of you working together to modify everybody's behavior simultaneously.

Cause-and-Effect Corrections

All puppies learn through cause and effect. Human babies do, too! If a certain behavior like jumping or barking gets your attention, is it any wonder that a puppy will do it again? Although I don't believe discipline is effective, some behaviors warrant discouragement. Here's where you use the cause-and-effect principles in reverse! When addressing an issue, there are three steps to remember. The reaction should be seen as

1. Coming from the environment, not from you.
2. Causing a withdrawal of human attention.
3. Your interactions should refocus the puppy's energy onto a displacement activity.

From the top. Using this cause-and-effect approach, all reactions to a given behavior must be perceived as environmental, not interactive. If you're using a side swipe or a spray-away correction, it must be done discreetly with a calm, detached body frame so that your puppy doesn't perceive your involvement or confrontation. His misdeeds must not be seen as attention-getting: even a quick glance can guarantee a repeat performance. No eye contact in Steps 1 and 2.

Step 3 is fun: redirecting a puppy to a better alternative. Here's an exercise I give my clients: create a chart that lists

(a) The current frustration
(b) An appropriate alternative
(c) The words necessary to communicate
(d) Any equipment that might be helpful in making your point

Jodi Buren

Corrections should be seen as causing a withdrawal of attention.

Here are some quick alternatives for many bothersome behaviors!

THE ENCOURAGEMENT CONNECTION

Behavior	Encourage	Words	Equipment
Jumping	Sit or fetch a toy	SIT, GET YOUR BALL/TOY	Toys
Chewing	Chew a bone or a toy	BONE/TOY	Bone/Toy
Nipping	Kisses or directed focus to the door, a toy, or bowls	KISSES or OUTSIDE WATER or FOOD BONE or TOY BED	Bells Peanut butter Cream cheese Yogurt
Bathroom	Go outside or on the paper	OUTSIDE, PAPER GET BUSY	Bells
Grab-n-Go	Bringing a toy	WHAT DID YOU FIND? THANKS FOR SHARING.	Toy Ball

Always encourage after you discourage. Help your puppy see what behaviors will get attention!

You may start to notice that your puppy begins to instigate Column B behaviors on his own. Yeah-pizzazz-underscore-highlight-click and treat-thank the heavens-shout YES!!! You are seeing the light at the end of the tunnel: don't ignore it. Get right down and praise that puppy. Interact with him. Let him know just how proud you are!

Defining Flags

At times I refer to a reaction as a "flag on the field." Yellow flags highlight a concern and a potential problem; a red flag is more serious.

- **No flag:** If there's no flag, it's a sign of normal development. Counter jumping is a good example. It's mimicking behavior.
- **Yellow flag:** A yellow flag goes up when behavior is manipulative. This puppy knows how to push your buttons. A behavior may have started out innocently enough; young puppies nip and grab objects, but after exaggerated interference, this puppy acts to get a reaction. He simply respects whatever gets a reaction.
- **Red flag:** When referring to aggression, anything more serious than a growl is considered red flag behavior. If you discover a red flag behavior, you need some extra help. Call a professional in your area, or set up a phone consultation with a listed professional. You need help to dissect your situation and understand how to address it.

HOUSEBREAKING 101

Here, the goal is obvious and universal. Housetraining frustrations, however, all have a personal twist. In some cases, the puppy really doesn't know any better. In other cases, a puppy values attention so highly, he'll eliminate right in front of you just to get you to look. This section's a mix of behind-the-scenes information (puppy thoughts) and basic tips so that you can accelerate to housetraining stardom.

Troubleshooting Tips

Here are a few considerations before we get started:

- **Bellyaches:** If your puppy isn't feeling well, etiquette won't be forefront in his mind. Frequent accidents (more than three an hour) or loose stools may highlight a parasitic invasion. Bring your veterinarian a stool/urine sample to check.

 **Collecting Urine**

The best time to get a sample is in the morning. Check with your veterinarian. Some vets like you to use a sterilized dish or syringe. Otherwise, use a clean Tupperware lid.

- **Free-flowing fountain:** Your puppy may be drinking too much water. Free access to water may be the root of your frustration, as restless puppies delight in finishing the bowl. Hot climates or long departures aside, if you're aware of your puppy's needs, limit the water to feedings and periodic drinks after play. (If you're a scatterbrain—and let's face it, we all have our days—don't risk dehydrating your puppy to save a couple of paper towels.)

- **Diet:** Plain, pure, and simple is best: varied foods will upset your puppy's stomach, as his intestinal tract is simple. Research top brands, or speak to your veterinarian or breeder to select a brand that is nourishing. When transitioning to a new food, gradually phase in the new food over an eight-day period.

General Guidelines

Before categorizing your issues, let's outline some general rules that will apply regardless of your situation.

1. **Attention is everything to your puppy:** Use an abundance of it to spotlight your pleasure when he cooperates. During the next week, limit your daily attention sprees to the moments that follow a proper potty.

2. **Necessary breaks:** Your puppy will need a bathroom break after eating, sleeping, and confinement and after or during play. In addition, if he's had a big drink, the rules of physics apply. What goes in will come out.

> ### 🐾 Give Your Puppy a Little Space, Literally
>
> No one would toilet train a child to use the neighbor's bathroom. Teach your puppy to make in your own space or yard. It has the added benefit of localizing his focus. As an adult, he'll localize his territory by his elimination spots. If they're scattered over a distance, he'll be mindful of all noises and events happening in his perceived territory. Down the road, this may lead to overexcitement or aggression when he notes a trespasser in his area.

3. **Confine your puppy:** House freedom is a privilege. It must be earned. If you can't supervise him, either crate him or confine him in a small room. When you're home, lead or station him, as discussed in chapter 2, as often as possible. The leash is not confining or torturous. Think of it as giving you the capacity to hold your puppy's hand and teach him gently.

4. **Pick an area:** For paper training, select one or more areas in your home. When selecting an outdoor area, pick one close to the door (the ideal is not more than ten yards). Walking back and forth gets distracting: your puppy may think "play," not "potty."

5. **Create a routine:** Use a word to highlight the focus, like OUTSIDE or PAPERS. Encourage your puppy to walk himself there when possible; it helps create memory.

Use a housetraining bell to encourage a signal.

6. **The signal:** Young puppies nip to signal their needs. Your routines will help them establish a pattern, and as they mature, they will develop other ways to tell you. Since standing at the door only works when you're there, too, encourage them to ring a bell. Hang a bell or a chime next to the door at their nose level. Tap it casually, saying, OUTSIDE, before opening the door.

7. **The right moment:** When you get to the area, ignore your puppy. You read that right. Ignore him until . . . he starts going to the bathroom. Now, don't go crazy. Stay calm and use trigger words like GET BUSY. (Eventually, this will prompt a potty any time and anywhere.) The puppy gets attention after he finishes.

Paper Puppies

If your goal is paper training, keep the papers organized! Scattering a piece here and there won't get the job done. Scattered paper—scattered thoughts—scattered pees and poops. Elementary. Place your paper or pads neatly in a corner. If you have a large home, place the main papers in one area but have other corner "toilets" in far-off zones in case of an emergency. If your puppy starts to eliminate, hustle him to the nearest patch, saying, "PAPERS," as you escort. As your pup matures, eliminate the other areas as you encourage him to the main area.

Addressing Specific Needs

Now it's time to address your specific issue, based on your puppy's age. Find which category you fall into to get the best training tips for your specific situation.

Specific situations require a specified approach.

Young Puppies (up to 5 Months)

If your puppy is less than 5 months old, he's considered a novice. No flag on the field just yet; you're only starting out. Begin by running through a quick checklist for this group:

1. These babies just can't hold it—their bladder muscles are just developing. Nearly all pups prefer to potty away from resting spots and hangouts. Help yours to build his bladder muscles by confining him. Use a crate or a small room when you're busy or gone, and when you're home, keep him with you on a leash or secured in the same room when you're unable to supervise his freedom and you suspect that his bladder or bowels may be full.

 Matchstick Trick

Take a cardboard match from a book of matches. Use cardboard since wooden ones can get stuck. Dip the unlit sulfur end of the match in petroleum jelly. Go to your puppy and offer him a delightful snack or some peanut butter (this may be a two person operation). While he's entranced with the delectable, insert the unlit sulfur end of the match in his bottom. This serves as a suppository. Now quick get her outside or tow her papers!!!

2. Your puppy will need to go out after he eats, drinks, plays, wakes up from a nap, or has been isolated. As he matures, his muscles will strengthen, and he'll prefer going to a conditioned spot to relieve himself, but every puppy is different so you'll have to be the judge. The following table structures the age of the puppy to his outing requirements.

AGE–OUTING CORRELATION

Puppy's Age	Number of Potty Breaks a Day
6 to 14 weeks	8 to 10
14 to 20 weeks	6 to 8
20 to 30 weeks	4 to 6
30 weeks to adulthood	3 to 4

3. Handle accidents calmly. No face rubbing, please. It nauseates. Assess whether you missed a signal or overlooked a scheduled outing; let it go. You'll do more damage to the relationship by yelling. If your puppy is over 16 weeks old and his accidents are frequent, calmly sit him by the area, point from his nose to the spot, and say, "This really disappointments me. Shame on you. Outside." Speak in a disappointed tone, and then escort him to his bathroom area.

4. Avoid cleaning up accidents in front of your puppy: he'll think you're ingesting it. Disgusting, I know, but his mom did it to keep their box clean, and you're just extending the ritual.

5. Make cleaning up efficient and easy. Have a paper towel roll and deodorizer (either 50 percent vinegar and water or a pre-made mixture from the pet store) in a set location(s) so that everyone involved can help out. Organization makes it simple.

6. Use the housetraining schedule I've created in the following table. Because this schedule accommodates an at-home puppy parent, you need to make the following modifications if you're a working puppy parent: get a helper to come in at midday until your puppy is between 8 and 12 months old; each day, bracket your departure with heavy doses of attention, play, and exercise; if you're forced to leave for long hours, buy a playpen (at a pet store) or gate him in a small room, designating an area for toys, a water dish, papers, and bedding.

 You Got the Look

Have you ever really, *really* had to go to the bathroom? Car trip, morning time when you're on the edge of wakefulness. Ever dribbled even a little? So you can relate! Don't be too harsh with your puppy. Make it a number-one priority to learn your puppy's "look"— and say, OUTSIDE, or PAPERS.

Caged Puppies

Pet store, kenneled, or shelter pups often have no choice but to potty where they play. In these instances, a crate may not be your best option. It may prompt a potty. You may keep your young puppy in an open-topped box at night, an enclosed room at night, and stations or leading to keep him with you when you're home. Get a friend or a neighbor's puppy to eliminate in his potty area to give him the right idea.

DAILY HOUSEBREAKING SCHEDULE

Time of Day	Potty Time
Early morning wake up	Go outside
Breakfast	Go outside after breakfast
Midmorning	Go outside
Afternoon feeding	Go outside after eating
Midafternoon	Go outside
Dinnertime (4 to 6 p.m.)	Go outside after dinner
7:30	Remove water
Mid-evening	Go outside
Before bed	Go outside
Middle of the night	Go outside if necessary

Do not crate a young puppy for more than six hours.
It's cruel, stressful, and confusing. Period.

Older Puppies (over 5 Months)

Over-5-months accidents may take on a more sophisticated twist. Although some puppies just take a while to figure it out, marking or attention-getting reactions highlight a flag on the field. Your puppy may be using his eliminations to make a point. Try to determine why, and then use the following tips to come up with a plan that is focused and compassionate.

- Errant soilers: An occasional backslide traced to a break in the normal routine (illness, kenneling, a forgotten outing, or houseguests of any species) is not uncommon. This puppy could also be suffering from an illness that increases thirst. If your puppy is on medication, ask your veterinarian whether there are side effects. No corrections are necessary, although don't

Testimony

My Whoopsie baffled me. She'd be good for days, then she'd have a piddle while stationed and look at me slightly confused. Initially, she did have a reoccurring urinary tract infection, but that was cured by 14 weeks of age. It took me a little while to fully understand, empathize, and work with her, but once I did, she made vast improvements. Here's what I discovered: Whoopsie loves interaction. She watches what's going on and likes to be where the action is. That said, she's also a bit lazy. She lumps around wherever we go, cheerful but not hyper. She lies down at every opportunity. I also discovered that she wasn't motivated into action by her needs: she'd go hungry for two days before standing by her bowl, or would get dehydrated before drinking from the toilet (mind you, these things never happened). It was only fitting that she didn't want to rock the boat when it was time to pee. She'd just squat and go. Although her initial responses didn't fit into any formula, a closer inspection gave me much more respect for who she is as a dog and helped me to housetrain her.

clean up in front of your puppy—it sends a mixed message. Go back a few pages to the "General Guidelines" (page 95), and keep your puppy under surveillance for a few days. Reemphasize the words and the routines.

- Attention getting: This puppy squats right in front of you with an innocent look on his face. He may even seek you out to show you what he's done. Yellow flag on the field! He so thirsts for interaction that he'll even potty to get it. The first question to ask is, is your puppy getting enough attention? When our daughter was born, our puppy Whoopsie felt mighty estranged. She definitely dabbled in a few dribbles. It was a convincing flag. We hired some neighborhood kids to play with her after school. If your life has gotten busy for whatever reason, either make time or hire someone to stand in. Review the guidelines, avoid discipline, and never clean up in front of your puppy.

 When Accidents Don't Count

Be reasonable! Don't blame your puppy if he's been left alone too long, he is sick, he tried to tell you (usually by nipping or fidgeting), or someone forgot to take him out. Your frustration overwhelms him and will inhibit communication.

Yes, you read that right. Don't discipline your puppy at all! It's a tall order, I know, but discipline is still attention, and it will satisfy. When it happens, don't look, talk, or interact with your puppy for at least thirty seconds. After that, take your puppy to his quiet area (crate, room enclosure, or station) for thirty minutes as you clean up. Help him see that this routine only results in isolation.

- Mischievous markers: As puppies mature, some develop a top-dog attitude. Although it will seem like they've gone from sweet and innocent to bullying overnight, it's a gradual change you may have been unaware of. Blocking you on the stairs or in doorways, racing out the door ahead of you, nudging for attention, or constant scratches at the door are all signs that your puppy is considering the top spot. Marking is a protective sign: puppies use urine to mark their territory and ward off intruders. A marking pup feels that it's his responsibility to defend. The most frustrating mark? The one in the center of your bed or couch (where your scent rests most heavily). This pup is generally 7 to 12 months old and prides himself on marking areas in the house. Here's a red flag. Not impossible to rehabilitate, but a definite project.

This is an authority issue. To resolve it:

- Get training. Lessons assert authority.
- Follow the guidelines. Word for word.
- Exercise, exercise, exercise: a tired puppy is a tired puppy.
- Use HEEL on your walks. No marking along the walk unless you yourself are planning to potty over the same spot where he marks. You're the leader now.

Refer to the guidelines in the "Tough Puppy" section of this chapter on page 123 for more suggestions on asserting yourself in your own home. If your puppy develops aggression in reaction to your taking charge, stop immediately and call a professional for guidance.

🐾 Cross-Training

Would you like your puppy to go outside when you're home but use the papers when you're out or during bad weather? It's doable in most cases. When you're out, put your puppy in a pen or a small room with the papers organized in one corner. When you're home, take them up and follow the bell-ringing door routine outlined previously. Repetition is the mother of skill. When winter winds blow and you just don't want to face the cold, gate your puppy in his enclosure with his papers.

WHAT TO CHEW?

Here's a lesson my teething daughter taught me: teething on shoes is satisfying. So is chewing on wicker furniture, paper products, cardboard boxes, and plants. The lesson was instantly clear: babies chew almost as much as puppies do. The key difference is that babies are under constant supervision, interference is immediate, and there are safe and age-appropriate alternatives. Furthermore, no one would consider yelling at or spanking a 6-month-old child for chewing on a sock, and I guarantee that if puppy parents were to apply these standards, the result would be similar. Of course, your approach should depend entirely on your puppy's age.

Young Pups (8 to 16 Weeks)

This is the explorative stage, not the manipulation stage where the rules shift ever so slightly. Be gentle with your puppy, and make sharing fun.

Curious and happy, a young puppy embraces life and explores every nuance: with his mouth. It's not naughty or disrespectful; it's a good sign of a normal development. Your goal at this age is to encourage sharing skills. When your puppy finds what he considers a treasure (yes, everything is a treasure to your puppy), teach him to show it to you. Avoid corrections, as this puppy is not old enough to comprehend your thoughts, and at most you'll communicate prize envy: that his treasure is a prize that everyone wants to steal.

To condition sharing,

- Any time your puppy has an object (good, bad, or indifferent), act really excited. In our house, we said, "Whoopsie, what did you find? Good girl!"
- As you're saying this, do one or more of the following:
  - Wear a snack pack with a treat and/or a clicker so that you have rewards available to you at all times.
  - Clap your hands and crouch down in a nonthreatening pose.
  - Find a treat cup and shake it as you approach your puppy.
- As he gives up the treasure, reward him and say, "Thank you for sharing!"

- If you're using a clicker, here's the perfect opportunity to use it. Click and treat as your puppy releases the object.

- Until your puppy is 6 months old, use an alerting sound like EP-EP when discouraging your puppy's interest. Curious, active puppies should wear a drag lead when supervised to enable your quick interference.

Objects are just objects to your pup!

This approach ensures that your puppy will welcome your interaction with his "treasures," rather than covet them alone or run from you.

The goal is cooperation, not confrontation.

If you approach your puppy when you're frustrated, it will overwhelm him. Just imagine me, another human being, approaching you in a huff! Your puppy will learn to run away and turn the whole thing into a game, or hunker down or cower in fear and be very confused about your relationship.

Older Puppies (16 weeks and older)

Alas, the manipulative stage. Fortunately, this lot can learn the concept of NO. This age group is aware of what gets your attention, and they don't care if it's negative or positive. If you focus on it, they'll repeat it. Have you been chasing your errant chewer? I can bet the book he's addicted to this game!

Time for a plan:

- Use a drag lead when supervising your puppy: a four- to six-foot lead on your puppy's tag or head collar. It allows interruption without direct interference. Throughout the day, work on a trigger word, GIVE, (as follows):
  - Create treat cups and place them around your home. If you're using a clicker, add one to each cup.
  - Whenever your puppy is chewing on one of his toys, approach him, shaking a cup, and say, GIVE.
  - Give him a treat and walk away. Do not take the toy.
- Do this same exercise with his food bowl: approach him, shaking the cup, say, GIVE, treat, and then walk away.

Now you'll need to make a decision. You have two choices: the *grab-n-show* or teaching your puppy the concept of NOPE. *Grab-n-show* teaches your puppy to bring you anything and everything he finds: the good, the bad, and the ugly. NOPE says don't take anything but your toys. Both have pros and cons. The first

Jodi Buren

Correct the object, not your puppy!

choice lands you with a reliable retriever who can be taught to carry just about anything: a helpful trait, I assure you. The con is obvious: occasional dog germs on your favorite shoes. If you value your possessions, it may not be your best option. Teaching the concept of NOPE and applying it to everything sounds irresistible to some, but it can overwhelm some puppies, leaving them coveting objects in your absence and challenging your authority when your back is turned. Make your decision, strike a balance as I'll instruct, and your puppy will accept your decision in the long run.

GRAB-N-SHOW

This concept is ideal for retriever-wannabes. The goal is to teach your puppy to deliver every object he finds—good, bad, or indifferent. A puppy taught the *grab-n-show* can eventually be discouraged from collecting certain objects, but not initially—if you discipline him, it goes against the goal of teaching him to feel positive about sharing.

To teach this trick, you'll need to place your puppy on a drag lead and use a snack pack or a treat cup (a clicker is ideal for this activity).

- Take your puppy into a small room or a hallway.
- Place a forbidden object on the floor, and wait until he picks it up.
- Shake your cup as you approach him and say, GIVE.
- If he's impulsive and darts away, stand on or hold his lead.
- Repeat this exercise for several days.
- Progressively move to more open areas, keeping a lead on your puppy to preventing darting. When working outdoors, put a long line on your puppy.

THE CONCEPT OF **NOPE**

Puppies who learn the concept of NOPE can also be taught to retrieve specific objects, eventually. If you teach your puppy the concept of NOPE, he'll learn that only his toys are acceptable to mouth. Have you ever said, "NO," to your puppy? Do you find yourself repeating it often, saying it louder and louder, thinking that intimidation might be the ticket? And yet you notice little retention or, in some cases, that the mischief is actually getting worse. Well, here's why: your puppy hears NO as a trigger word for confrontational play. Grabbing a specific object guarantees interaction. So, we need to restructure your delivery. To teach it properly, you'll have to change the word slightly so that it bears a new meaning. Rig the following situation:

> ### 🐾 Of Course!
>
> All puppies enjoy holding things in their mouths: their mouths are equivalent to our hands. Exploring is fun. Dramatic reactions are perceived as confrontational play or prize envy. If a puppy grabs a shoe and a chase ensues, his conclusion is that shoes must be valuable. A smart puppy will learn to grab the shoe when backs are turned or the room is empty.

- With your puppy out of sight, place a shoe or a paper towel in the center of the floor.
- Bring your puppy into the room on a leash.
- The instant he alerts to the object, tug back on his leash and say, NOPE, in your normal directional tone. Do not yell or modify your voice!
- Next correct the object. You read this right. Correct the object: pick it up and shake it, stomp on it, saying, BAD SHOE, BAD SHOE.
- Stay focused on the object. It, not your puppy, is bad.
- Walk by it. Walk by it again and again.
- If your puppy shows interest, repeat this from the top. If not, praise and redirect him to his station: "Let's go find your BONE/TOY!"

🐾 Giving Good Correction

Remember the three ingredients of a good correction:

- It must be seen as coming from the environment, not from you: the leash tug.
- It causes a withdrawal of human interaction: yell at the object, not at the puppy.
- Redirect his attention toward a displacement activity: "Get your BONE."

Throughout the day, use your foundation words to direct your puppy. If you're concerned about house freedom, use the leading techniques to condition better manners. Lead your puppy during the day as often as possible. When his mind wanders to untouchables (trashcans, the dishwasher, and litter boxes included), pull back and say, NOPE. Correct only the most tempting objects, as yelling too much is overwhelming.

Getting no respect? Ask yourself these questions:

- Am I staring at the puppy or the object? Stare at the object.
- Is my timing off? If the object's in your puppy's mouth, you're too late. Remove the object and start over.
- Are you using an appropriate teaching collar? You need the right tools to communicate. Go back to chapter 2 to review your choices.

MOUTHY MARVINS

Nipping, mouthing, play-biting—call it what you like, it's the most misunderstood behavior. The more mouthing is disciplined, especially early on, the more agitated and confrontational or, if you've got a shy puppy, confused and nervous a puppy becomes. To discover better solutions to mouthing problems, we'll divide puppies according to their age and comprehension abilities.

Young Puppies (Under 5 Months)

These little ones get nippy and fidgety because they have need-pressures, like human babies, that they neither understand nor know how to relieve. Nipping is nothing more than your puppy's attempt to reach out to you for help, like the crying of a baby. Discipline only confuses his bonding instincts and mental growth. Instead, use the Needs Chart (page 47) to help your puppy learn better ways to communicate. Understanding his needs will help you quickly decipher how you can help. Using your words and routines, help your puppy identify a pattern. For example, say, "OUTSIDE," as you take your puppy to the door for a potty break.

If you've tried to redirect and your puppy is still badgering, think back and ask yourself the following questions:

- Is yelling common in your household? Yelling encourages confrontation.
- Is he jumping in relation to the nipping? Have you been shoving your puppy when he jumps?

 Pressure Points

To remove objects from your puppy's mouth, place your hand over his muzzle and gently squeeze the area above and just behind his canine teeth. If your puppy growls, get help. Growling is a red flag behavior.

- Is your puppy nipping specific people, like the kids or company? He may be picking on the weakest links.
- Have you been confrontational in your corrections?

If the answer to any of these questions is yes, you've actually taught your puppy confrontation. A loud household will do it, too. It revs up everybody. New house rules:

- Teach "kisses" by spreading butter or peanut butter on your hand.
- Fit your puppy for a head collar, and attach a drag lead when he's supervised. It allows calm interference.
- Print out your Needs Chart, and share it with the household. Consistency is calming.
- Pull his head away from your hand quickly and say, NOPE. Next, encourage KISSES, offering him your palm. Good puppy!
- Three strikes and you're out: if your puppy just won't quit, crate him calmly with a chew toy.
- Spray away correction: Using a small spray bottle or a canister of mouth spray, discreetly spray the body part that your puppy is nipping. Do not face off or spray your puppy's face: it's mean and is seen as interactive. Remember, good corrections are seen as coming from the environment, not from you. When your puppy withdraws, say, YES, and encourage, KISSES!

Older Puppies (Over 5 Months)

By this stage, puppies are maturing. Most have a handle on their needs and show it by going to the door or the papers to eliminate or standing by their dishes when hungry or thirsty. Nipping begins to have a more hierarchical focus. Is your puppy

- Nipping when you stop playing or to instigate play?
- Nipping you from behind?
- Nipping you to control handling?
- Nipping when play starts getting out of hand?
- Nipping at people in motion?

These are all indications that your nipping has moved into a mature phase. The buck must stop here. In some cases, early seeds of aggression are being sown. From now on, your puppy's teeth must never touch human skin. Not anyone's for any reason. Ever. To impart this message to your wayward puppy,

> ### 🐾 Slap Jack
>
> Do you know the game where you lay your hands on top of your opponent's? Then they try to slap your hands before you yank them away? What if I laid my hands atop yours, but when you went to slap me, I didn't move? Didn't flinch a muscle. Didn't even look at you. Would that be fun? Would you want to play any more? Not likely. When your puppy nips you, if you pull your hand away, you're playing the canine version of slap jack.

- Fit him with a head collar and a drag lead when you or your family are together with him.
- Use the term EXCUSE ME often to communicate your importance. Review its many uses on page 156, and go out of your way to get your puppy in your way so that you can say, EXCUSE ME. It's the most passive way to communicate leadership.
- Quit playing tug-of-war or wrestling games. They're confrontational, and they encourage mouthing.
- Play *two ball toss*, *soda bottle soccer* (see chapter 5), and other games involving not one, but two toys: stay focused on your toy so that it becomes the coveted prize (when your puppy stands calmly, throw or kick your toy and go for the other one). Enroll in a class, or follow the lessons outlined in this book. A little education is a great thing.

When the nipping does surface,

- Ask yourself if there's a need. Always check. Correct the nipping (refer to the advice that follows), then overemphasize the routines and the words. In time he will prompt the need himself, ringing a bell to go out, standing by the water dish, or putting himself to bed.
- Teach or review KISSES by rubbing your hands with butter or cream cheese. If your puppy becomes overzealous with his licks, say, THAT'S ENOUGH, and pull him away or walk away.

If satisfying a need just doesn't help and KISSES is falling on deaf ears, you'll need to consider what's motivating your puppy:

- **He's trying to get attention:** Ignoring may be the simplest solution. If this is impossible, tuck mouth spray in your pocket and each time he nips, spray the body part he's nipping, *not his face*. The body part. Not your puppy. All other interactions are seen as attention. UGH!

- **He's bullying:** This pup needs more direction. Period. The lack of structure has left a top-dog void that he's all too happy to fill. Being a puppy, he hasn't learned diplomacy. Instead of a gracious ascent, he's attempting a hostile takeover. Use a head collar or a Good Dog collar (page 31). Attach a lead to a teaching collar, and supervise him.

  - Use confinement to structure his behavior: Either lead him directly, station him, or isolate him in a crate or a small room. Full freedom has left this pup with a swelled head.
  - When he nips, take the lead and issue a quick sharp tug as you say something sharp like, SHHTT, or UNACCEPTABLE!
  - Immediately follow with another instruction like "HEEL" (follow me) or GET YOUR TOY (take it elsewhere).
  - Sign up for a class or use this book to structure lessons. This puppy needs your direction to feel safe. It's not his fault no one took charge. Fortunately, it's not too late!

Pull his head away from your hand, not your hand away from his mouth.

JUMP-A-HOLICS

Are you sharing your home with a jumper? A knock-you-down, muddy-paw-prints-on-the-couch, embarrass-you-in-front-of-your-visitors jumper? Well, I can relate, having been around quite a few. It's overwhelming. Shortly, we'll establish a *Four-Paw Rule*, but for now let's take a closer look.

The top four reasons puppies jump are

- To get closer to our faces
- To investigate a surface they can't reach
- To get our attention and to play
- To assert power

Physical corrections or chaotic exclamations signal confrontational play and send a "repeat" message. Though some people can overpower a puppy, most can't, and a puppy will quickly learn who the weakest links are. Smarter techniques are just ahead.

Reaction Techniques to Try

You need an appropriate reaction when your puppy jumps in specific situations. Read through the following, and try each a minimum of ten times to see what's most effective.

- **Close Shop:** The fastest way to extinguish attention or greeting jumping is to show your puppy that jumping leads to less facial interaction, not more. To *close shop*, fold your arms in front of your face, and repeat this posture any time your puppy jumps, whether you're sitting or standing. Don't look down until your puppy has all four paws securely on the floor. This one works great for puppies of every age.

- **Side Swipe:** (Your puppy must be 14 weeks old to practice this one.) Here you're going for the "slipping on the ice" feeling. Attach a drag or a short lead to your puppy's collar. When he jumps, grab it and give him a sharp tug to the side. Don't look at or scold him. Follow this cause-and-effect correction with a direction to get a TOY or SIT for attention. This reaction is good for greetings, attention getting, jumping up to investigate counters, and confrontation.

- **Reverse Yo-Yo:** Secure your puppy on a drag lead, and step on it so that your puppy can jump only a few inches before he's pulled down. Tie a knot in the lead for identification. This works for attention getting, greeting, and overall excitement.

- **Spray Away:** Use a small spray bottle, mouth spray, or, in extreme cases, the blaster (which blasts citronella spray) to create a safety zone between your bodies. Do not aim at your puppy's face. I repeat, do not aim at your puppy's face. Don't interact or explode angrily. It's another cause-and-effect reaction. The "effect" is that when your puppy jumps at you or at company, a noxious vapor is released from the atmosphere. When he stops jumping, redirect his energies with a toy or a direction such as HEEL (if you're walking) or SIT (if he wants attention). This method works well to influence confrontational, greeting, or attention-getting jumpers.

Situation-Specific Techniques

In addition to the reaction techniques listed previously, put a game plan in place ahead of time. Here are some ideas:

For greeting or play jumpers:

- Decide what you will encourage during the greeting ritual. My top three are either to get a toy, sit for attention, or go to a predesignated station.
- When your puppy's calm, encourage SIT (positioning him and *bracing* if necessary) or toss a favorite toy for him to play with until he's calm.
- If you come into the house and your puppy is crated or gated, ignore him 100 percent until he's quiet—let him know that calmness, not hyperactivity, buys freedom. (The first few times it may take up to twenty minutes for him to calm down.)

For company jumpers:

- Create a *greeting station*. Physically tie a leash to a nearby banister or door frame, allowing your puppy to observe but not interact until he's calmed down.

- You'd never let another human bolt out ahead of you to overwhelm visitors: don't let your puppy! Teach him to WAIT behind you (page 150). Use a leash and a training collar if his enthusiasm demands.

- Ask your company to ignore your puppy until he settles down. Don't count on it, though. Persist.

 **Bracing**

Clip your right thumb over your puppy's collar (thumb pointing to the floor). Spread your fingers across his chest evenly, and, if necessary, rest your left hand on his waist muscles (just behind his ribs). Now he really can't jump!

- If your puppy is a toy fiend, place a basket of them by the door to redirect his enthusiasm. We did this with Whoopsie, and now she comes to the door bearing gifts.

- When the excitement simmers, brace your puppy and then prompt him with, SAY HELLO: Which to your puppy will mean sit still.

For confrontational jumpers:

- Fit your puppy for a head collar, and attach a drag lead. The pressure over the nose and the neck elicits submission naturally. When your puppy confronts you, calmly use the leash to get in control of his head.

- Don't retaliate. Even if your intimidation is successful, he'll pick on those less powerful.

- Give him exercise and lots of it. A tired puppy means a happy family.

- Structured exercise walks are exhausting. Teach your puppy to HEEL (page 172), and practice on long power walks. Remember what the human phrase equivalent is for HEEL? "I'm the leader, follow me!"

- The *three strikes and you're out* rule applies: after two corrections and if your puppy misbehaves a third time, lead him into his crate or a quiet room, leaving him alone to focus.

For furniture fanatics:

- The big decision for you at this point is, do you want to have your puppy on your furniture? Your dog will do whatever he learned as a puppy, so you have to decide now: couch or no couch? Bed or no bed? Your puppy won't suffer either way.

- Even if you want your puppy to come up, it's nice to have him ask permission. Each time you bring your puppy to the couch or he comes on his own, tell him to SIT. Make calm eye contact with him, and pause varying amounts of time before you say, OKAY UP-UP! Cuddle to your heart's content!

- Do you prefer that the paws stay on the floor? Don't feel guilty. Provide your puppy with a nice mat or a bed near by. Each time you bring your puppy to this area, or he comes to say hello, point to his spot and say, "Go to your MAT." Withhold your affection until he is calmly sitting in his area. If he jumps up, very calmly curl your index finger under his collar and tug him to the side. If it's becoming habit, secure a hand or a drag leash to his collar, enabling you to make a more detached correction.

At Home with Sarah

Whoopsie Daisy, our Labrador Retriever, is a furniture dog. Nothing satisfies the family more than a group snuggle. There is a catch, however: Whoopsie must always ask permission. She's not allowed up unless she asks politely. And how does she say please? By sitting in front of us and pouting, with her most soulful expression. Most of the time we say, UP, UP, but occasionally we say, NOT NOW, which signals her to go to her bed.

COUNTER CRUISING

Metaphorically, counter cruising is like a 2-year-old wanting to help her mom crack eggs. Mommy do, baby do. For the child, not only is the coordination lacking, but raw egg is unsafe. Yelling, however, would be cruel. Praising her interest while giving her a displacement activity is the more appropriate way to handle it.

Although you may not be thrilled to hear it, counter cruising is a great sign that your puppy is developing normally, a prime example of bonding. You focus on the counter tops all the time, and your puppy has been watching you since he was just a half pint. Suddenly, his legs have grown long enough that he can finally reach up. Oh, Joy—the things that he can see, taste, and smell! Can't you relate?

What confuses your puppy is your reaction, which is typically shouting, shoving, and/or racing in from another room. This only spotlights the activity, and clever cruisers learn to be crafty: to scope when your back is turned or when you've left the room. They learn other skills, too, such as the quick snatch, the gulp, and the run and hide.

The first step to resolving this issue is to take pride in the creative, determined energy of your puppy and to understand that no matter how many times you admonish him, he doesn't have a problem with his behavior. In fact, it's exhilarating. That is, until you enter the scene; you become the downer. You can teach your puppy better habits, although you'll have to redirect your own energy.

 The Concept

The right frame of mind is helpful here. We're going to teach your puppy that what's on the counters is bad, not that he is. What's up is unsafe and must be left to the leaders of the group.

Catching the Thought

Here is your chance to make a great impression. Rig the first few situations for quick interference.

- Go to the counter without your puppy, and put a temptation close to the edge.
- Bring your puppy in on his training collar and leash.
- Walk to the counter.
- The moment your puppy alerts to the counter, tug back on his lead and say, NOPE, in a directive tone. Do not yell.
- Correct the counter! Slap it and look ferocious! Look at the counter, that is, not at your puppy. You want him to fear the counter, not to fear or challenge you.
- Calmly direct your puppy to his play station, and when you get there, take a minute to play with his toys.
- This technique works wonders with coffee tables, high chairs (without the baby), dishwashers, etc.
- Practice only two situations a day. Properly timed and directed sessions are quickly understood.
- Throughout the day, correct any interest in the counter. If your puppy even looks like he's checking out the counter, interfere with a quick NOPE and a sharp clap of your hands or a stomp of your foot. Then direct him to his play station or toys.

Caught in the Act

It's a sorry sight: a wrapper torn all around, while your puppy looks so pleased with himself. The truth is, he is pleased. Ripping paper to shreds, dismembering a turkey . . . it's very empowering to a weak, confused, energetic puppy. Don't be too hard on him. You're too late to make a lasting impression. Though your frustration may bring a look of "guilt," it's not really guilt, it's fear. I'm sure you don't want to scare your puppy. The only one to correct, in fact, is yourself for leaving the object within reach. If you continue to correct him, he'll hone his craft. Your interruptions will be perceived as *prize envy*. He'll learn to think around you.

If you've got to get something away from your puppy, do it calmly. Go to your puppy with a toy or a treat cup for a cheerful exchange. Use a catch phrase like "Spoons are not for puppies." (Chicken, pacifiers, the remote control . . .) "Bones are for puppies!" Then help him find a bone. Your puppy should welcome your approach.

🐾 Got a Clamper?

If your puppy clamps his jaws when you're trying to remove an object, pry them open by pinching the skin covering his canine teeth. If your puppy growls, call a professional to help you deal with the aggression. You've got a *red flag* issue.

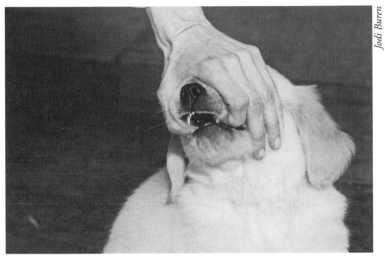

Jodi Buren

Pressure point to open the jaw gently.

If you are in the room with your puppy and suddenly his paws are on the counter or he's taking a napkin from someone's lap, leave a drag lead on his collar to enable quick interference. The pronounced tug should give your puppy the feeling of slipping on ice. Redirect him to his station and toys, securing the lead if necessary.

After the Fact

It's too late. Register your mistake, and take note of it. Haven't you ever done something when you thought no one was looking? Sometimes it's fun to see what you can get away with!

A final word on counter cruising. It seems to be a favorite pastime of adolescent puppies, on par with a human teen's ignoring his parents' requests. There are three key points to ensure this habit doesn't stay with you forever:

- Keep your counters clear. Finding nothing isn't exciting or memorable.
- Chill out. Intense reactions guarantee repeat performances.
- Create play stations with puppy toys so that your puppy will have his own area. Tie the toys down if they get lost.

LOUD MOUTH

This is one behavior that should take no one by surprise. People talk. Dogs bark! At least, most do. How much they bark, and when, are the variables that depend on breed, age, and your response. Of course, nobody likes to hang with a dog who barks uncontrollably, but few realize that this habit starts in early puppyhood. To resolve a "problem barker," look at things from his perspective: the why, when, what, and where.

- *Why?* There are as many reasons a puppy barks as there are reasons children talk. To get attention. To protest. To effect change. Just to hear themselves. Many utterances are instinct drawn: the guttural woof of a 4-month-old Rottweiler in response to a sound in the night can take even the puppy by surprise.
- *When?* This is also revealing. Is your puppy barking when you're home or away? When you're on the phone or speaking with someone, or when he's isolated from you or outside alone? Is he alerting to a noise or a sight? Does he bark at the door or on your walks?
- *What?* Finally, ask yourself what's prompting the vocalization. Isolation? Boredom? Lack of attention? Is your puppy trying to mimic yelling or musical sounds? Is it more environmental—is he barking at something or someone (a sight or a sound)?
- *Where?* Next consider where your puppy barks. In the car, in the crate, or at home? Is it happening in one specific room or at a window or a doorway? Inside, outside, on your property, or off?

Once you've considered the previous questions, read over these six categories of barking and see where you fit in.

- **Attention getting:** This puppy more than wants the spotlight: he needs it, either to feel safe (an insecure puppy) or to feel respected (a bossy fellow). In the midst of self-identification, he's too young to figure life out for himself and needs reassurance from you in the form of constant reflection. Naturally, 100%, one-on-one attention is best, although even a short glimpse will satisfy his need. Your "other life," whether that involves talking with someone else or busy work, leaves this puppy feeling disconnected and stressed. If barking works, even if it only begets negative attention, it will be repeated. Indefinitely.
- **Protective:** This pup thinks he's your protector and your guardian: alerting you to visitors and protecting you from perceived threats are top priorities. Though you may want him to mature into a dog who barks at intruders, you probably don't want him threatening your house guests.
- **Playful:** This comedian is all about fun. Even if barking rouses flagrant disapproval, the interaction is noted as confrontational play. The play escalates, and the barking continues!

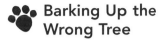

- **Frustration:** Puppies, like babies, are social creatures. People and dogs thrive on interaction and reflection, especially as babies (or pups). Bouts of isolation when you're home are beyond comprehension: "Why the separation?" Stints outside are no fun: there must be two to play! As a puppy matures, he will tolerate isolation and perhaps even enjoy the time alone. If forced to suffer isolation during his early stages, however, his unmet need for reflection will not be satisfied, and he may displace his frustration through chronic barking. If it works to bring you back, it will continue. Indefinitely. As this pup matures, he'll have an insatiable demand for reflection (since it was not provided during the critical time) and will continue barking when frustrated by isolation.

> **Barking Up the Wrong Tree**
>
> **Fact 1:** Yelling is translated into barking, across the board.
> **Fact 2:** Yelling at a barking pup will encourage more barking, as you're seen as either backing him up or confrontational, which may lead to aggression.
> **Moral:** Don't yell at your puppy. There are other, more creative approaches.

- **Sound or motion:** This passionate puppy is attuned to everything! Acute hearing and/or visual sensitivity go far beyond the demands of the average household. Terriers, also known as sound hounds—bred to sense the motion of a tiny mouse under a woodpile—are no longer praised for their strengths. A herding dog, bred to alert to a tiny hoof step in a herd of sheep, just aren't appreciated for their rapid eye response. When you yell as a result of your puppy's barking, he perceives *you* to be barking, and it only intensifies his reaction.

- **Startle:** Timid, nervous, or undersocialized puppies bark when startled by a person or a noise. It communicates their inner confusion. Though it's tempting to soothe, please don't—your interaction will reflect their emotion and will not direct them.

Solutions

Attention getting: This puppy learns quickly that the surest way to get your attention is to bark. Whether your reaction is negative or positive doesn't matter: if you stop what you're doing, and look to him, he'll bark again—guaranteed!

- First things first: is your puppy getting enough attention? Your pup might have a valid gripe.
- Use the lessons outlined in chapter 5 to hone up on your leadership skills. Direction ensures safety, and safety a sense of calmness.

- Increase the exercise, and find some puppy friends. Play dates aren't just for kids anymore.

- Ignore those early barks. No acknowledgment whatsoever. If you can ignore the first three bouts of barking, your puppy will try something else. I speak from personal experience. Whoopsie barked at her dinner station through two full meals. It gave everyone a headache. She got the message early: barking doesn't work. When she finally chewed her bone, we lavished her with praise.

- Buy earplugs if you have a hard time ignoring your puppy. Again, I speak from personal experience.

- If ignoring is proving impossible, try a distracting object when the behavior is predictably at its worse. A peanut butter–like spread stuffed inside a hollow toy can work miracles.

- A startle approach with a penny can or a spray (using a water gun or a blaster) may work, although you must be discreet. Your puppy must think the reaction is coming from the environment, not from you.

- Another technique I like is to use a *head collar* and a leash. Secure it to your side or onto an immovable piece of furniture. A gentle pull will tuck your puppy's head into a quieting position.

- If your landlord is threatening eviction, you may try a citronella barking collar, although this may only be used in conjunction with other behavioral techniques.

Protective barking: Avoid yelling at this puppy; he'll perceive your yelling as barking and your mimicry as backing him up. This barking is instinctive (part of his genetic blueprint). Our goal is not to eliminate it but to shape its focus. The ideal? That your maturing dog barks to alert and finds you, "his leader," for further direction.

- Bring him to your side, and reward him enthusiastically.

- Leave your puppy on a leash when supervised. Keep a treat cup handy or in your pocket.

- When he alerts to a noise, praise him.

🐾 Keeping Them Calm

When greeting company, direct your puppy to his *greeting station*. Organize an area within view, and secure a station lead if your puppy won't stay. Protection breeds need order to feel calm.

- If he continues to overreact, stand tall and say, SHHT, as you tug the leash. Completely ineffective? Try a Good Dog collar or a head collar.
- Teach BACK TO ME by saying these words as you clap, wave a toy, or shake his treat cup. (Practice first when he's undistracted.)
- If it's the doorbell, go to the door together (hold the leash), and instruct him BACK to your side or to a specific *greeting station* (see the corresponding box).
- Set up situations asking a family member or a friend to ring the doorbell three times at thirty-second intervals. If your puppy alert barks a couple of times and then looks to you, praise and treat him. If he continues, tug the leash and refocus him with BACK.

Hone up on your obedience. Take a class to ensure proper social etiquette. Protection puppies are powerful and determined: help yours shape a positive worldview.

A good protection dog always takes his cues from his owner and family.

Playful barking: This outgoing puppy has a hard time taming his enthusiasm. If not headed off at the barking phase, he may escalate into rough play. Vary your approach accordingly.

- Often, this puppy is tired and needs to be settled for a nap.
- Divert his attention with stimulating toys or an interactive run. If this escalates his hyperactivity, end the play session.
- Try to calm him with comforting long strokes: the soothing effects of a mother's tongue.
- If this pattern continues, attach a head collar and a leash to settle him when stimulated.

Frustration barking: Related to attention getting, this barking generally results from over-isolation.

- Exercise and training are important. Tired puppies are more relaxed.
- If isolation results from poor manners, use the leading and the stationing techniques described in this book to civilize your pup. A welcome puppy is a happy puppy.
- Directions to WAIT and STAY are important. Both indicate that your separation is temporary.
- Stage departures. Station your puppy with a mat and a bone. Leave for a few minutes. If he barks during any or all of your absence, don't worry. Return to the room as planned, and ignore him until he quiets down. Greet calmness with gentle, quieting pats.

- Gradually increase your timed departures as his tolerance increases.

- Avoid rescuing a barking puppy. Your reinforcement won't help either of you.

- If you've got a marathon barker, you may try a cause-and-effect sequence to discourage him. Either discreetly stage a spray correction (he mustn't know you've returned or are watching him), or try a commercial citronella barking collar.

Sound and motion: Things that you or I might never see or hear become life-shaping events for these puppies. Serene companionship is nearly impossible if the barking is left unabated.

- Lessons are a must, as they teach your puppy to put you above outside distractions. When everything is distracting, getting your puppy's focus is a real plus. If you can pinpoint a time of distraction that really sets your puppy in motion, work your puppy outside of his *Red Zone* (the distance from the distraction at which he can stay focused on you). Slowly inch closer to the distraction. If food is a strong drive, use it to encourage your puppy's attention.

Jodi Buren

- Can you block off your puppy's access to areas that are most stimulating? I know a Wheaten Terrier named Duffy who went totally bonkers when the school bus arrived in the afternoon. Lessons helped, and so did blocking the access to the front room from 2:30 to 3:30 until he had a better handle on his impulses. Sometimes the most obvious solutions are the most effective.

- When you're home with your puppy, keep him on leash. Correct any alert barking with a quick tug and NOPE, and quickly refocus him on an appropriate distraction toy. In my house I said, KILL THE DUCK (politically incorrect, I know), and my terrier would shake her duck around. Clever girl!

A blaster-leash tug combo may be your best bet.

This Is the Captain Speaking . . .

Imagine yourself on a very turbulent plane. So turbulent, in fact, that you're scared to death. Do you want the pilot sitting next to you in a state of shock or up in front flying the plane while saying calmly, "Please sit down and fasten yourself belts. Everything will be okay." For your puppy, SIT and STAY will be just the thing he'll want to hear.

- A discreet blast of citronella spray from behind can also be an effective deterrent. Refocus your puppy immediately on a toy.
- Play the *swing toss game* from chapter 5 to give your puppy an outlet for his energy. Investigate other toys that slowly dispense food as your puppy plays with them, such as the Buster Cube and Jolly Balls. They're great for puppies with high prey drive.

Startle barking: The temptation is to caress and soothe this puppy. Don't. Please. Your empathy will be misconstrued as fear (your body is small, your voice tone feeble, and you're crouching behind him).

- Act confident and sure of yourself. Don't miss a beat.
- Direct your puppy with familiar words to help him feel safe.
- Be an example of calm. He'll follow your lead.

DYNAMIC DIGGERS

Digging is great fun! It's up there with tearing a pillow to shreds. For some puppies, it's a passing phase; for others, a lifelong addiction. How you manage it will either spotlight the activity or take the edge off your puppy's enthusiasm. Here are some standard dos and don'ts.

- Never garden in front of a young puppy. He'll want to help.
- Give up yelling and chasing your puppy. You're reaction is seen as *prize envy* and is entertaining—your puppy will want a repeat performance and will dig to get it.
- No after-the-fact outbursts. Save your responses for a more creative approach.

Think of digging as a puppy's natural expression of unadulterated joy. Unearthing dirt, breathing the smell of Mother Earth—oh, the power of his mighty paws! Here's some tips for keeping those paws in check:

- Set aside an unused patch of dirt, build a sandbox, or find a digging area at a local park. Then . . . go dig with your puppy. Play hide-and-go-dig with biscuits and toys. If it's his favorite pastime, share it with him—give him a release!

- Take your puppy's stools and plop them into old holes with ¼ cup red pepper (a spice). Cover the holes up.

- Avoid leaving your puppy outdoors alone for a couple of weeks. It's boring. In order to amuse himself, he might dig. It's a mind-freeing behavior and an adrenaline rush. If you must, leave him with a few interactive toys: a rope toy tied to a banister or a tree, a hard, indestructible ball, and a satisfying chew.

- When outside with him, engage him in activities that he could play on his own: *swing toss game*, *soda bottle soccer*, the ones listed earlier. If he's tempted to dig, attach a long line to enable you to discourage him *from a distance*. If you get too close, it's seen as interactive. Refocus to an appropriate digging location or activity.

POOPIE PALATE

Try not to visualize it, even as it's happening. The truth is that your puppy enjoys poop. To him, few things are tastier. A relaxed approach is best. Over time, this habit—like mud, sandboxes, and Bazooka gum—usually loses its flair. Here are some ways to ward off this habit:

- **Don't compete.** Shouts, shooing off, running toward him—these actions make you look like a formidable challenger. I know, I know. You don't want to eat it, but your puppy won't see it that way. You'll only draw more attention to the poop.

- **Try the long line and head collar combo.** If he's discovering poop while running free outside, attach this winning combo. Each time he finds a pile, tug on the line and say, EP, EP, EP. Quickly run in another direction, redirecting him to a ball or a toy.

- **Gentle discouragement.** If your puppy finds a pile of poop, calmly clap your hands, saying, EP, EP, EP, as you turn away from him. That's right— as you turn away from him. Your turning away signals that you're off to a new adventure, prompting a following response. Pick up a stick or a toy or shake a treat cup to encourage your puppy along. Time will dull the thrill.

- **Overkill.** Is your puppy obsessive about poop? Does he scan each open area and remember where he found it yesterday? If nothing you do to discourage him is helping, you may want to try this technique. Although I haven't tried it personally, I've gotten word that it can be a miracle cure. Here's what you do:
  - Leave your puppy inside for this step. Go out with a bucket and gather as much poop as you can find.
  - Dump your bucket near the house.
  - Feed your puppy a hearty meal and follow it up with some favorite treats.
  - Take him out, and when he finds the enormous collection, don't interfere. Let him feast. Better still, walk away and play with one of his favorite toys.
  - If he looks at you, don't look back. This will tell you if the behavior is an attention-getting ploy.

    He'd be eating it anyway, so you'll just make it easier. Often, this approach creates quick revulsion. Of course, some puppies finish it and go out hunting for more. Keep your fingers crossed!

TOUGH PUPPY

It's quite startling the first time you see your puppy with the hard eyes and the gleaming teeth that signal aggression. You may feel furious and insulted. You will feel angry, if not at your puppy directly, then at the powers that be. You'll feel confused and perhaps afraid.

To take nothing away from your feeling, aggression is not as uncommon as many people think. Even puppies get frustrated and defensive. Especially in a loud or defensive household, aggression is a sign of a puppy who cannot handle his frustrations. Without words to convey emotions, he relies on species tact. A firm eye or a snarl in a group of puppies would be an instantaneous communication. How you cope and redirect this behavior determines how your puppy will deal with these feelings as he matures into adulthood.

Of course, some aggression is not natural: it's a marked sign of a genetic aberration. This can be seen in pure breeds that are line-bred (breeding family members to one another) and in puppy mill puppies whose genetic wiring has suffered stress.

These categories outline the different forms of aggression. Although delving into the nitty gritty of your puppy's reaction will open your awareness and stir your thoughts, I strongly suggest you find a professional to help you. Left

Balancing Three Factors

To determine how serious your problem is, consider these factors:

- **Breed:** Know your puppy's natural genetic inclinations. Retrieving breeds are historically bred for gentle, permissive dispositions; it's far more alarming to see one of these growling over a possession than to hear a growl from a feisty, instinctive, or dominant breed, like a Jack Russell Terrier or a Rottweiler.

- **Age:** Puppies under 20 weeks should not exhibit signs of aggression. Though a play growl is common, any hard stares or belly growls are *red flags* on your playing field. Call for professional help. As your puppy matures, aggression parallels the onset of adult hormones (7–11 months). This section will give you an understanding of how aggression evolves, as well as tips in handling it and preventing these displays, although early professional intervention is necessary once you note aggression.

- **Temperament:** Aggressive puppies are independent thinkers. Most often, they're headstrong and bold, confident to explore and conquer on their own, and satisfied to give direction if you're slack. There is also the flip side: puppies who act overtly fearful or petrified of everyday situations—so fearful, they're unable to absorb human direction.

unchecked, the intensity that brought on the aggression will sharpen, and your puppy may be a difficult companion to trust.

- **Spatial aggression:** A puppy who defends objects, food, passageways, and/or resting areas.

- **Protective aggression:** Defending the home and/or people.

- **Displaced aggression:** Frustrations are displaced onto the closest outlet, usually a dog or a family member. Some puppies displace on inanimate objects (like a pillow) as well.

- **Hierarchical aggression:** This pup is making a bid for top-dog status and will use aggression to make his point.

- **Containment aggression:** This pup shows aggression when confined, i.e., on a lead or behind a fence.

- **Predatory aggression:** Over-the-top reactions to moving targets.

- **Fear-induced aggression:** Visualize a puppy so petrified that his tail and ears are laminated to his body. Aggression may seem unlikely; however, these puppies are panicked for their lives. When these puppies bite, it is often without warning.

- **Psychotic aggression:** This is marked by dramatic temperament swings. It's like Jekyll and Hyde. Frightening.

Aggression 101

Following are quick summaries of what triggers these forms of aggression and some tips for preventing and dealing with it. The first step is realigning the hierarchy: it must begin with people and end with your puppy. He must know that each member of his household holds seniority and must be respected. Even if they babble and sleep in a crib.

SPATIAL AGGRESSION

This puppy is simply trying to tell you that what's his is his. His food, his objects, his sleeping space. It's not unnatural, although it's unfortunate. Somewhere along the line, he got the message that your relationship was confrontational, not cooperative. (If you witness this reaction immediately or during the onset of hormonal maturity, it has a strong genetic component.) Games like tug-of-war and chasing or rough-housing all convey a competitive message. If a young puppy is yelled at and/or chased for having inappropriate objects in his mouth, he will grow to perceive these as objects of value. In time, he may guard them.

To prevent and rehabilitate, you'll need to fit your puppy with a head collar and a drag lead (left on during meals) to enable easy handling and keep a treat cup and a clicker handy to signal your positive intentions.

1. Shake a treat cup and reward your puppy until he associates the sound with a reward.

2. Approach your puppy with the treat cup while he is eating a meal. Stop above his bowl and toss in several treats. If he growls as you approach him during a meal, stop and toss him a few treats before you leave.

3. Repeat Step 2 until you can stand over him and drop treats into his bowl.

4. At this point, approach his bowl speaking happy praises but *without* shaking the cup. When you get to his side, toss a treat into the bowl and leave.

5. Next, try kneeling down as you shake the cup, and toss a treat into his bowl.

6. When you kneel and toss a treat into his bowl without tension, try placing the treat into his bowl with your hand.

7. After you offer your puppy a handful of treats, try stirring the kibble with your hand. If you're successful, continue this once every other day for a week.

8. Next, after offering a handful of treats, try lifting the bowl. Give it back immediately and leave. Repeat this once a month only.

9. Repeat this entire process with prized objects, like bones or toys.

> ### 🐾 Proper Meet and Greet
>
> Puppies who are isolated during greetings or visits may develop *frustrated territorial aggression (FTA)*. FTA often leads to exaggerated reactions. In a normal group of puppies, the leader permits or denies entry to a visitor, who is then "sniffed out" by the rest of the pack. Isolation frustrates this normal process and encourages a more aggressive response the next time the doorbell rings.

PROTECTIVE AGGRESSION

A host of situations can lead to protective aggression. Here's a short list:

- When delivery people or passersby approach and leave the home territory, a reactive puppy assumes that he scared them off.
- When his people are home and they react to a territorial response by yelling or physical handling, the puppy perceives their heightened responses as backup or signs of distress.
- When a puppy reacts aggressively in a car or a yard, he is warning all intruders to stay away. Because they do, he considers himself victorious, and his territorial aggression is reinforced.

Call a professional to help mend your difficulties. In the meantime,

- Use a head collar (page 28). It allows calm handling and full head control.
- Have two lessons with your puppy each day. Keep him behind you at all thresholds and when meeting new people.
- Use a treat cup or a tube of peanut butter to help your puppy associate outsiders with a positive reward. Yes, peanut butter now comes in a tube. Most puppies love it. If you tape a bell to the tube, it will have special meaning. After your puppy has calmed down, encourage visitors to offer the tube to your puppy.
- Stop yelling! Just quit all theatrical interventions: they add more negative energy to an already tense situation. To calm your puppy, you must set the example.

DISPLACED AGGRESSION

This type of aggression occurs when immediate frustrations, such as an inability to chase a cat or challenge another dog or get at the postman, are displaced onto other pets, family members, or inanimate objects. This pup has the weight of the world on his shoulders. The pup is task-oriented and intense; frustration comes easily when he is prevented from following through on an impulse. It borders on an obsessive/compulsive disorder. Address this problem immediately. The pup needs to learn how to displace his intensity onto appropriate targets.

- Throughout the day, emphasize a displacement activity. Use a trigger word repetitively: "BALL! Get your BALL."
- Start lessons today. Sign up for a class and/or use this book. Your pup needs clear, consistent direction.
- Once you've determined your puppy's hot button (chasing an animal, retrieving a toy, another dog), figure out his Red Zone: the distance from the animal or the object at which he is unable to control his frustration.
- Work just outside that zone, using a clicker and other food- or toy-oriented techniques to keep him focused.
- Gradually move closer to his distraction.
- If the situation arises suddenly, protect yourself. Use a product like the blaster, which blasts citronella spray, to dissuade. Use a head collar and a drag lead for quick control.

If your puppy has bitten, call a specialist immediately. This puppy should not be around children.

HIERARCHICAL AGGRESSION

This pup is making a bid for top-dog status and will use aggression to make his point.

- Use the trigger word EXCUSE ME (page 156) frequently when your puppy gets in your way. This is the most passive way to communicate your leadership.
- Ignore all of his attempts to get your attention, including but not limited to barking, pawing, head butting, and whining.
- Have short five-minute lessons two to five times a day. Go through all the directions he knows. If he's growls when you direct him DOWN, don't force it. He has issues. Get professional help.
- If your puppy responds to DOWN, repeat it throughout the day.
- Avoid stare-downs unless you initiate them, in which case make sure your puppy breaks eye contact first.
- Once a day, enforce a thirty-minute quiet time, either by stationing or by anchoring.

CONTAINMENT AGGRESSION

This pup shows aggression when confined, i.e., on-lead or behind a fence. This behavior is common if a puppy has been confined in a populated environment and has undergone stress. Containment at a shelter or a pet store often triggers this reaction as well. The cage or the crate protects a puppy from challengers, and any displays are reinforced as self-protecting. The same scenario gets repeated on-lead. Pups who walk in front often strain at their collars, putting their bodies into a defensive stance. When in range of another dog (often in this same position), the puppy must determine what's in his protective interest. Based on prior feedback, the reaction will be defensive. What follows doesn't help the situation at all. If the "attack" is mutual, both dogs are dragged along past each other by their owners—and the cycle of containment aggression continues. UGH!

- Fit your puppy for a head collar or a Good Dog collar today.
- Teach HEEL and reinforce it: this says, "I am the leader. Follow me!"
- No yelling or physical reactions. Both are interpreted as situational, not instructive.
- Lots of lessons. Join a group class today.
- Discover your puppy's Red Zone.
- Work just beyond that distance with clickers, treats, and toys.
- When you sense your puppy's tension rising, tug the lead as you say, NOPE. Redirect with HEEL and distract with positive lures if they're effective. Speed up, stay focused ahead, and don't slow down.

PREDATORY AGGRESSION

Predatory aggression is another instinctive behavior from times when puppies were wolves and hunted for survival. Most puppies still possess a chasing instinct.

Although we have suppressed the drive to kill in most breeds, some (Nordic breeds and terriers especially) instinctively chase and, in some instances, kill small game.

If you have a chaser on your hands, you have your hands full. Their instincts are strong. Focused play gives them an outlet, but you need to be present with other animals or children to discourage interactive chasing rituals.

- Work through the basics in chapters 4 and 5. Once your puppy has mastered them, take him to new places where you'll seem more worldly and in charge.

- Determine your puppy's Red Zone: the distance at which the distraction does not affect your puppy. Work outside it initially. Gradually reduce the distance as your puppy's focus improves.

- Use a training collar that issues a sharp cause-and-effect correction. The chain collar or the self-correcting collar can work well if used appropriately. The instant your puppy alerts to an animal or an object (watch for his ears to pitch forward), quick-tug the leash and say, NOPE! Refocus with a familiar STAY or HEEL.

- Play the *swing toss game* to re-channel your puppy's impulses. Take a plastic gallon milk jug and remove the lid. Slather peanut butter or cream cheese on the inside and the outside of the opening, and tie the handle to a ten- to fifteen-foot rope. Go into a field (either fenced or with your puppy on a long line), and swing the toy around. Toss it into the grass or the bushes, keeping it moving until your puppy is spent. If he likes to tug, tie toys to trees or stair banisters to encourage him to tug on something that won't come loose.

FEAR-INDUCED AGGRESSION

Keep your puppy on-lead when you expect company. Hold your puppy's lead while you act confidently in new situations.

- Teach your puppy that you're not weak. Practice lessons twice a day, focusing on words and exercises from chapters 4 and 5.

- Consider using the head collar. When a puppy is scared, the steady pressure across his head is more reassuring than a neck jerk or a harness hold.

- Lead your puppy around your home and neighborhood to show him you know how to run the show. Reinforce WAIT at all thresholds and use EXCUSE ME if he crowds you.

- Create comfy play stations with mats and toys and a pre-secured leash. Practice thirty-minute quiet times during the day. When your puppy is stressed, keep him by your side. Familiar words like HEEL, STAY, and WAIT are reassuring.

> ### 🐾 A Puppy's Choice
>
> Puppies can control the level of damage they inflict when biting. How hard and where (body, arm, or face) are conscious choices. To put this in human terms, an angered person chooses how to confront the issue: from words to physical posturing to a push or a punch.

- Set an example by staying relaxed. The calmer you are, the cooler you are as a leader.
- A large part of the problem is that the fearful puppy feels no one has control of the situation. Keep your puppy on his leash, and act confident and secure in new situations. Encourage everyone to ignore him until he comes forward. Use your treat cup to encourage a more positive association to unfamiliar situations.

PSYCHOTIC AGGRESSION

This aggression is remarkable. Seen as young as 8 weeks, it comes from deep within your puppy's psyche and is very difficult to influence. Get help immediately.

ERRATIC VICIOUSNESS

At unpredictable intervals, this puppy growls fiercely from his belly. It may happen when his owner passes his food bowl, approaches when he's chewing a toy, or even walks by him. At other times, the puppy is perfectly sweet—a "Jekyll and Hyde" personality.

FEAR BITERS

This puppy shows dramatic fear or a startled bite response in nonthreatening situations, such as someone turning a page of the newspaper or moving an arm. He can act extremely confused or threatened when strangers approach.

SEPARATION ANXIETY

Separation anxiety peaks at 9 months, so if you're experiencing it early, pull up your chair. It'll get worse unless you make it better. Ninety percent of puppies experience this at some level. How you handle it influences the duration, the potential destruction, and their abilities to cope. The problem is similar to a teenager's behavior: in the human world, teenagers are separating from their

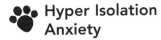

parents emotionally but are still unsure of the world that beckons them. Most kids don't take their turmoil out on the couch. Your puppy might.

If your puppy were living in a wild pack of dogs, his ninth month would herald new responsibilities. Traveling with the pack, he would be expected to participate in group activities. The anxiety our pets feel stems from the thwarting of their innate instinct to begin traveling with us 24/7.

> ### 🐾 Hyper Isolation Anxiety
>
> This is anxiety that occurs when a puppy is isolated. The concept of isolation is foreign, causing rising concern, which creates anxiety, which explodes into hyper behavior when you're both reunited. It quickly becomes a vicious cycle as the hyperactivity begets more isolation.

When helping to remedy anxiety issues, I categorize the personality of the puppy first. If your puppy could talk, which of the following three statements do you think he'd utter?

1. **"You're my guardian . . . and I miss you."** (Separation anxiety in its mildest form.) This puppy stress whines, may bark when initially left alone, and is excited when reunited with you. If he's left to wander freely, there might be some destruction but nothing over the top.

2. **"I'm your guardian . . . how dare you leave me."** This puppy thinks he rules your roost. That you're his responsibility. Your departure is extremely disrespectful: how can he protect and direct you when you walk out on him? Resistant displays as you're leaving, incessant barking, destruction when left alone, and hyperactive homecomings are signs that your puppy is quite frustrated with the situation.

3. **"I'm your guardian . . . but I'd rather not be."** This puppy has taken charge by default, not by desire. He directs you only because you don't direct him. When you leave, his exalted position is put to question: how can he protect and oversee you when you're gone? Stress sets in like a thunderstorm. He worries. This puppy may chew himself or pace nervously when you're gone. He'll be the one looking out the window, chewing his paws or gnawing the moldings. Whining, pacing, desperate vocalizations and howling, along with periodic bouts of protective barking, will be his lamenting song. When you return, you may not be able to console him. He may spend the rest of the day Velcroed to your side, demanding attention every three seconds. "Do you need me? Do you love me still?—it's been too long. . . . tell me you love me."

To resolve separation anxiety, there are some universal concepts:

- When your puppy demands your attention, ignore him. Teach him SIT or DOWN, and use it before each loving interaction. It will become a habit.

- Avoid being puppy-trained! You're sending your teenager-puppy the wrong message: that you need him to organize your life. When you leave, he won't be able to shake the stress.

- Start organized lessons. This communicates structure and balance and reassures him that you're the one to watch. When you're not there, lessons will help reassure him that you're on patrol.

- For now, contain your puppy using a crate, a playpen, or a small gated room when you go out. Freedom to pace only intensifies his angst.

- Your goal is to leave the house and trust your puppy not to eat the walls. It's a more pleasant scenario for your puppy, too. Follow these steps:

    1. Reread stationing on page 29, using a chain lead if your puppy chews through nylon. Station your puppy with a bone for half-hour stretches after an outing and some exercise.

    2. Initially, stay in the room but mill about, moving calmly. This mild separation may cause some anxiety. Ignore your puppy until he settles down. Don't lose heart if it takes days to happen. Buy earplugs if the whining or barking are hard to ignore, and turn up some classical music. No eye contact, no touching. When the time is up, unhook the lead and continue to ignore your puppy if he's stressed or hyper. Focus on a calm puppy, and that's what you'll have, even if the process takes weeks (which it rarely does).

    3. Practice short departures. Station your puppy, and leave the room for a minute. If you're greeted as though you've been gone a year, ignore him. Think of this as the 8-to-10 zone described on page 43. Wait until your puppy settles to rest or chew his bone before you acknowledge him. Yes, it may take twenty minutes initially, but it won't be long before he can tolerate your disappearance. Continue to leave the room—come back, leave—come, leave—come. If you're puppy is hyped up or vocal, ignore him. Totally. Your goal is to help him contain your separation calmly. If he's still resting or chewing when you return, you may go over for a five-second reassuring pat. Congratulations.

    4. Lengthen your departures. Eventually, start leaving the house. Come and go, for minutes at a time.

Note what sets your puppy off. Is it the moment you leave the room or go to the closet or fetch your keys? Periodically, carry your keys or wear your coat without leaving. What happens?

Prevention and the Cure

- Keep all your departures and arrivals low-key, even if you're just going to the bathroom.
- When you have to leave, secure your puppy somewhere safe and go. Dim the light in the room (to encourage napping), leave a favorite chew toy rubbed in your palms to leave your scent, and turn on calming music to drown out incoming sounds.
- When you go, don't look back.
- If you're in an apartment and eviction is pending, consider a citronella no-bark collar. I've had positive reviews. Otherwise, stick it out.
- When you return, ignore your puppy. You read that right. Ignore him until he is 100 percent calm. If you come in like gangbusters, the message is wild. Any time your puppy thinks a sound might be you, he'll get hyped, and when it's not you, the disappointment will be crushing.

Separation anxiety is normal. Extreme cases signal a hierarchical issue, which can elicit an out-of-body experience. A puppy can go into a state of near shock, resulting in bodily harm, excessive destruction, or panting. If your puppy is getting worse, speak with your veterinarian. There is a pharmaceutical drug that can help if used in conjunction with behavioral methods.

LEASH LUNGERS

Imagine if I grabbed your shirtsleeve and forcefully pulled you across the floor. What would you do? The asphyxiating leash walk is not much of a thrill for your puppy, either, so let's remedy this situation ASAP!

- Work inside or out in an open area.
- Attach your lead to your waist or hold the center of the lead in both hands, at your waist level.
- Walk forward, calling out your puppy's name and LET'S GO. If he scampers ahead, call to him as you turn sharply around and walk in the other direction. Repeat this over and over until either you fall

Jodi Buren

Throw your voice to alert his attention

down in a dizzy stupor or your puppy starts following your lead. And when that happens, exclaim a hearty YES and give him a big hug (click/treat).

- Call his name as you turn. The motion of your voice will pique his interest.
- Use this same technique in increasingly more distracted areas.
- For the true test, work in the most distracted environment you can find. Each time your puppy is focused more on the surroundings than he is on you, call his name and change direction.

MULE WANNABES

Here's a situation where pulling does not come into play. This puppy won't move: passive resistance that's solid as a rock. And it's quite effective. The most common response is to walk back, coax, and carry. Some people try a dramatic beg. Our ideal falls somewhere in between:

1. Gather some props. A treat cup, favorite toys, and a clicker, if you ascribe to that, are good for starters.
2. Resist the urge to look back when your puppy puts on the brakes. Attention reinforces behavior, even just a quick glance.
3. Call your puppy to you: kneel forward on a knee as you clap your side and/or shake your treat cup. Face the direction you want your puppy to follow.
4. When your puppy gets near you, praise him warmly (click and treat).
5. Walk out the extent of the leash, and repeat the same procedure over and over. Eventually, it won't take you an hour to walk down the block!

Note: For some puppies, gentle, steady pressure can coax them into motion. If you're concerned about your puppy's neck, fit him for a head collar or a no-pull harness.

RUNAWAY PUPPIES

Losing sight of a puppy is heart-wrenching. Have a puppy ignore your call or react to COME by running away from you is definitely one of life's chief frustrations. If his checking in with you is an afterthought (whatever the reason), you may have taught COME as a command of separation, not togetherness. How? Imagine that you're a young pup exploring and learning about the world. Suddenly, your companion is staring at you, repeating an unfamiliar word again and again. Since eye contact reinforces behavior, you (the puppy) freeze. You stare back. What

 **Microchip**

Your veterinarian can speak to you about an identification chip that is injected into your puppy's left shoulder/neck region. It enables other professionals to scan your puppy (like a holiday package) and send him home.

🐾 Long Line

Using a long line when playing outdoors quickly influences your puppy's choice to stay within reach. On a six-foot lead, many puppies learn that togetherness is asphyxiating: if the leash were released, they'd be off. This holds true for the flexi-lead as well. The long line, a twenty-five- to fifty-foot lead in an open area, gives your puppy freedom as you stand nearby offering praise and treats for his return.

follows is overwhelming—whether you're yelled at, chased, or grabbed, you will quickly learn that COME means "run away."

Fortunately, all is not lost. If you use the right approach, your puppy will have a new view in no time. Invest in a long line, and break out your snack pack/clicker as you practice all the lessons in chapter 5 and play the following games to convince your puppy that togetherness is best.

Keep a snack pack full of treats or toys at quick disposal to ensure that your puppy's return is met with enthusiasm and rewards. Condition the "check-in" by rewarding every return and encouraging your puppy to come back to you by playing the following games:

- **Run-away-come game:** If you chase your puppy as he's running away, he'll perceive that you're simply backing him up. Not the goal, I know. It's time to turn the tables. With your puppy on his long line, practice running away from him. Using a treat cup adds sparks to any game!

- **Toss your voice:** This is a handy way to get your puppy's attention. Toss your voice in the opposite direction, swinging your head away from him as you call his name. This will perk interest in what you're doing and guarantees an exuberant reunion. You're the one to watch.

- **Treat cup name game:** Stand apart from a partner, and call your puppy back and forth. Shake the cup as you call your puppy's name, and reward him the instant he returns.

If the unthinkable happens and your puppy does run away, stay calm. Feeling frightened and hysterical is natural, but it will not help your puppy. Make several calls to the police and neighbors, and drive around, shaking his treat cup and calling his name. When you find your puppy, lavish him with love. Corrections will dampen the reunion and will guarantee that he won't come so fast the next time.

Jodi Buren

Play the run-away-come game with a long line and a treat cup.

> 🐾 **Walk *This* Way**
>
> When calling your puppy, walk or run in the other direction. That's right—don't even look at him. Think of me calling you into the kitchen: would you want me repeating, "KITCHEN KITCHEN COME INTO THE KITCHEN," and running at you, shaking you to stop watching TV and come this second? Or would you want me to call you enthusiastically as I walked into the kitchen?

WHINE-A-LOTS

My dog Whoopsie never ceases to amaze me. As I'm writing this section, she is doing something that she has never done before. She is whining. It reminds me that I forgot to set aside a section for this most irksome behavior. Why is she whining, you might ask? Well, I can't say with 100 percent accuracy, but in general whining is a sign of stress: a dog caught between desire and demand. Whoopsie either wants someone to play with her or she wants to go out. She has put herself in DOWN-STAY, so until I get a further clue, there isn't too much I can do to help her.

If you've got a puppy who whines, here's your hit list:

- Corrections don't help. It's involuntary—a dog trapped between impulse and expectation.
- Earplugs do help. Seriously.
- Target the specific trigger. For example, if it occurs when someone puts on a coat, coats should be a worn in the house until your puppy desensitizes to this activity.
- The remedial lesson? Teach your puppy to STAY, and practice this lesson a lot. He needs help learning to contain those impulses!

Oh, by the way, Whoopsie just wanted to play ball. I waited until she stopped whining.

DOORWAY DRAMAS

A telltale sign of a hierarchy going awry is often revealed at the front door. If your puppy pushes his way out and/or barges past you when company calls, you're an afterthought. There's no debate. Can you imagine if a friend did that? No matter how excited the friend might be, it just wouldn't be cool—to say nothing of the danger. Many doors open onto streets or near driveways. All is not lost, however. This one's easy enough to restructure. The trigger words are WAIT and OKAY.

- Put your puppy on his leash/teaching collar.
- When you come to the door, bring him behind your heel and instruct, WAIT.

- If, as you open the door, he lurches forward, give him a quick tug back as you say, NOPE.

- Re-instruct WAIT.

- Keep it up until you can relax the leash and he's still. You get a bonus point if he looks up. He's looking to you for permission.

- Say, OKAY, and either release him if you're staying indoors or walk out ahead of him.

> ### 🐾 Other Thresholds
>
> At every door in life, one of you must lead while the other follows, whether at your home, visiting the veterinarian, or going into stores or other friends' homes. Your puppy will feel calmer if the home rules apply everywhere.

- Repeat this five times during this first trial run, and make a habit of it from now on. Soon enough, your puppy will be doing it automatically—what I call a default behavior.

For the next week, leave a drag lead on your puppy when he's supervised. When the doorbell rings, either lead him to a greeting station or step on the lead so that he's contained. Either choice teaches civility. In both cases, use "WAIT" as you open the door; no one should acknowledge your puppy until he's calm. No one pets or interacts with him until he is calm.

> *Remember the company covenant: in most cases, they're coming to visit you, not your puppy.*

Door Wide Open

Can you teach your puppy to stay inside even if the door is wide open? No, I'm not kidding. Whether in your home or your car, this lesson saves lives and calms households.

- Secure a three-foot station lead six to ten feet from the door. This can be his greeting station if you've already set one up. (If your puppy chews his leash, buy a chain lead for this project.)

- Hook him on it, instruct, WAIT, and go out the door, *leaving it wide open.*

- Do something, anything, for up to five minutes: unpack groceries, get the mail, garden.

- Don't look back, pine, or explain yourself.

- Gradually increase the duration.

- Real life: if you're having a guest or a delivery, secure your puppy before you open the door. If you're expecting movers, construction workers, or anything that would require the door to be left ajar, secure your puppy and give him a bone or a toy. You're helping him contain his impulses and civilizing him all at once.

- He may bark, whine, and throw himself on the floor in protest. Make sure he is safe from harm, but otherwise ignore him until he's calm.

This is a lesson that some learn quickly, and others take time. I had a refrigerator delivered when our Whoopsie was 4½ months old. Although she whined for the first thirty-seven minutes, she chewed her bone the rest of the time. Unfortunately for her, the service men didn't like puppies, but it was a wonderful lesson in containment.

Car dashing is another dangerous game. Read up on training puppies to have good behavior in the car in chapter 7, and follow a similar routine.

MOUNTING DRAMATICS

Mounting behavior carries a different meaning, depending on the dog's age. With young puppies, it's either a dominance signal or an attempt to feel more in control of an otherwise stressful situation. You can differentiate which option applies, based on their attitude the rest of the day: are they self-assured or passive? In some cases, it's just unexplainable, like the Golden Retriever mix who would stand next to the couch and air mount for several minutes. A puzzle. One of life's many.

If your puppy is mounting inanimate objects, ignore it. It's odd, but dominating a defenseless pillow won't interfere with your day. If it's you or the kids, that's a different story.

Under 4 months: Take your puppy's collar, or drag lead if one's attached, and firmly side swipe him to the floor, saying, EP, EP, EP. Walk away. Don't make a scene, as it's seen as confrontational. If the behavior continues, fit your puppy for a head collar and attach a drag lead to that. Head collars give you power, whereas neck collars create retaliation. If your puppy's the shy, retreating type, mounting only to gain more self-confidence, help him find another way. Notice what sets him off. Direct him with a trigger word like HEEL or SIT-STAY or UNDER to give him the security of your leadership.

Older than 4 months: The buck stops here. At this point, mounting has more to do with top-dog status and possessiveness: an attempt to dominate or gain control in a chaotic situation. Whether it's you, your kids, or the company that's being mounted, the behavior is unacceptable. To resolve this, enforce two daily quiet times and thirty minutes to an hour of leading each day, using the following trigger words:

- **EXCUSE ME:** To enforce your spatial significance. Review page 156.
- **WAIT:** Grant or deny permission to go through doors, up or down stairs, through thresholds, etc. You're the leader, the captain, the social director, the

protector, or the guardian. Pick a metaphorical image that works for you.

- **BACK:** Whoever stands in front is in charge. This directs your puppy back behind your feet.
- **LET'S GO:** Where you go, he follows.
- **SIT:** Say it once and reinforce it.
- **DOWN:** The same rules apply. Position if necessary.
- **THAT'S UNNACCEPTABLE!** Leave a drag or a hand lead on your puppy's training collar when you're supervising him. If he's large and overbearing, consider a Good Dog or a head collar: both empower your position and direction. The moment you sense that your puppy's ready to mount, take the lead and snap it down firmly as you stand very tall, stamp your foot, and say, THAT'S UNACCEPTABLE! Calmly crate your puppy for twenty minutes to an hour, and then go about your daily tasks.

> ## 🐾 Red Flag
>
> If your puppy growls at any of these instructions, find a professional to help you proceed.

HERDING HABITS

Herding puppies are born, not made. When will you know if your puppy's got the drive? If a moving slipper or an animal can impel him to utter disarray, your puppy may soon graduate to bigger and more dangerous targets.

Impulse control is your objective here. It's not a question of whether he will chase; it's teaching him what's acceptable. First, provide an outlet—a behavior you can cheer. An instinct this strong cannot be snuffed out. Second, when your puppy is old enough (5 months), teach him the concept of NOPE.

A Positive Outlet

Whether your puppy was bred to herd sheep, cattle, or other livestock, the urge takes hold when he observes horizontal motion. In a perfect world, each pup would have his very own lamb or calf to keep busy; however, there are suitable stand-ins. As you find a positive alternative, use a trigger word to elicit the response (e.g., TOY or BALL):

- Take an empty half-gallon or gallon plastic milk jug. Tie it to a five-foot to fifteen-foot rope, enabling you to swing it. Slather something creamy (peanut butter, cream cheese, butter) on the inside and the outside of the lid (cap removed). Take it into a large room or an outside space, and start swinging. Swing left, swing right—just below your puppy's line of vision. Toss it into the brush. Give it to one of the kids, and let them start running around and around, the bottle dragging behind them. The slather

Jodi Buren

Rig a run-by!

should keep the puppy from grabbing and tugging. Let him tackle and hold the jug from time to time to avert frustration.

- If your puppy is less than 12 weeks old, tie a toy onto a four- to six-foot lead and secure the end to your ankle. Proceed with your projects, lugging the puppy around behind you. If he tugs endlessly, try the slather approach listed previously.

- Go shopping. Buy a lot of toys that simulate motion. Find one that your puppy likes, and buy a few of them. After your puppy has successful chased one, bait and toss or kick another one. (Please don't expect him to retrieve it: you'll need another breed entirely.) Keep this up until you're both pooped.

Differentiating

Although you can't eliminate your puppy's instinct to chase motion, you can help him differentiate between what's acceptable and what's not.

- Before your puppy hits the age of recognition (5 months), use EP-EP to discourage chasing. If EP-EP is ineffective, use a drag lead to enable interference without interaction by stepping on or pulling the lead. EP-EP is most effective the moment your puppy's considering the chase, which you can gauge by his locked gazed and crouched body position.

- If it's the kids your puppy's after, station him in a room where they're active. As they get riled, your puppy may whine or bark. Ignore it or sit with your puppy calmly, teaching him the fine art of observation.

- Head collars work miracles, especially when used before the age of 14 weeks. When a neck collar is pulled, it may elicit a stronger reaction as the puppy will feel trapped, frustrated, and egged on, whereas with the head collar, the head is gently redirected toward you, conditioning a checking-in response before he darts out.

The Concept of NO

Here's where the real learning takes place. Our goal is lifesaving: letting your puppy know what's acceptable to chase and what isn't. An unchecked passion for chasing can quickly put your puppy in harm's way.

1. Find the right training collar. If your puppy is older than 4 months, the head collar may not be useful. A marvelous conditioning tool, it is not as effective in extinguishing instinctual behaviors. For this job, I suggest one of three collars:
   - Check chain: ¾ cloth, ¼ chain
   - Original chain collar: all metal
   - Good Dog pinch collar

   Please refer to chapter 2 for a thorough explanation of each.

2. Set up situations.
   - If your puppy is razzed by squirrels in the backyard, toss out some corn nuts and go out when the squirrels are gathering. Bicycles, kids, cars . . . go find them.
   - Walk toward the distraction with your puppy on-lead and at your side.
   - The *very instant* your puppy alerts, tug back and say, NOPE. If you're ineffective, be quicker and sharper with your body language, standing very tall.
   - Next, tell your puppy, BACK and WAIT.
   - If you've been playing toss with a specific toy (or bottle), have it lying about and direct him to a toy or a ball to displace his frustration.
   - Keep your puppy in the situation for five minutes. If it's the children you've set up, have them run back and forth. If it's traffic, stand and observe. Squirrels, lizards—well, you get the idea. Flood him with the stimulation until he begins to contain it.
   - After leaving the distractions, take him back for a chasing game with his favorite toys.

> ### 🐾 Poison!
>
> If your puppy has ingested poison, call the Poison Control hotline (1-900-680-0000), and follow their recommendations. Some poisons should not be regurgitated. Although you will pay a nominal fee, you won't be put on hold.

INEDIBLE INGESTION

If your puppy's palate extends beyond everyday kibble, he may have a life-threatening compulsion in need of immediate attention. Although a sock may not tickle our taste buds, if your puppy finds it tempting, it's a *red flag*. It, and objects like it, can block the digestive tract. Not good. Another scare is the puppy who is so in love with eating that a bag of poison is just as tempting as a fresh cut of meat.

- Talk to your veterinarian about the best way to induce vomiting.

- Discourage the grabbing of objects by rigging situations and yelling at the object exactly as described in the chewing section of this chapter.

- Don't yell at your puppy. Your frustration communicates prize envy and encourages a "gulping" response in attempts to hide the evidence and keep the prize.

- Use your treat cup to teach him to show you what he grabs. Practice this skill with all objects, good or bad. Shake that cup, kneel down, and say, GIVE, cheerfully when he's near you. With an extra dose of enthusiasm, your puppy will bring the object to you, rather than keep or eat it. (If your puppy is hesitant, let him drag a lead when you're supervising to enable your indirect control.)

- If your puppy is obsessed with swallowing something specific—a sock, for example—supervise him at all times. You may proof a playroom when you're interacting with him. Fit your pup for a head collar, and set up situations as described in the chewing section to develop a weariness of socks. If you're still unsuccessful, find a behaviorist and work through this problem together.

- Watch the poops. There's no better way to monitor your puppy's health than to check the consistency of his stools. A simple glance will be informative. If he hasn't pooped within a twenty-four-hour period, take note and inform his veterinarian. X-rays are a common procedure when pica (the formal term) is suspected.

Chapter 7

Enjoying the First Year

Although you've probably had the realization already, I'm going to come right out and say it: raising a puppy is a project. Your puppy will infiltrate all aspects of your existence, will alter your thoughts, and will require consideration and energy. That said, if you raise her well, your puppy will weave her way into your life's fabric in ways a person could not.

However, you have to get through the first year. You'll forget your days of frustration a year from now, but the first ten months can be an emotional roller coaster. In this chapter, I will walk you through all the stages of your puppy's first year, from the angelic weeks to the pressures of puberty. Each of the five sections will be broken down into smaller parts that tell you what to expect and what to teach, as well as answer common questions.

If you have an older puppy and are reading this chapter, you do have the option of reading through the first sections to pick up tidbits that you can incorporate into your routine, or you can simply flip ahead. Sidebars are always reserved for special highlights, so take a peek at those, too.

OH-SO DEPENDENT (8 TO 12 WEEKS)

Nothing is more delicious than a baby pup, freshly weaned from her mommy, cleaving to your side with pure love and affection. The world beyond is overwhelming, safety and nurturing are all she longs for: you become her savior and her salvation . . . at least for a little while. Although her fall from grace is inevitable, you've got a few weeks to witness the wonder. Each nuance, from the flight of a butterfly to the sound of your laughter, is fresh and open for interpretation. You are your puppy's role model and example. If you exhibit confidence, you'll be her idol, too—she'll grow emotionally strong under your direction. You are a powerful influence at this stage.

Having said that, I must remind you that you are a dog . . . at least to your puppy. She is looking to you to interpret her world and to set up life routines that help her

🐾 Sticking It Out

There will be one stage that baffles you. That makes you feel frustrated and tired. That puts you at odds with this puppy you love so much. Promise me you won't give her to the neighbor. Mark the days on your calendar. It will be over soon enough. Stick to the program, invest your time in your lessons, and up the exercise and the socialization—a tired puppy makes a happy household!

to meet her basic needs. Though she's capable of learning a lot right now, her brain is still developing, so go easy and don't overwhelm her with lessons. Stay focused on her basic needs (page 47), and teach her the words and the routines that pertain to each. Don't correct her: she's simply too young to understand, and you'll only succeed in frightening her. I've heard it said that "my puppy knows," but I can assure you, she does not. After all, a 6-month-old child would be petrified if you yelled at him, too, but neither the puppy nor the child would understand you.

The best course of action in this stage? Be supportive.

My suggestion for this stage is that you provide as much reflection time and mirroring as your schedule will allow. Reflecting involves doing exactly what she does—without insisting that she follow your plan. If she wants to check out the closet, get on all fours and go with her. If you don't want her to chew your boots, pick them up. If she wants to play ball, find a second ball and play next to her, (allowing her to take yours if she wants it). If you take her into a field hoping she'll fetch but all she wants to do is chase butterflies, make the butterflies your high priority. Mirroring involves getting into her head and mirroring her energy level. If she's sleeping, lie next to her and relax (watching TV or reading a book). If she's calm and wants to cuddle up, stay calm, too. If she's excited and wants to play, guide her toward acceptable releases. These are the final weeks of her brain's development. Make them as peaceful as possible.

🐾 Right vs. Wrong

Imagine that you're walking a young puppy when a loud siren goes off and frightens her. The human reaction would be to kneel down and soothe her. But the right response to give a child would be the wrong response for the puppy. She'd perceive your high-pitched voice and lowered posture as fearful, which would intensify her anxiety. Yet another example is the puppy who is lifted when approached by a larger dog. Although it's understandable, it teaches her to fear and react defensively with other dogs. In this situation, the puppy should be left on the ground (even if she shrieks), and her people should interact and show her how to play by example by reaching out, petting, and playing with the other dog until she feels safe enough to join in.

> **Encourage More Than You Discourage**
>
> Promise me (and your puppy) one thing. That you'll always encourage a positive alternative after you've discouraged your puppy. End on a high note. Redirect and reconnect.
>
> - "NOPE, don't chew that. YES, chew this."
> - "NOPE, don't jump on the counter. YES, go play with your toys on the mat."
> - "NOPE, don't nip my hand. YES, give me kisses."

What to Expect

- Distractibility: Don't be crushed if your puppy is not paying that much attention to you. Although this is a critical socialization time, there is a lot to take in. Focused bonding comes later.

- Brain development in high gear: Her brain will be in overdrive. Your puppy's brain is still developing and is hardwiring every experience, so make sure all of your interactions are calming and reflective.

- Open mouth, insert . . . everything! Of course, she'll put things in her mouth—all puppies do—and that includes you. She will nip you as if you were a dog.

- The developing sphincter (bladder muscle): Her bladder will be just as young as she is. She'll piddle the instant she feels the urge—her bladder muscles are the last to mature.

- Rumplestiltskin: Your puppy will sleep a lot. Don't be surprised or concerned. Again—it has to do with brain development. The most efficient wiring takes place when she's asleep. Sixteen to eighteen hours a day are not unusual. Let your puppy rest as much as she wants, and create a cozy nest for her away from the hubbub.

> **No Great Strides**
>
> Gauge your expectations. This is not the age to do a lot of training or to discipline your puppy. In fact, the pressure will only create more confusion down the line. Similar to disciplining a 6-month-old child, corrections overwhelm and frighten this puppy. Although a tough puppy may fight back and a reserved pup will look like she "knows," it's their only defense. Better to befriend and bond with your puppy during this stage. During the next stages, you'll be able to effectively communicate your disapproval without losing your temper.

What to Teach

8 WEEKS (OR OLDER)

Words of the Week

NAME: Of course, your puppy's name will be the word of the week, rather than the word *NAME*. Here are some surefire techniques to guarantee a welcoming association to your puppy's name:

- Each time your puppy finds you, say her name and touch her lovingly.
- If she enjoys her meals, say her name as you put her bowl to the floor.
- Repeat her name as you hand her a toy or a bone.
- Once she has made the treat cup association, call her name as she alerts to the sound.
- Her name should bring happy thoughts! Try something else when it's time to isolate, medicate, groom, or do anything that's considered a drag.

KISSES: This all-important word helps teach your puppy early on that skin is best for licking. Whenever your puppy is licking you, repeat, KISSES, in a clear, directional tone. To encourage kisses, rub a frozen stick of butter on your hand.

GET BUSY: Say this phrase as your puppy is peeing or pooping. Eventually, you'll be able to prompt her, but for now we're angling for early association.

Things to Do

Create a play station. Place a mat in a corner of her free room (gated kitchen, mudroom, or bathroom). Place her toys on the mat and her bowls close by. If possible, tie a few toys onto an immovable object to ensure that they stay put! (See chapter 2 for more information on stationing and leading.)

Customize your own Needs Chart. Using the sample chart form on page 47, customize your own Needs Chart, and share it with everyone in the house. Constancy in word, time, and routine will help your young puppy feel safe and nurtured.

Jodi Buren

Mimic the soothing effects of the mother's tongue. Your puppy identified her first Mom through smell and touch. Every day Mom would clean off each puppy and soothe them with the pressure of her tongue. Simulate this effect by stroking your puppy firmly a couple of times a day as you mutter in soft loving tones.

Soothing effects of the mother's tongue.

Make a treat cup. Place your puppy's kibbles or broken-up treats in a cup or a plastic container. Shake it as you simultaneously offer a treat. Soon your puppy will make the connection.

Games to Play

At this point, the *toy along, tag along* game (page 87) and the *treat cup name game* (page 77) are fun games to help you bond with your puppy.

9 WEEKS (OR OLDER)

Words of the Week

SIT: Don't overdo this command—just a few times a day will do. Say this word . . .

- When your puppy is naturally moving into the position.
- As you lure her into the position with food or toys.

YES: Everyone likes to hear this when they do something right. Each time your puppy is being good, give her a cheer. A sharp YES is more pointed than "Good Dog!" Follow each YES with a click and a treat or some lovin' attention!

OUTSIDE or PAPERS: Each time you bring your puppy outside or to the papers, associate these actions with this direction.

Things to Do

Use a collar for the first time. Attach a lightweight nylon tag collar. If your puppy itches or seems intensely distracted, remove it after twenty minutes. Put it on a couple of times a day until she's conditioned to the feel. For some puppies, it's like wearing bracing.

Create a Weekly Fun Chart. Here's a fun way to get the family involved. Refer to page 208 for some clever ideas, and make some time to create a personalized Fun Chart for your puppy.

Make a clicker association. If you're tempted to try the clicker, this is the time to make the association. Read about it in depth in chapters 2 and 4, and check out references online (I've got numerous hot links on my site, www.dogperfect.com). The sound of the clicker is used to photograph moments and behaviors that you'd like to see again. For many puppies, it accelerates learning exponentially!

Games to Play

The *elevator up and elevator down* game (page 73) is great for this stage.

10 WEEKS (OR OLDER)

Words of the Week

MAT: Spend time emphasizing this direction. Soon you'll be able to lay down a mat or a bed and your puppy will go to it happily.

- Feed your puppy on or near her mat. Say, MAT, as you walk there with her food or water dish.
- Shake your treat cup and say, MAT, as you run to it from different angles.
- Say, MAT, as you offer her a toy or a bone to chew.
- Mimic the soothing effects of the mother's tongue (stroke her firmly) while she's on her mat. Cradle her there, too.

BONE or TOY: Each time you offer your puppy a bone or a toy, add a directional word and praise her for taking it. Soon you'll be able to call out, TOY, and your puppy will search for it. This also helps your puppy remember what is hers.

EP, EP: Your puppy is too young to understand the concept of NO. It would be like yelling at a 6-month-old baby. Think of this sound as guidance. It says, "Oh, no, that's not good for you." You can tug a collar or a drag lead for emphasis, and then redirect your puppy to an appropriate alternative.

Things to Do

Socialize your puppy with objects. Each day lay something unique in her play space. A closed umbrella, an open umbrella, the vacuum, an upside-down garbage pail. Be creative. Your puppy will not "see" these things with her eyes; she will see them with her nose. She may be startled; resist soothing her. She'll put more faith in you if you act confidently by going to the object and "pretending" to sniff it. Sniff every inch of it. Leave it there until your puppy has hardwired its shape, texture, and odor into her memory. If you're walking your puppy outside, follow the same protocol. Think of yourself as a dog, and go investigate every inch of everything . . . with your nose!

Condition your puppy to handling. This is a four-star exercise. It can make the difference between a puppy who is relaxed when handled to one who is uncomfortable or defensive. With a treat and/or a delectable spread in hand, examine your puppy. Touch her ears, check out her gums, lift her tail. Talk softly as you do, telling her what a wonder she is. As you examine her eyes and touch her paws, let her know how happy you are to know her. This is also the time to introduce your puppy to grooming tools. Don't use them—simply let her smell them and lightly feel their touch.

Use a drag lead. Attach a short (three- to four-foot) lightweight nylon leash to your puppy's tag collar. Let her drag it when supervised. If she's uncomfortable

Jodi Buren

Early object conditioning.

with the weight, leave it on for several five-minute intervals until she ignores it. If she chews it or carries it about, you have two options: ignore it or soak it in a distasteful solution. My mantra? Pick your fights.

Games to Play

The games *soda bottle soccer* (in chapter 5, page 86) and *grab-n-show* (page 74) are great choices at this stage. Remember, soccer for puppies must be played with more than one bottle! And the best way to encourage the grab and show is by running away from your puppy when she has something and/or shaking a treat cup!

11 WEEKS (AND OLDER)

Words of the Week

COME: Ahh . . . the all-important direction! Start by saying this word only when you are physically touching your puppy. That's right; teach this one as a direction that highlights togetherness, not separation. Here are a few ways to practice:

- Each time your puppy naturally approaches you, say, COME, as you caress her head lovingly.
- Shake your treat cup. Say, COME, as you pop the treat into her mouth.
- Wave a toy. If she decides to run over, say, COME, as you give her the toy.
- Pretend you're a dog, and do things that might excite her curiosity, like playing with sticks or digging in the grass or the carpet. As she approaches, say, COME, and pat her.

WAIT and OKAY: WAIT says: "Stop and check in with me, your protector, before proceeding." OKAY says: "Yup, the coast is clear."

- With doors: Stop as you get to your door. Shake a treat cup to encourage her focus, and/or hold your puppy by the collar or the drag lead and say, WAIT. If she lurches forward, give her a quick tug, saying, EP, EP, and repeat, WAIT. Pause until she cooperates. Then say, OKAY, and lead her out or release her.

- With the car: The car is a dangerous place for a puppy. Structure each experience, and start teaching her manners now. Restrain her for starters: either in a seat belt contraption or a crate. She must also learn one door and one seat or spot. As you open the door to let her in, teach her WAIT. Pause, then say, OKAY, and then tell her, TO YOUR MAT. Coming out of the car is even more important. Insist on a solid WAIT (from two to twenty seconds) before releasing with OKAY. If your puppy won't cooperate, hold her back or secure her lead until she calms down.

Things to Do

Lure your puppy into position. Using your puppy's food or toys, practice guiding her into different positions. Remember to place the lure less than one inch from your puppy's nose. The goal is to get your puppy to move to a place or a position without any physical direction (from the leash or your hand) and to let your puppy establish the confidence that she can learn something new on her own. When practicing the following skills, remember to keep the lure close to your puppy's nose and move the object very slowly. When she moves into the targeted position, say the direction and mark the moment with a YES or a click, then reward her with the lure.

- **SIT:** Bring the lure from your puppy's nose up and back toward her ears.
- **DOWN** (on or after Week 12): Move the lure slowly from your puppy's nose to the floor, right between her paws. If your puppy is unfamiliar with this word, say it after she's moved into position.

  Once your puppy has caught on, teach her to sit up from a down or go into a stand by moving the lure up from her nose very slowly and saying, SIT, as your puppy brings herself up to a sit.

  Play the *puppy push-up* game for further reinforcement!
- **STAND** (on or after Week 12): From a sit position, bring the lure straight out from her nose.

Condition your puppy to textured surfaces. Let your puppy experience different surfaces: from grass to gravel and grates. If you're not going out, bring what you can in. Spreading sand, gravel, and the like in a crate tray will serve the same

Jodi Buren

Sit, Down, Stand.

purpose. Lead your puppy into the area with a treat cup or a toy. If she seems startled, kneel down and investigate the area with your nose. Yes, your nose. Act like a confident older dog, and she'll have total faith in your abilities to guide her.

Introduce your large or giant-size puppies to stairs. (Please note: hollowed wooden steps are the pits—the depth perception is terrifying, and the slippery surface is hard to grip. If possible, find some solid carpeted stairs to start with.) Assign one person to guide your puppy's body down, and others to shake treat cups and call out from above or below. The guide should carry your puppy midway and gently cradle her ribs, helping her maneuver her legs through the action. Repeat the process no more than three times; end with a snuggle or a game.

Games to Play

Push away come (page 88) and *clicker tag* (page 76) will be fun games to play at this stage. Practice *push away come* when your puppy is relaxed, and *clicker tag* when she's more zestful!

COMMON CONCERNS AND QUESTIONS

Our 9-week-old is peeing and drinking constantly. Although I carry her out every half hour, she still has accidents!

The housetraining may be a simple issue. There are a few things you can do. You can teach her a specific route to the door, saying, OUTSIDE, but avoid carrying her; she must learn to navigate to the door on her own. You may try having her urine tested because she might have an infection (refer to page 38). Hanging a bell by the door and tapping it is another great strategy, as it gives her a way to signal to you that she needs to go out. Also, monitor her water. She may be drinking bowls of it just to amuse herself. Give her water with food and when she looks thirsty. If you are leaving her alone for more than four hours, leave water with her and a piddle pad, and expect accidents.

Our 11-week-old Shetland Sheep Dog has wild spurts of energy twice a day—generally, after he's been isolated. He bounces off the walls, racing around, nipping at everyone's ankles. When we try to catch him, he barks at us and scoots away. Then when we finally catch him, he nips our hands! What are we doing wrong?

Don't play into his frenzy. Consider a head collar, and attach a drag lead to it or any other collar to enable interference without interaction. To divert the ankle nipping, teach everyone the *Stand Like a Statue* technique (mentioned in the appendix), and use the spray away correction (see the appendix) to assign an unpleasant reaction to it, rather than give him more attention. Remember to encourage after you discourage. Teach your puppy to refocus on a game like *soda bottle soccer* (see page 86).

Our 10-week-old Dachshund freaked out when a loud garbage truck drove by our house. Now she won't leave our porch. Help!

Poor dear. She's in the midst of what's known as a fear impression period. Her brain is hardwiring various types of stimulation, and it's easy for her to get overwhelmed. Keep her away from the road. If the porch is as far as she'll go, play there. If a truck passes by, divert her attention to a favorite game or sing to her. Act confident and unperturbed. As the weeks pass and her confidence grows (following your example), slowly reintroduce her to roadside walks. Kneel down and bring her under your legs when a loud vehicle passes, using a direction she's familiar with to help her feel safe. WAIT is a good one. Avoid picking her up: it puts her up high and in front of you. You'll look more afraid. A low voice, clear direction, and a sense of calm are what you need.

We have two dogs—one 2 years old and one 12 weeks old—but the 12-week-old puppy won't leave our 2-year-old dog alone, chasing and biting her constantly. Our 2-year-old's warning growls aren't effective, and aside from separating them, we don't know what to do. Our 12-week old puppy doesn't acknowledge either one of us and doesn't respond to his name.

By the time your 2-year-old asserts herself, your 12-week-old puppy is already wound up and takes her actions as confrontational play. Your puppy needs more direction from you. Using a head collar (preferably) or the small Good Dog collar, secure him to your side and lead him whenever your older dog is in the room. He may thrash about initially: just keep up the pace. If he likes his food, deduct half from each meal and use the rest to motivate his cooperation and focus. Slide him treats for everything initially, from walking with you to responding to directions. Direct his play using any of the games listed for this age section (see chapter 5). Top on my list would be the *toy along, tag along,* and *swing toss* games. When you reintroduce the two dogs, keep the puppy on a drag lead, attached to whichever collar you chose, and supervise the interaction. Try to keep it toy-focused. You can also try spraying a distasteful solution on your older dog's body: a great cause-and-effect correction. Finally, ensure that your 2-year-old dog continues (at least for now) to get all the royalties: fed, greeted, and treated first. If she growls at the puppy, shame him and either lead or isolate him for fifteen minutes. Read "Two Puppies: Twice the Fun or Double Trouble?" in the appendix at the end of the book.

My 8-week-old Great Pyrenees Mountain Dog is really sweet
but doesn't seem very interested in me or my boyfriend.
She's chewing on wires, too. How do I stop that?

She's so young!!! Don't worry about her attention just yet. In fact, the more you try to get her to focus on you, the less she will. Your constant attention is translated differently: she sees your eye contact and high-pitched loving tones as signs of an insecure puppy in need of direction. Instead, make some treat cups, pretend to eat from them, and play with her toys. Interact with her only when she approaches you. Use her name each time you give her rewards. As far as the wires go, don't make a fuss: you'll only draw attention to it. Have bottles of distasteful solution around, and spray the wires calmly as she's chewing them; she'll consider other things to chew.

Our puppy cries in her crate all night long. We can't get any sleep.

Poor you. Been there, done that. First of all, it will help if she's sleeping near someone's bed. The pack theory predominates. *If* it's out of the question or she still cries, try these remedies:

- Buy or make a snuggle puppy. Even just a stuffed dog might make her feel less lonely.
- Make sure she's tired out and has eliminated before putting her to bed.
- If she's making in her crate, you may need to wake once or twice in the night to take her outside. In this case, don't make these excursions interactive. Take her to her area, then back to her crate.
- Try tucking a blanket over her crate to give it more of a denlike feeling.
- Music is worth a try; classical is ideal.
- If none of the previous suggestions help, try putting your puppy in an open box and lay your hand over her for comfort.

SELF-ASSURED (12–16 WEEKS)

Oh, no . . . some creature is taking over your puppy. She's sassy. She doesn't come immediately. She ponders your direction. She's bold, she's brave, she's hard to impress. She'll march right up and demand attention. What's happening? She's growing up—these are all marvelous signs of normal development. You should be proud of yourself—during the first weeks, you have succeeded in giving her a sense of security, and now she's showing it off.

At 12 weeks, her brain is fully developed, and she's ready to learn.
This is the best age to begin lessons, as she's old enough to remember but still too young to take all matters into her own paws. And she'll learn things, whether you teach her or not. If you don't teach her, she'll teach you. Has your puppy begun a training program for you? Here are some signs:

- She solicits your attention (and gets it) by jumping, whining, pawing, and nipping.
- She grabs your clothing and carries it around the house (while you're still in it!).
- She's taught you how to tug and wrestle during walks.
- She marches right up to company and isn't happy unless she's the center of attention.
- When she wants a biscuit or a bit of your lunch, she'll bark at you for it. Advanced human-trainers will just help themselves.

Don't despair. This is a fascinating age as long as you position yourself as your puppy's captain and teach her how best to organize her space and activities. The love of learning is surfacing. She'll dig your leadership, and together you'll set the foundation for the months ahead.

What to Expect

- Your puppy's confidence is growing . . . in her surroundings, in her impulses, and in your relationship. Curiosity and memory retention are also coming into play. The consequences can work for or against you, helping to shape cooperation or defiance. If you face her self-assurance with an extra dose of patience and empathy, you'll be allied. If you melt in frustration, you'll be locking horns and her naughty habits will get worse.
- She's easily distracted. Please don't diagnose ADD if your puppy's attention span is less than a nanosecond. It's normal. Now that her brain is wired, she's ravenous for experience. Each of her senses is geared for absorption and keyed into stimulation. Distractibility is a given. And yelling or repeating yourself won't help a bit. She'll just tune you out, making later lessons a chore.
- She'll bond more with you. If you're calm and consistent, you'll notice an increase in eye contact. She'll watch you when she's calm. And the less you look to her, the more she'll look to you. It's that team captain metaphor all over again. You'll notice her bonding in big and little ways, from the times she runs up to your legs when startled, to the times she looks up when confused. Cop a confident attitude, and her adoration will glow. Although she's getting more confident herself, the still-novel nuances will spell emotional instability if you're not there to guide her.

What to Teach

12 WEEKS (AND OLDER)

Words of the Week

EXCUSE ME: Be mindful of your space this week. Puppies like to get in the way. Aside from their trying to get attention, it also helps them to determine whose space is the most important. Be clear now, or your puppy may grow up to be an annoying adolescent who gets her thrills slamming into your side at full speed. Not fun! Whenever your puppy blocks your path, trips you up, gets on the wrong side of the leash, or simply gets in your way, say, EXCUSE ME, and either shuffle through her or move her aside with the leash. Don't be impatient. Soon your puppy will be moving with her tail wagging.

DOWN: Some puppies take this direction too seriously. Yes, some see it as a submissive posture or as incredibly boring, but with a little ingenuity on your part, you can bring levity to their perspective. Here are some surefire techniques:

- Start luring her down with a treat or a toy (read the previous description for the particulars). Lure her often, using a clicker or a sharp word marker like YES to highlight the moment of cooperation.

- Use pressure points to guide your puppy down without making her feel threatened. (See the following list "Use pressure points" for the particulars.) Sound markers will accelerate her understanding.

- Puppy see, puppy do. Kneel down on all fours, then lie down as if you were a puppy. If you're feeling spry and spunky, roll on your back. The camaraderie is comforting.

- If your pup has a hard head, break DOWN into four parts.
    1. Lowering her head
    2. Relaxing her haunches (or shoulders)
    3. Moving her feet forward
    4. Lowering her body into the down position

 **Be Gentle!**

Pulling your puppy's legs out from under her is very scary. It would be like my asking you to sit and pulling you up by the ankles. Gently put her into position using pressure points or luring her and letting her work her way down on her own.

Praise each step individually, building her success rate over ten to twenty repetitions for each step. Once she's a wizard at Step 1, push for Step 2, then 3, and then 4. Although it may take you a week to get a solid DOWN, you'll have her eager cooperation!

Things to Do

Take her to puppy kindergarten. Soon your puppy will have all her shots. This is an ideal time to scout out a puppy kindergarten in your area. Before you sign up, speak to the instructor or the facility running the program. Do your philosophies align? Here are some questions you might want to ask:

- What is the age range?
- How many puppies are in the class?
- Have they all had their inoculations?
- How much of the class is free play?
- What do you teach them?
- Do you separate the puppies according to size?
- What is your philosophy?

Try bracing. This technique is a real wonder. It helps your puppy learn the Four-Paw Rule and how to contain the impulse to jump. Take your right thumb and slip it over your puppy's collar, fanning your fingers out across her chest. With your left hand, brace her waist with your thumb and forefinger. Remind her to SIT as you, your family, or others greet her.

Use pressure points. When tempted to push your puppy into a position, avoid pushing on her skeletal frame. She'll resist you. Instead, use pressure points in her muscles to gently guide her.

- **SIT:** Squeeze her waist gently with the point finger and the thumb of your left hand. Grasp her tag collar, and lift at her jaw line as you ease her into a sit. If she resists, tuck her tail between her legs with your left hand.
- **DOWN:** The pressure point for down is in-between her shoulder blades. As you press that point, gently lift a front paw and ease her into position (the tripod effect).
- **STAND:** Place two fingers of your left hand along her thigh or belly. If necessary, pull forward on her collar to steady her into position.

Games to Play

Tunnel down (page 78) is the best game to play at this stage.

13 WEEKS (AND OLDER)

Words of the Week

LET'S GO: This one urges your puppy to follow you. Mental imagery is important here. When introducing this direction, be very proactive. You're the coach calling your puppy downfield. LET'S GO. Praise any cooperation, and reward (click or say, YES) your puppy often. She'll think you're too cool. As she grows more comfortable with the leash, you may hold it, increasing the distance and the duration of her cooperation. Treat her a lot during the first few days, gradually lengthening the distance between each reward.

INSIDE: Long term, this is a great direction to call your puppy into your house or to direct her to any door. Teaching it can be a lot of fun. Think of the door as home base! Here's how:

- Take a treat cup or a favorite toy. Stand outside the door. Shake or wave the toy as you run toward the door. As your puppy follows, shout, INSIDE! Then praise, reward, and release her. Yes, release her with a phrase like GO PLAY!

- Repeat the sequence three to five times, and then end it with a yard game. You don't want her to think that INSIDE dead ends outside fun.

- If the weather's inclement or you have a few inside moments to drive this lesson home, start the game inside, saying, INSIDE, as you run to the door! Though it might seem confusing to you, your puppy is simply learning that when she hears this direction, she is to run to the door.

- This is a perfect time to use a clicker. Click the instant your puppy reaches the threshold, and treat her immediately.

Things to Do

Walk her on a leash. As your puppy conditions to the drag lead, begin to pick it up and follow her around. As she grows comfortable with your presence, begin to apply pressure here and there. Once she acclimates to this, do silly things to get her to follow you: shake treats, bounce a toy along on a string, skip, dance . . . ! Praise her and say, LET'S GO, as she follows you. If she puts on the brakes, kneel down and encourage her to follow. Resist the urge to pick her up . . . you'll be puppy-trained in no time!

Introduce her to new rooms. When introducing your puppy to new rooms, bring her mat and some favorite chew toys. Satisfy her needs, playing some good energy-releasing games so that she's calm. Sit on the floor with her and pet her lovingly.

Games to Play

Hide-and-seek and *follow the leader* (page 73–74) are games that help reinforce concepts taught at this stage. (*Hide-and-seek* is like the kids' game, but to help your puppy find you, you can shake a treat cup!)

14 WEEKS (AND OLDER)

Words of the Week

GIVE: Spend the entire week obsessing on this word. Seriously. It's a word you'll use every day, and in some instances, it may save your pup's life. The goal is to condition your puppy to share and show you everything she finds. If she finds a ball, a squeak toy, a rotting squirrel, a knife, or a trap, you want to be the vision that pops into her mind, the first person she wants to show. Think I'm wacky? It's not out of reach. Just follow these steps:

- Never scold your puppy for having something in her mouth. Aside from being too late to influence her decision to grab it, you'll only be conveying prize envy: that what she has is valuable because you want to take it from her.

- Spread treat cups around or carry treats in your pocket for easy reach, and each time you remove an object (regardless of its identity) say, GIVE, and pop a treat into her mouth. When approaching her, shake a cup, click, or talk lovingly. (You will teach her the concept of NO shortly, but now is not the time.)

- If she approaches you with a toy, either let her keep it, scratching her ears and telling her that she's wonderful or pop a treat in her mouth as you say, GIVE. Always give her toys right back. Let her see that GIVE is not a dead end.

- Also approach her with a treat cup during a meal (one time every few days) and say, GIVE, as she spits out her food and looks up.

Things to Do

Practice lead-abouts. Once or twice a day for five to ten minutes, hold or secure your puppy's leash and walk about your home. Use words she's most familiar with, and carry rewards that will highlight your travels. Reward cooperation often!

Introduce stationing. Choose one area to station your puppy. Bring her to the spot (decorated with a familiar mat and bones), and tell her MAT and BONE. Show her to the area, and sit nearby. If she's content, secure her to an immovable object as described on page 32. At this stage, you should stay next to her.

Games to Play

Have some fun during this stage, and help solidify the concepts you're teaching by playing games like *say please* (page 76) and *clicker advance* (page 73).

15 WEEKS (AND OLDER)

Words of the Week

BRING: Another all-important concept-direction combination. Make it fun, and you'll have cooperation that will last a lifetime. Reference GIVE from last week if you haven't already. Spotlight all mouthed objects with praise so that your puppy will feel comfortable sharing her treasures. Here are some ideas:

- Take your puppy out, and toss her some toys. When she picks up a toy, call her name and literally run away from her! If she chases you with the toy in her mouth, say, BRING, and reward that: stop short, turn and face her, and exchange a treat for the toy. Good girl!

- Also practice in small rooms or tight hallways. Toss the toy, and praise your puppy's interest. Kneel down and look at the floor, or turn and scurry a few paces in the opposite direction. As your puppy moves toward you, say, BRING. Gradually increase the distance.

BACK: Here's a gem. This directs your puppy back behind your heels. A perfect way to communicate your leadership, it's invaluable when greeting people or dogs or reminding your puppy to watch you for direction at home or when out and about. As it requires some fancy footwork (backing up is not a canine-friendly move), practice it first in the quiet of your home. Just follow these steps:

1. With your puppy on a leash, take a treat or a toy and bring it back from just below her nose to under her chin (tucking her head down).

2. If she sits automatically or turns around, put a hand under her belly or hold the leash steady.

3. The moment she backs up—even just one step—say, BACK, and reward her. Repeat this until you're able to sequence at least six backward steps.

4. Now practice it in the quiet of your home while standing and holding her leash. Does she follow the transition? You've graduated to the "real world." Go ahead and try it with company, although you should be ready to guide her. Reward all cooperation, especially in the beginning!

Things to Do

Practice with doorbell setups. Everyone's experienced a wild, obnoxious door jammer. These puppies (soon to be dogs) go ballistic whenever someone comes through the threshold. If you'd like your dog to be the exception rather than the rule, follow these steps:

1. Have someone sneak out and ring the bell or knock every twenty seconds for five minutes. Don't answer the door; don't make a scene. Let your puppy condition to the sound.

2. Create a greeting station and send your puppy there when reality "knocks" (pun intended), as you open the door and welcome your company. Wait until she's calm to introduce her, bracing her as you do.

3. When you come in, don't greet your puppy first thing. Good manners start at home. Stay cool for a few minutes, especially if she's manic. Reconnections should be calming.

> ### 🐾 Doorbell Strategies
>
> Hyper red alert to the doorbell starts early on. If you stoke your puppy up with phrases like, "WHO'S THERE?" or "LET'S GO GET 'EM!" don't be surprised when she starts throwing herself against the door and knocking you out of the way as you open it. When someone comes to the door, treat it as you would with no puppy present. Go to the door and answer it. If your puppy's hyper, create a greeting station and ignore her until she's calm.

Introduce stairs to small puppies. If you carry your puppy up and down the stairs, she might develop a complex—either learned helplessness or royalty. Either way, it's one lifelong habit you'd best not get started. To teach your little peanut how to navigate the stairs, follow the same protocol outlined for the bigger pups during Week 11.

Games to Play

Puppy push-ups (page 75) and *bait & toss* (page 79) are great games for this stage.

COMMON CONCERNS AND QUESTIONS

> *Our puppy, 15½ weeks old, is a lot of fun and we all love him, but lately he's gotten this habit of blocking us on the stairs and whenever he wants attention. When we ask him to SIT or DOWN, he pivots in front of us. What's up with that?*

He's just trying to assert himself. Don't take it too seriously. Avoid looking at him when he does this, leave him on a drag lead or a short leash, and simply say, EXCUSE ME, and BACK, as you shuffle through him. When giving him a direction, use pressure points to brace him or rotate him back into position. Then, and only then, praise him verbally from an upright position.

> *Our puppy walks well on his teaching lead for about a quarter of a mile. Then he just stops and sits down. He won't budge an inch. I end up carrying him home every time. Now it's a habit.*

This is not uncommon. It could be passive resistance or learned helplessness or just a self-willed streak. Try to avoid carrying him—it will become a lifelong routine.

With a treat cup, kneel down in front of him at the end of the leash, using a click-and-treat system when he moves forward; string along a scented toy (put some peanut butter in a water bottle)—whatever it takes to break the cycle. If he's choking himself, consider a head collar.

Our puppy won't go into the down position. When we try to push him down, he gets very nippy, and my daughter just gives up. I keep telling her she has to win, but he's beginning to look scary.

Scary is not good. He perceives this direction as a confrontational threat. Make sure he responds to you before your daughter handles him, and call a professional on the first signs of aggression. Also, don't be too forceful. You want him to like working with you and playing on your team! Try playing the *tunnel down* game with irresistible treats and toys. If your puppy is mad for his meals, split the meal in half; have your puppy go down under something like your leg or a chair. Pretty soon, it will all seem like fun. Another trick is to split the DOWN into four sections:

1. Lowering his head
2. Leaning forward
3. Moving his paw forward
4. All the way down

Praise or click and reward each section twenty times before requiring the next sequence of behaviors. It may take a week or so, but your efforts will pay off.

Our Corgi just freaks out on the stairs. I know you encourage that we introduce him to them, but our stairs are slippery.

As a rule, herding breeds are leery of slippery floors. My first suggestion is that you carpet your stairs. Next, remember to cradle him up and down by holding his midsection securely and moving his legs through the action. Have a friend or a family member above or below to coach him on with treat cups and toys. Start with three steps at a time.

Our little female Bulldog won't GIVE up anything she steals. Toys, yes; paper towels and socks, no. She's not interested in her milk bones; she clamps her jaw and just plants herself. Have you ever tried to squeeze the jaws of a Bulldog? It's impossible. Her eyes get very hard and determined.

Funny little helmet head—I can see that it would be hard to squeeze her mouth. To prevent any mischief, let her drag a lead so that you can interfere without grabbing her (which makes her more defensive). First, try the jollying approach: help her associate a clicker with something irresistible—steak wouldn't be out of the question! The moment you see that she's got an object in her mouth, approach her cheerfully, saying, GIVE, as you click and present her with the food. If that doesn't work, here are some other suggestions:

- Using a calm posture, try prying her jaw—where her teeth end. Say nothing as you're doing it, but praise her if she releases.
- That said, I'd have tiny spray bottles of water or a distasteful solution handy, and if she gets "bully," spray the corner of her jaw very discreetly.

All the while, work on her association to the word GIVE and to sharing. Use your clicker constantly to help her make a positive association to sharing.

Our puppy, 13 weeks old, whines and fusses when we secure her at her play station. She lurches out to the end of it and isn't happy until we are back at her side. What are we doing wrong?

Make sure you stay with her for a while! Moving away too quickly may leave her feeling trapped and stressed. Check the length, too: station leads should be no longer than three feet. A longer tether allows nervous pacing. Create a cozy space with a mat and toys, and stay with her until she's secure. Leave her gradually. If you leave her for a minute and return to a hysterical puppy, ignore her. Reconnect with her when she's calm.

It's hot where we live, and our puppy pushes her mat aside and prefers the tile—is that okay?

Most definitely. Breeds with heavy coats are known for this, too. Let your puppy define "comfort" while you define "location."

LOOK AT ME NOW (4–6 MONTHS)

Though your puppy still looks young and innocent, you may be experiencing more of the mind games associated with older pups: you call and she'll race off. You give her a direction, and she'll look up as if you've never met. You want to show off your living room exercises, and she'll act like she's never heard the direction before. Once again, don't be discouraged. These are all signs of a puppy who is developing normally. Rejoice!

What to Expect

- Your puppy's attention span is developing. When you've got her attention, you're likely to keep it. That said, she's likely to be distractible and nervous in new situations. It's all part of growing up. She's separating and becoming herself while still clinging tightly to you. The transition may lead to emotional instability. Like childhood, the stages of puppyhood are confusing. Empathize and practice patience. This stage will pass, and you'll have more to look forward to.

Attention Getter

Is your puppy starting to bark at you just because? You're occupied on the phone or with the kids or at the sink and suddenly you're startled by a sharp woof! If your puppy could speak, would she be shouting at you for a back massage or some play time pronto? If it's any consolation, she's right on time. This is the stage where her psyche is developed and strong enough to make demands. You must decide, now, who is calling the shots and teach her more civilized ways to get your attention, like sitting quietly.

- You may have a puppy who is overly theatrical and/or vocal. For these puppies, drama is a wonderful way to stay center stage. Some puppies actually revert to previously resolved issues like nipping and jumping. It's just one more attempt to ditch civility. If you lose your center, you'll lose respect. Your puppy will view your frustration as wimpy and uncool. You'll be viewed as a hothead who can't confidently assert direction. Don't go there. An extra dose of patience and structure will serve you well during this stage. Take it all step by step and day by day because some days you'll worship your puppy and bless the forces that brought you together; other times, you'll rue the day.

What to Teach

4 MONTHS

Words of the Week

STAY: This direction requires concentration—don't handicap yourself or your pup. Practice in a quiet room at a time when you'll both be able to concentrate. Post-meal, post-pooping, post a good romp. Although you can use food as a constant motivator, I find that it sometimes distracts from lessons. Introduce this direction in two different ways:

- Have a lesson. A short three- to five-minute lesson will do. Bring your puppy to your side and attach a leash. Fold the leash neatly in your left hand, and hold it above her head. (Check the collar; it should be relaxed.) Flash her with an opened palm and say, STAY, in a clear, confident-sounding tone. Pivot in front of her and look to her forehead, not her eyes. Pause for a few seconds, return back to her side, pause again, and release with OKAY as you swing your arm out and step forward. Repeat this sequence no more than six times, and end with an on-the-floor cuddle or a fun game.

- Use your signal and direction with treats and toys. Say, STAY, just before you offer your puppy a treat or a toy. Flash your signal (opened palm), start with short pauses, then release with OKAY as you toss a treat. It's a fun way to increase your puppy's concentration.

> ### 🐾 Staying by Your Puppy's Side
>
> Like learning to count to three, structuring early lessons is pivotal. Think of it like teaching a child to count three figures. Would you scatter them on a page? Sideways, diagonal, and upside down? Or would you line them up neatly in the left corner with a line underneath? Same idea. Start and finish your STAY exercises at your puppy's side.

COME (front): Most puppies learn COME as a command of separation, often yelled during happy exploratory moments, shattering their fun like a clap of thunder at the pool. When the tension escalates or a chase ensues, COME indicates time for play or a cause to fear. Let's turn the tables on this all-important direction. Teach COME as a direction of togetherness:

- Throughout the day, walk up to your puppy, signaling, with your arm out in front of you and your palm up, by drawing an imaginary line from your thighs to your eyes as you say, (NAME), COME.

- Encourage your puppy to sit in front of you and make eye contact after this direction is given.

- Treats or toys (and clickers) will drastically increase your puppy's behavioral memory.

- Mark the moment she connects with a sound marker (YES, pats, and/or click and treats).

- Help her to see that COME is about reconnection and rewards.

> ### 🐾 Under the Microscope
>
> Examined closely, the direction COME is equivalent to a team captain's "HUDDLE!" It involves three sequences:
>
> - Name association: When you call, your puppy should be psyched, looking up as if to say, "That's me—what's our next adventure?"
> - Racing toward you: When you call out, you'd like your puppy to charge toward you as if she can't wait to reconnect!
> - Reconnection: The most important step is the physical reconnection; without it, your puppy may just keep on running!

Varying the 3 Ds

As you repeat these lessons, you'll notice your puppy's curiosity pique. She'll remember the sequence. She'll get it. You'll both feel proud. Now it's time to vary the 3 D's:

- Distance: Gradually inch back. Don't aim your sights too far: you must build her success rate! If she begins to break repetitively, come in closer; you're probably moving too fast.
- Duration: Vary the pause both when you're standing in front of her and when you move back to her side. She's a clever creature: If you're too patterned, she'll figure it out and pre-empt you!
- Distraction level: Eventually, your pup will have to contain life's distractions. For now, you'll introduce her to the concepts of sound and motion. Wave an arm, jiggle your leg, moo like a cow. Be creative and gradually increase the intensity.

NOPE: Is NO a common utterance in your household? Are you tired of shouting it over and over? Most pups learn NO as interactive, not instructional. Fortunately, it takes only some slight tweaking in terms of timing to make this direction clear. The first step is to **pick one temptation** (for example, one sock, one paper towel, one shoe). For more hints, flip to the section "What to Chew?" in chapter 6, "The Not-So-Perfect Puppy." Avoid shouting at your puppy if she's already stolen or destroyed something. You're too late, and your frustration will come across as prize envy: not cool. Here's how to do it right:

- With your puppy out of sight, place the temptation in the middle of the floor.
- Bring your puppy on a lead toward the object.
- The moment she alerts to it, pull the lead back sharply and say, NOPE, in a clear directional tone (no more yelling!).
- Correct the object—"Bad tissue, shame on the tissue!"—without looking at the puppy.
- Continue to walk by the object until your puppy shows no more interest.
- Redirect and reconnect; for example, ask your puppy to FIND YOUR BONE or say LET'S PLAY BALL!

Things to Do

Use a teaching collar. In chapter 2, we discussed each collar in intimate detail. Flip back to that section for the full scoop. The right teaching collar should leave your puppy feeling that walking near you is the safest, most happy place of all.

- Head collars: This wonder collar works well on puppies of all ages and breeds, although for the strong-willed set, it's heaven sent.
- Neck collars (chain correction collar, martingale): These work well for easy-going puppies who are sensitive to sound.
- Good Dog collar: This pinch-and-release collar is a tremendous asset for pain-insensitive puppies who won't tolerate the head collars.
- No-pull harness: Although this collar won't "train" your puppy to walk at your side, it will prevent pulling and may condition positive walking skills over time.

Practice point training. I love point training. Long term, it's an invaluable communication tool. For now, you can introduce it as a game, and practice it in any free minute: during commercials, while you're on hold with an operator, while you're waiting for dinner. . . . Pointing is advantageous all around. You'll be able to direct your puppy silently with the flick of your finger, and your puppy will be able to depend on your direction in all situations. See "Point Training" in chapter 4, "Puppy Parenting Styles," to get all the details on how to point train your puppy.

Games to Play

Run-away-come (pages 76) is a great game for this stage.

 Look What You Can Do!

The long-term goal of this lesson is to use the point of your finger to direct your dog. Eventually, you'll be able to use it to do other things, including

- Send your puppy to her mat.
- Teach complicated lessons such as COME and DOWN.
- Send your puppy up the stairs.
- Point your puppy off the couch.
- Direct your puppy back away from visitors or toward them for a structured hello!

5 Months

Words of the Week

STAND STAY: Although the application might not jump right out at you, there are so many. STAND STAY is great for grooming, wonderful to still your pup for a pat, or (for the larger crowd) to help steady you as you stand. It is the first level of containment: the ability to hold still. (Sit is the second level, and down, the third.) You can introduce it using the method of luring:

- From a sit position, bring the lure straight out from her nose.
- When grooming or toweling her paws, use peanut butter or cream cheese spread on a vertical surface at her nose level. Say, STAND, placing your hand gently on your puppy's inner thigh to steady her as you groom her.

You can also introduce STAND STAY through propping:

- Kneel next to her, perpendicular to her side.
- No eye contact—she'll want to play and lick you!
- Pull her collar out straight forward as you press on her thigh with your fingers, saying, STAND.
- Relax your body, resting your fingers or hand on her belly if she fidgets.

Yet another great method is bribing. Place a spreadable treat (such as peanut butter) on a vertical surface at your puppy's nose level. Bring her to the area and say, STAND STAY as she licks it. This is a wonderful time to condition grooming or medicating.

DOWN (with a straight back): During Week 12 lessons, you introduced the direction DOWN in a fun and playful way. The next step is to help your puppy assimilate the direction like any other—it's just a direction that you, her leader or captain, will give her when appropriate. No overtones, no threats, nothing too domineering, just a direction. Here's what you do (initially, it's kosher to use a treat or a toy to encourage cooperation): kneel on the floor or sit in a chair with your back straight. Then lift your arm above your head and point signal while instructing, DOWN. Keep your back absolutely straight; just move your arms. One of three things will happen:

- She'll go down easily—immediately release the treat and praise her.
- She'll look down with a confused expression (she's accustomed to your facial accompaniment). Try luring her again. If she's still resistant, use pressure points to position her.

- She'll brace her body and refuse to cooperate. Break down the posture into four parts as described on page 156, praising and treating at each step until she's sold.

  Practice these steps for three days, then introduce the direction STAY, pausing between the position and your reward. DOWN (point and lure), STAY (pause), and OKAY (release and treat)!

Jodi Buren

The three sequences of DOWN.

NOPE: Here are three ways to encourage your puppy's understanding by increasing the temptation:

1. Repeat the same sequence described on page 105 with a plate of food. Stomp near the food and say, BAD COOKIES, or whatever.

2. Ask your spouse, friends, or kids to sit on the floor and have a sandwich. If your puppy approaches them, pull her back and say, NOPE! Walk by or stand and talk with them. Correct any of her attempts to sneak over. Although it may seem cruel, life is one big fat gigantic distraction (for all of us), and social and happy are those who learn self control.

3. Sit on the floor yourself and nosh. Remember, eye contact invites your puppy to the feast, so no looking. Fold the lead up, and hold it in your left hand. If your puppy rushes forward, quick-tug to the side and say, NOPE. Provide a mat and a bone as a displacement activity. Once you can do this, your puppy will be welcome everywhere!

Things to Do

Introduce grooming skills. Now's the time to condition lifelong grooming skills. Having grown up with my beloved Shawbee, a husky mix who thought the bath was life's greatest torture, and who had to be sedated for anyone to clip her nails, I could not emphasize this exercise more. Here are some tips:

*   Find a spread that delights your puppy: peanut butter, cream cheese, yogurt. Pick one.

*   Let your puppy lick this reward as you introduce her to the brush, the clipper, the drying towel, and the bath. Yes, the bath. I rubbed peanut butter around the bath's edge, and let my puppy Whoopsie lick it off as we scrubbed her. Now we can't seem to get her out of the tub!

Create signals. Signals help to create visual focus. Like young children, many puppies learn signals before words. Use them as you introduce your directions. Here's my list:

*   **SIT:** Use a pointed finger, drawing up from your puppy's nose to your eyes.
*   **STAY:** Extend a flat palm, like a police man flashing STOP.
*   **DOWN:** Point from your puppy's nose to an imaginary spot on the floor between her feet.
*   **COME:** There are two signals for COME: raising both arms as if in a football cheer, and pointing a direction as the puppy comes near you (the same one used in the COME (front) exercise—see the section "4 Months" on page 164).

- **HEEL:** Simply point and tap your arm to your left leg (or right, if you've got your puppy to that side).
- **YES:** A full-fisted, raised-arm gesture that let your puppy know she's spot on!
- **GO** (GO TO YOUR MAT, GO SAY HELLO): a point that directs your puppy to a given area.

Provide long-lead freedom. Is your puppy beginning to ignore you? Has she given you the teenage equivalent of the eye roll? Don't worry—this is another good sign of normal development. Chasing her around as you scream at the top of your lungs won't help the matter any. Full freedom, however, can put her in harm's way, especially if the area is unenclosed. Long line to the rescue! (Refer to page 182.)

Games to Play

If your puppy is paw expressive this is the time to introduce *wipe your paws* and *paw and high five* (see chapter 5).

6 MONTHS

Words of the Week

WAIT and OKAY: We introduced these words early on, as they pertained to doors and thresholds. Take them one step further, and use them to teach food and stair containment.

- Food: It isn't polite to grab anything from anyone, regardless of species. Civility is within your puppy's grasp. Hold the lead securely in your left hand, and offer a treat or a toy with your right hand. If your puppy leaps forward, quick-tug back and say, NOPE. Redirect by saying the direction WAIT, and hold the toy very still until your puppy sits calmly and watches you for direction—then say the direction OKAY!
- Stairs: You might as well go the distance. WAIT ingrains civility, but in the case of stairways, thresholds, cars, and curbs, it also reinforces your position. It reassures your puppy that you're watching out for her: WAIT while I check things out and make sure we're safe." With your puppy on a leash (or dragging a lead), say, WAIT, at the bottom or the top of the stairs. Pause (varying the time) and say, OKAY. If she barrels ahead of you, go back to the beginning. This time when you say OKAY, next say, EASY, calmly, tugging the lead back if she gets too excited. Now ask other people to distract you. Have the kids go ahead of you down the stairs. Ask a friend/family member to run up the stairs quickly as you remind your puppy she has to WAIT until the coast is clear. Civility rules! You wouldn't let a kid knock down Grandma; your puppy shouldn't either!

HEEL: The human phrase equivalent here is "I'm the leader; follow me!" Though it may take a while for both of you to synchronize, eventually you'll be maneuvering as one down a crowded street or while you watch the kids on the ball field. As all directions do, this one reassures your puppy that you're watching out for her.

Practice heeling in circles in an open, quiet place (inside or out). Clear an area to walk in a counterclockwise circle. Position your puppy next to you at your left side, head and feet facing in the same direction: your puppy's paws lined up with your heels. You're welcome to shake a treat cup or bait your puppy with a treat or a toy. It may over-distract her, however, making learning more difficult. You be the judge. Then follow these steps:

- Relax your arms straight, keeping your left thumb behind your thigh. Quick-tug the leash back whenever your puppy pulls from your side.
- Call out your pup's name, saying, (NAME), HEEL, in the same tone you'd call out to a friend to follow.
- Walk in a cheerful manner, head held high and shoulders back, to communicate the right attitude.
- Praise your puppy for walking with you with YES!
- Quick-tug the leash if your puppy's attention starts to stray.
- Stop after each circle by slowing your pace and reminding her, HEEL.
- Place your puppy into a sitting position (to do this, grasp the base of the leash with your right hand and use your left hand to squeeze her waist).
- Practice five circles, two to four times during the day.

Things to Do

Practice out and about. Everyone wants a well-adjusted puppy, a confident, well-mannered companion whose happiness radiates. Although lessons are helpful, socialization is just as important. Like anything, however, how you socialize your puppy is key. One of you must take the lead; let it be you!

- Exiting the car: Your puppy should be secured as you drive, for your safety as well as her own. Don't rush to exit the car or rev her up; the ensuing excursion will be a fiasco. Instead, be cool. Exit the car in a normal fashion. Go to the door closest to your puppy and instruct, WAIT, as you open the door. Reinforce it. If your puppy is overstimulated, wait a few minutes before releasing her from the car. The moment she hits the cement, instruct, HEEL, and bring her to your side.

 **Why HEEL?**

The root of this direction? I'll give you a hint. It directs your puppy to walk right next to a certain body part . . . your heel!

 **An Off-Leash Rusher**

If you're rushed by an off-leash dog, stay calm. As calmly and as quietly as you can, discourage your puppy from facing off or making eye contact, by picking her up and holding her head to your body or by holding the leash tightly as you hustle away. Eye contact will excite or aggravate the other dog, over which you have absolutely no control. Calmly walk out of his or her perceived territory as you say a quiet prayer to yourself. I've had countless encounters, and calm exiting works every time.

For the rest of her life, you want her to come to your side automatically; now is the time to start enforcing the habit.

- Greeting people: Your popularity is about to experience a sharp rise. Don't be alarmed; socialization is good for both of you. Just remember—you are your puppy's voice. If she's overwhelmed, you need to come up with a few zingers to back people off or, in some instances, solicit their help by asking them to offer your puppy toys or treats. If you've got a wild child, you're about to experience firsthand just how hard people are to train. Many people may actually encourage the jumping. You mind the jumping, so emphasize the Four-Paw Rule. Wait until your puppy has settled down, bracing her if necessary, before you okay any pats.

  If you're not sure whether your puppy is good with children, don't use strangers as guinea pigs. Brace your puppy, and explain that she's in training. Everyone will respect you!

- Greeting other dogs: Some puppies flip out when they see other dogs, going so bonkers they'd disown you in a nanosecond. Others get overwhelmed. Regardless of who's on the end of your leash, you should follow some guidelines. First, don't let your puppy drag you over: if the lead slips, your puppy will bolt. Long term, this puppy won't be trustworthy off-lead. If she does bolt, bring her BACK and instruct, HEEL. Also, be sure to ask the other puppy's parent if you can let them play together. If so, release her with OKAY, GO PLAY. When it's time to go, call your puppy back to HEEL, and on you go. However, if there's no interest on the other end of the lead, simply say, NOT NOW, and march on.

- Crossing the street: At every curbside, at every street your puppy must pause and look to you for direction. Street Smarts 101.

- Entering buildings: Whoever enters first is the leader. Let it be you. Let it always be you: you'll both be calmer. WAIT and OKAY work beautifully.

Practice bracing in public. Dog people are magnets. Make your début, and your popularity will suddenly soar. Socialization is invaluable. If your puppy is having trouble sitting still, brace her as described during Week 12. Stay at her side, and kneel just in front of her. Remind her to STAY as everyone's ogling.

Games to Play

Use the *wiggle-giggle-freeze* and *hidden treasure* games (pages 78 and 74) to reinforce concepts learned at this stage.

COMMON CONCERNS AND QUESTIONS

Whenever I pet my puppy, Zoe, or offer her food, she gets so excited I can hardly calm her down. She gets really jumpy and starts going at her leash. HEEL and STAY are out of the question.

Your Zoe sounds spirited and fun. Do you remember the difference between praise and petting? Praise focuses her attention on you; petting focuses your attention onto her. Petting signals play. Also, if she's so food-motivated, you may have to avoid using treats for the time being. Make sure you're feeding her enough, and if that pans out, just jackpot her (give her a big handful) at the end of your lesson.

When can we start using a teaching collar with our Labrador? I used a choke collar on our last dog, but she pulled anyway. How do I determine what will work best with her and our three children, ages 3, 5, and 7?

The children are still too young to walk Sadie in trafficked areas or perhaps even walk her at all. Make sure she's well mannered on the leash before letting them out with her unsupervised. Regarding collars, a head collar could be your best bet; it's similar to walking a horse on a halter. Where the head goes, the body will follow. If you wanted to use a neck collar, you have options: I'd have you try the check chain first. If she's sensitive and responsive to the noise of the chain, that's all you'll need. Your other option is the Good Dog collar, which simulates the scruff shake of a more dominant dog each time you pull on the lead.

Our Bearded Collie, Jack, won't let me groom him or clip his nails. He nips at me, and it's getting worse. I bought him a special grooming table, and when he sees me setting it up, he runs off and won't come. Any suggestions?

It sounds to me like reactionary aggression. This is an impulse reflex to perceived or experienced discomfort or pain, as if someone suddenly sliced off the end of your toe. He obviously is not a fan of the table. Try grooming him on a bed for a while (putting a big sheet down if you're concerned about the mess). Make a lifelong habit of staying calm and firm, using tones and familiar directions to make him feel safe and directed. STAY pops to mind. Use WAIT if he's more familiar with that direction. Use soft, loving tones to praise him when he cooperates. Also, use a familiar bone or a peanut butter–stuffed toy to engage him while you work. If all this is to no avail, muzzle him. It's not the end of the world, and you're protecting him from his own impulse. And once you've successfully clipped or de-matted him, he'll see that it's not as life threatening as he once perceived.

When my kids are running by or we play the** wiggle-giggle-freeze **game, our 5½-month-old puppy, Tim, jumps up and knocks the kids down (ages 7 and 9). He thinks it's a riot. Lately, he's started grabbing the kids' mittens and hats and racing all over the yard with them. When he calms down, he can be a real angel.

Your puppy is having a ball. I'm sure your kids scream and sometimes chase him, so it's one gigantic free-for-all. You're right to play the *wiggle-giggle* game. It will help with his self-control; however, before you play another round, let's set some ground rules. Tim needs to be fitted with a training collar. Read through your options, and try them out to see which is most effective. Next, set up a run by with the children. Read the particulars in "Predatory Aggression," in chapter 6, "The Not-So-Perfect Puppy"; correct any impulse to chase with a quick leash tug and NOPE! When Tim can contain his urge to chase them in the living room, test it outside on the long line. The next time you play the *wiggle giggle* game, secure a drag lead onto Tim's collar to enable a quick correction from behind.

My puppy doesn't look at me very much. I keep trying to encourage his focus (we learned LOOK UP with a clap), but that seems to backfire. Any suggestions?

Don't try so hard. Your efforts communicate confusion. How would you feel if I stared at you so often? Also, bag the phrase LOOK UP; it's having a reverse effect. Instead, resort to activities that would spark his curiosity, such as shaking a treat cup (and pretending to eat the treats yourself), playing with a few of his toys (as you completely ignore him), or running in silly circles in the yard. When he looks to you, click or praise and reward that.

Our Portuguese Water Dog used to come whenever we called her in. Now she stops and stares and goes back to whatever she's doing. If we chase her, it becomes a gigantic game. It's so frustrating!!!

Been there, done this, too. First, resist using COME to call her in; it's a downer. Teach her a word like INSIDE by playing a game. Shaking her treat cup or waving a favorite toy, run to the door, shouting, INSIDE. Race her there, don't ask. If she refuses, put her on a leash. Reward her at the door, and let her run back outside. Run back and forth a few times, making a high time of it. Now when you put her out, chaperone her on a long line. Play with her for a while, then suddenly exclaim, INSIDE, and race to the door. If possible, let her go back out. The next time she refuses to come to the door, and it will happen, ignore her. Walk back inside, and shut the door. Stand by the window, shaking the treat cup and pretending to eat the treats, or play with one of her toys. It's a stage. Welcome to adolescence.

HOT SHOT (7 TO 9 MONTHS)

Ahh . . . the age of hormones. Your puppy is about to go through a major transformation. It's called growing up! Do you remember this? Hormones, rebellion, confusion, curiosity . . . puberty. An exciting time, but not always pretty.

At around 6 months, your puppy experiences an onslaught of hormonal urges: Dominate! Submit! Explore! Hide! Approach! Retreat! If she were a teenager, she'd get an unusual haircut and would laugh at your clothes but would still be a little nervous when you're not home. And on top of this, growing pains add the awakening of breed-specific instincts, telling the herders to herd, the hunters to hunt, the guarders to guard, and the pullers to pull . . . it's utter canine chaos, and she's still cutting her baby teeth!

So here we have a puppy—who looks very much like a dog—pumped full of hormones, high spirits, and anxiety. It's no surprise that she may give you the puppy equivalent of a teenage eye roll when you give her a direction.

You may wonder if you'll be able to tell when your puppy is shifting into this stage. You will. Trust me, which is why lessons are critical now. Without them, your puppy may not outgrow this stage, condemning you to life with an eternally pubescent dog. Surely, you've met adult dogs who jump, mouth, mount, and generally misbehave at every opportunity. These dogs are stuck in an early stage of development: Peter Pan puppies in the flesh. Don't let this happen to your dog!

What to Expect

- The most telling sign of this stage is unpredictability. It's like having two different dogs in your home—the precious angel who gazes up at you with adoring eyes, and the wild-eyed demon dancing just out of reach with your shoe in her mouth. The one you show off on outings, and the one you say belongs to your brother. The one who makes you smile, and the one who makes you cringe. And the ease and speed at which she can transform herself are truly amazing. As if the last stage wasn't exciting enough!

- She'll try to train you. Now that she's in training, your eager little student will try to use all her hard-earned knowledge to train you. On-leash, your puppy may be a real crowd pleaser; but off-leash . . . that's another story. You'll find yourself shouting, repeating directions, pleading, offering bribes, giving in. Ah, puberty—such a joy. Call your parents right now, and apologize for yours.

Avoid Saying NO So Often

I know this may not be on the top of your daily priority list, but spend five minutes mimicking your puppy. Yes, mimicking her—the her you love. Be selective, choosing the behaviors you truly find endearing, like when she's resting her head between her paws after a long day or when she's nosing a toy around the living room floor. Mimicking these activities draws attention to them, and it reminds your puppy on a daily basis that there is so much you really, truly love. It's a wonderful way to avoid the NO trap so common with this stage. Give it a whirl.

What to Teach

7 MONTHS

Words of the Week

BRING and GIVE: If you've been using these words and concepts all along, combining the two won't be a gigantic revelation for your puppy. I recommend doing it when she is feeling playful. Take her into a hallway or a confined room. Toss a toy, and as she grabs it, run away from her and say, BRING! Turn and face her as she nears you: either click or shake some treats and say, GIVE, simultaneously. Gradually, bring this game into more open spaces.

SIT-STAY: By now, you should be living-room champions. It's time to push the envelope just a bit. Here are some exercises to practice:

- Tug test: Instruct, STAY, and pivot two feet in front of your puppy. Tug steadily forward on her lead. Signal and remind, STAY, when necessary. If she breaks, step in closer and ease up. Build her success rate as you encourage her containment.

- Disappearing act: Remind, STAY, close to a corner. Hide half your body, then return and release. Next time hide your whole self for a quick instant. Mix it up, gradually increasing the time she can focus without watching your face. Next, stand behind her, which introduces the challenge of her not watching you. Start walking around her. If she breaks, touch her head for reassurance. Then pause at her tail, steadily increasing the duration.

- Temptation city: Life is full of distractions—bring them on! Each time you introduce a new

Using life's distractions to steady your stay.

Jodi Buren

one, stand at your puppy's side, holding the lead above her head. Write a list of ten distractions, such as a dog walking by, the doorbell ringing, or tossing a ball inside or outside, in order of their intensity (from lowest to highest distraction for your puppy), and work through the list at your puppy's speed.

If your puppy can't hold herself together, brace her, holding her steady with your hands on her collar and waist. As she grows more reliable, gradually move away.

Things to Do

Start vocal tossing: This is a fun little exercise. First, a human similarity. Imagine that I wanted you to join me in the kitchen from the living room where you were reading the paper. When you didn't respond immediately, would you rather I (a) run at you hollering your name, snatching the paper from your hands, and dragging you with me by your shirtsleeve? Or (b) simply turn as I call your name, saying, "Come into the kitchen. I've got something to show you!"

You pick. Now play the same game with your puppy. Call her name as you swing your head away from her. Instead of her feeling like you're closing in, she'll be curious as to what you've found and where you're going! Your voice should trail. See her ears perk up! Now jog away from her as you call out. It should inspire playful feelings of togetherness. (If she's unimpressed, add a treat cup to the mix!)

Games to Play

Hidden treasure (page 74) is best played to reinforce this stage's concepts.

8 MONTHS

Words of the Week

HEEL: Feeling dizzy from the earlier HEEL exercises? Well, okay then—it's time to bring this direction into the real world. The first few days everything may look and feel a little sloppy. Don't be disappointed. You're in good company. I once tripped on a bench, and I've walked into countless trees. My suggestion is that you stay focused on the prize, that happy day when you and your puppy will walk together side by side, no reminders necessary. Here are some tips:

- Start in a moderately distracting environment, like the peripheral edge of a parking lot.
- When possible, do a few familiar circles.
- Gradually move into busier locations, and keep your puppy's enthusiasm in check.

- When necessary, use the tush-push by sliding the leash behind your back and pushing back with your tush. This relocates the weight of the correction to your tush, which is much more solid than your arm.

- Stop frequently, and praise often.

- Use treats, the clicker, or toys if you find them helpful.

DOWN: Remember our goal? That your puppy view DOWN as a simple exercise on par with SIT or WAIT.

> ### 🐾 Hands-Free Heeling
>
> Go back to your early circle exercise. Tie the lead around your waist, or toss it over your shoulder. As you circle around, drop the lead from your hand and slap your side. If your puppy forges ahead, let her go. Just as she reaches the end of the slack, quick-tug the lead and say, "NOPE." Redirect your puppy back to your side with "HEEL." Praise, mark, and reward cooperation!

Although the initial overtones relate to trust, in time it will be a calming, lifesaving direction that you'll use each day, regardless of the environment or the distractions. If you've mastered the DOWN (with a straight back) direction from the section "5 Months" on page 168, you're ready for the final leg: DOWN from a standing position. Here's how you do it:

- Put your puppy on a leash, and take her to a quiet room. Slide the leash under your foot discreetly, stand tall and say or signal DOWN.

- As you say it, you may bend at the knees but not the back (don't curtsey). If your pup needs a hint, slide the leash up slightly to remind her. Do not crane her neck; the lead should apply only light pressure.

- If she's still resistant, position her gently, and praise away.

- Practice three to ten commands, mixed in with all the other words like HEEL and STAY.

Things to Do

Begin doing attention exercises. Your communication here is that your puppy pay more attention to you than to her surrounding environment. She can and should be attentive to surrounding activities and noises but should always focus on you. Try this exercise as a setup. Ask a friend to help.

- Bring your puppy to a HEEL position. Secure the leash to your waist, or hold it midway, leaving three feet slack.

- Ask your friend to approach at a 90-degree angle.

- When your puppy alerts to the person, call her name out and dodge to the right.

- If your puppy follows, great; if not, she'll get a sharp tug. Praise her for being with you regardless.

- Repeat the exercise until she's more focused on you than on your friend.

- Now have your friend hold some food or tap some pans together, or have your friend approach with another dog. How many sequences does it take until your puppy is paying more attention to you than to what's distracting her?

Once you've perfected the art of the attention exercise indoors, take it outside. Any time your puppy is distracted by a stimulus (a bike, a car, a dog, and so on), simply say her name cheerfully as you dart (with a slack leash) to the side. Repeat the exercise as often as necessary, and refine it as her focus improves (if you're standing with her in a store and she's distracted, call her name and take a short baby step away). Praise her to the moon if she's focusing without reminders.

Try signaling only. Signaling sparks visual curiosity. This is especially great when you're striving for off-lead control! In an earlier exercise I had you blending signals with directions. Now try to separate the two. When you begin this exercise, overemphasize your signals. If your puppy ignores you, quick-tug the leash and say or signal, NOPE. When she responds accurately, say and signal (or click), YES. Reward her cooperation. Eventually, phase off saying YES and NOPE, using signals for those as well. Each day emphasize three directions in a formulated and fluid medley (for example: SIT-STAY-HEEL, DOWN-STAY-COME, and so on).

Games to Play

Try *combat crawl* and *break dance* (see pages 80 and 79) for this stage.

9 MONTHS

Words of the Week

COME: Here you're going to bring all three steps of the COME sequence together. Outside or in, stand behind your puppy, varying the distance with her regular leash, long lines, or a flexi-leash.

1. Call out your puppy's name. If she doesn't listen, say, NOPE, as you quick-tug the leash. Praise her the moment she looks to you.

2. Now say, COME, and throw one or both arms above your head. If you're agile, run back a few steps as she comes, and reel in the leash. (If she runs past you or gets diverted, say, NOPE, and give a quick-tug.)

3. When she reaches you, signal up in COME (front style). The finished picture should be her sitting in front of you, looking up.

Jodi Buren

Come 1, 2, 3!

STAY: Out-of-sight stays are a sure sign that your puppy is internally focused on your direction: she doesn't need your visual presence to reinforce her attention. That said, this response doesn't just happen; it takes practice!

- Secure your puppy to an immovable object.
- Instruct, STAY, and go to a nearby corner or tree. Remind her to STAY with a signal and disappear. Count backward from fifteen. If your puppy has broken, walk to her calmly, reposition her, and pause for another ten seconds before releasing her.
- If she succeeded, praise her very calmly.
- Practice two more out-of-sight exercises if all goes well.
- Gradually increase the amount of time you're able to "hide," as well as the distance from your puppy.

> ### 🐾 Like a Good Story
>
> The direction COME has a beginning, a middle, and an end. The beginning starts with calling your puppy's name. The middle should show your puppy running happily toward you. The end is when she sits in front of you and looks up. Though it's tempting to blow off the ending, don't! You'll end up with a puppy that runs to you but keeps on going!

As an added bonus, station your puppy in the house and instruct, STAY. Leave the room for varying amounts of time. Release her when she's calm and trusting in your direction.

Things to Do

Introduce the long line. Clip this one onto your puppy's tag collar, and allow her to roam freely for a few minutes. Remember, the less you look to her, the more she'll look to you. Look interested in other things, and she'll find you irresistible. Here are a few exercises to practice on the long line, with the goal of off-lead control clearly in view. Bear in mind, however, that some breeds, such as terriers and hounds, should *never* be let off-lead.

- The Check In: Each time your puppy chooses to check in, reward her!
- NAME: Pick up the end of the line, and call your puppy's name. (Quick-tug the line if she ignores you.) Say, YES, or click and treat when she checks in.
- WAIT: When your puppy is moving away from you, stand next to the long line, say, WAIT, and step on the line. The moment she pauses to look back, say, YES, and release with OKAY!
- SIT: Enforce this at close range to start: two feet, four feet, six feet, and so on. Instruct, WAIT, and then SIT. Praise her cooperation, or position her calmly.
- DOWN: Follow the previous sequence using DOWN instead of SIT.
- HEEL: Occasionally, call your puppy back to your side. Simply slap your side, call her name and HEEL, and reel her in if she needs some direction.
- COME: Stand behind your puppy periodically, and run through the stages of COME—beginning, middle, and end!

Help your puppy's developing conscious awareness of your otherness. Does this sound silly to you? Seemingly an impossibility . . . too anthropomorphic? Well, seeing and doing are believing—trust me. During Week 4, you began to introduce the word NOPE to the exercises your puppy knew. Integrate NOPE as a direction that in essence means "Wrong, try again," and do the attention exercises described in "Things to Do" in the section "8 Months" on page 179, as well as the following exercises.

- SIT: Give the direction. Your puppy should respond within one second. If not, quick-tug the leash and say or signal, NOPE. You may restate the direction one time. If your puppy does not respond, position her crisply.

- STAY: After positioning your puppy (in a sit, a down, or a stand) and directing, STAY, be mindful of any of her motions to move. If she fidgets, say, NOPE, and tug the leash to the side when possible. If she moves out of position, escort her back and reposition her crisply without repeating the direction. Remind her to STAY, and move off. If she breaks again, reconsider your distance or the distractions: one variable must change. Reposition her but stay closer to her side; consider holding the lead.

- DOWN: It's the same deal as sit. Direct her once. If there's no immediate reaction, give a quick-tug and NOPE. Position her if necessary, crisply, without physical tenderness or eye contact. Her ignoring you shouldn't result in more attention.

- HEEL: HEEL says, "Follow me!" Your puppy should focus more on you than on her surroundings. That means no sniffing, no nosing about. Just watch her ears—they're the antenna. Are they angled toward your leg—great, praise that! Are they pitched forward, while she's looking off to the side. Whoops—that's not good. Off-leash, your puppy would be racing off. Incorporate NOPE each time your puppy's attention strays. After each NOPE, remember to remind her to HEEL, and praise her for that.

🐾 Redirect and Reconnect

NOPE is the middle piece in any direction. First you direct, saying, NOPE, when attention wanders, and then redirect and reconnect. Repeat (redirect) or position your puppy and praise (reconnect) her cooperation.

- COME: Your puppy must fully understand and love this direction before you incorporate NOPE. Otherwise, you'll run the risk of tarnishing her enthusiasm. Review each section of the COME exercises if you're unsure. Come is a three-step direction: your puppy must know each step before practicing this next sequence. To fully incorporate the concept of NOPE, we'll apply it to every step.

  - Come Step 1—Name Alert: When you call out your puppy's name, she should look up with enthusiasm and interest. If she'd rather not, stand at the end of the lead and call her name as you turn from her. If she ignores you, say, NOPE (in a confident directional voice). As she's reminded and looks, say, YES, and cheer her. Repeat this sequence solo until you're both on the same page.
  - Come Step 2—Call Back: This step calls your puppy back to you, like football players gathering in for a huddle. Stand behind your puppy, and call her name. When she looks to you, say, YES, and run back as you call, COME. Say, YES, and praise her as she runs to you. Reel in the slack as best you can (it's easier to do if you keep your arms low). If she diverts her attention or races by you, give the leash a quick-tug and say, NOPE! Redirect her to COME, and praise her cooperation.
  - Come Step 3—Come (front): No sequence is finished without the reconnection. As your puppy comes toward you, hold your hand out in your come front signal. If she races by or crashes in, say, NOPE, and direct her into position by signaling and maneuvering her with the lead. Give an enthusiastic YES for every full sequence. Brilliant!!!

Begin practiced departures. Whether you're in the midst of your puppy's separation anxiety or you're hoping to avoid it, this exercise is a surefire bet. It not only teaches your puppy to relax when you're apart, but it also works to remind her that your rules stand, whether or not you're presenting sight. Here's what you do:

- Secure your puppy to a familiar station.
- Leave a bone or a toy.
- Remind her to STAY, and leave the room.
- Come in after one to two minutes but completely ignore her, whether she's whining, jumping, or howling to the gods. Wait until she calms down. Then approach and pat her.
- Continue making short departures until she's coping.

- Gradually increase the time, following the same protocol.
- When she's a pro, leave her at a station once a day for up to thirty minutes. I use this outside the local Pizza Station (the local hang)—everyone knows who's inside!

Games to Play

Here's where you can really have some fun! By now you know what makes your puppy's tail wag, so play games that highlight her passions. Got a barker: play *volume control and the mathematical puppy;* if your pup loves to carry and retrieve, *four-footed fax* has her name written all over it! Sniffers will love *treasure hunt;* chompers will like the *swing & tug;* and for the entertaining crowd try tricks like *roll over!*

> ### 🐾 Direction vs. Discipline
>
> The tone for NOPE should be directional. You are not disciplining your puppy; you're simply providing direction. It's the same as if I asked you to pass the salt, and you handed me the pepper. I would never stand up and shout, "You stupid idiot! I wanted the salt!!!" Calm direction and patience bode well for your dog's off-lead focus.

COMMON CONCERNS AND QUESTIONS

My Cairn terrier won't come, at all. I get so mad, and it's not like she's defying me; she just darts off after a squirrel and disappears for up to five minutes. The whole time I'm shouting hysterically because I'm so scared. I can't even look at her when she comes back.

Expecting an instant recall from a terrier is like expecting an avocado to taste like an apple. Your puppy is from an instinctive line. Terriers, in general, don't value your wishes the way a Golden Retriever would. That said, be very careful letting her off-lead. Accidents happen in the blink of an eye. In a safe enclosure, practice the following:

- Never look at Dotty when you're calling her. She'll translate your voice tones as back-up barks, and it will heighten her prey drive. Throw your voice in the opposite direction in a tone that says, "Hey, look at what I've found!"
- Don't waste your energy being frightened or mad. Easier said than done, I know, but both emotions put out negative energy fields. She'll avoid you.
- Confidence is key. It's an attractive quality. Work on long-line exercises, and develop her awareness as she matures.

The first time we left our puppy loose in the house, he took one of my husband's slippers from the closet, but he didn't destroy it. It was kind of cute—he was sleeping with it when we came in. My husband got really angry—and I'll admit that he looked guilty. Now I've gone back to isolating him, but I really don't want to any more.

Tell your husband that his puppy missed him terribly, and that's why he took his shoe and cuddled with it. It may be a lifelong habit, and since there's no destruction, what's the harm? I find it endearing. If it really aggravates him, tell him to shut the shoes in the closet and scent a toy (by rubbing it in his hands) before he leaves. Then discuss after-the-fact corrections: they intensify separation anxiety and lead to destruction. For now, isolate Ted for a couple of weeks. When you test his freedom, clean up the house, portion off a room or two (condition freedom slowly), and leave him for fifteen minutes. Ignore Ted when you come in, reconnecting after he's calm. If there's destruction, let it go and clean it up when Ted's out of the room.

We worked with our puppy on the GIVE, and she's very good. BRING isn't happening. We brought her into the hall, but she didn't feel like playing so we quit. Any ideas?

Play right before her favorite meal. Go into a bathroom and get her pumped up: shake the toy and excite her. Toss it in the air and the moment she catches it, click and treat. Gradually toss it out from your body. When you bring the game out of the room, start with short tosses and if she doesn't bring it, stand up confidently and walk away. I find that playing a hybrid *toss* plus *run-away-come* game is helpful, too: say, BRING, instead of COME, running short distances to start.

The YES NOPE timing is hard for me. And since I walk in an unrestricted park with our puppy off-lead, I feel completely ignored. Is there any way to reinforce these directions without a long line?

No, you really need a line for security and reinforcement. Think of the NOPE as a hot-wire correction: you're not trying to pull him, you just want to give him a reminder. A quick pop, then let it go. And YES should be said the instant he looks to you. Investigate the clicker—your puppy may respond well to it!

We've worked with our puppy a lot, and she loves her clicker. However, when we left her with a pet sitter, she wouldn't let the woman get near her. She actually jumped the fence and ran away. It took almost a day to find her, and she was hard to catch even then.

Your puppy sounds like she's family proud and doesn't transfer her loyalties well. I can assure you that she was insulted by being dropped off at a stranger's house and left high and dry. Here's what I want you to do. Wherever you're planning to leave her next, go there soon. Buy an hour of the person's time. Take your clicker. Introduce them. Go through a lesson, and play your puppy's favorite games. When the day comes to leave her, go early. Walk her around, explain the situation by drawing mental images (I'm serious), and then take a few minutes to reintroduce her to the caretaker.

WHO'S THE BOSS? (10 TO 12 MONTHS)

This stage means different things for different people. Some pups become more aware of your weaknesses and continue to highlight them in a last-ditch attempt to be the leader. Others have exhausted all options and are content to follow your lead. If your puppy remains skeptical of your direction, be consistent. Persist in making your point clear. Consider investing in group or private training—it will be money well spent.

Now think for a moment. If you asked your puppy to describe you, what would she say? "Fun to be around, confident, cool," or would she wag her tail nervously and say, "Impatient, easily fooled, unsure." She has an opinion—she's learned to read you well. Make a good impression: stand tall, be patient but clear, and don't be afraid to have some fun!

What to Expect

- By now, your puppy is starting to calm down. She manages better on her own. She chews her bone. She responds immediately to your direction. She doesn't assault your visitors. She's almost perfect!

- Sometimes she ignores you. Every now and then, she runs right by you when called to come. Occasionally, she'll fidget out of a DOWN-STAY or will face you when she ought to be at your side. Please understand: she wants to behave, but her teenage genes are relentlessly telling her to make one more glorious attempt for top-dog status. To that end, she begins a subtle campaign for control to ensure that you're strong enough to contain her. You may not think that a sloppy sideways sit is a very big deal, but your puppy makes a little mental checkmark every time you let her get away with it. It's her conscious mind taking hold.

   Here are some other surefire signs that you're being "puppy tested:"

   - She shifts positions before responding to SIT or DOWN.
   - She faces away or pivots in front of you during HEEL.
   - She blocks your path and/or slams into your leg on the COME command.

 **Putting You to the Test**

At this stage, your puppy's world is being shaped by two conflicting forces: the desire to please you and the urge to test her leader once more just to make sure you can walk your talk. Don't take it personally! Once your puppy understands that you most certainly do mean what you say, you'll be in the driver's seat. Here are a few rules of thumb:

- Remain calm. Don't let your puppy see that you're angry or frustrated. All teens, regardless of species, derive perverse pleasure out of your discomfort.

- Never lose. If your puppy is challenging you on a direction and she is on-leash, stick to your point until it's clear that your directions don't have an option clause. If your puppy is off-lead and she ignores you or defies a direction, ignore her and withdraw from the situation. A graceful retreat is not a failure.

- Raise her awareness. She's capable of learning that some behaviors are right and others are wrong.

What to Teach

10 Months

Words of the Week

HEEL: Is this direction beginning to fall into place? Are you styling as you and your puppy float down the street as one? Well, good. Now you're ready for two new exercises:

- HANDS FREE in public: If you've got your leash around your waist, slide it around your left side so that the knot or the clip rests on your tailbone. As you're moving along, drop the lead, slap your leg, and remind her to HEEL. Walk on confidently. If you drop your shoulder or glare at your pup, she'll be confused. Speed up if she lags or slows, and tug if she thunders ahead. Remind her to HEEL, and don't forget to praise her focus!

- Short-Lead Handling: Go back to your circles, to your quiet space. This time attach a short one- to eight-inch lead to your puppy's buckle collar. Hold onto it as you start out, letting it go for short stints as you walk on confidently. Any change in pace or posture may be

 **Stiff Back?**

If your puppy is too short for you to hold on a short lead, thread a lightweight lead through the one-inch short lead and hold it loosely. When it comes time to let go, thread the leash out discreetly.

misconstrued as a warning signal, causing your puppy to hesitate or bolt. Keep yourself relaxed, gracefully reaching for the short lead if your puppy darts off. If she races off, go to her calmly and let it go. You need more on-lead practice before getting too fancy. Next time, practice in a smaller area as well.

Emergency DOWN: This direction has saved two of my dogs, and countless clients have called to tell their tale. I'm rather partial to it. It takes a few weeks to perfect, but with slow and steady progress it will develop. Your puppy must master the standing DOWN before you can expect this response. Here's what you do:

- Stand next to your puppy.
- Suddenly direct DOWN in an emergency voice.
- Kneel down as you direct and position your puppy quickly if she looks startled or confused.
- Pause a few seconds, then release with OKAY and praise her lovingly.
- If you're using a clicker, mark each DOWN and reward her with food. (Phase out treating within five days, or you may become treat-dependent.)

This direction hearkens back to pack mentality, when the leader would make a warning signal that would send all to seek cover. Soon your pup will catch on and will begin to respond with urgency. Gradually extend your distance from her and vary your position: in front, off to the side or behind: when she hears this one you want her to hit the dirt instantly! This exercise is stressful, however, so limit your practice to two DOWN sequences every other day.

Use the emergency DOWN when necessary. It's not a trick!

Jodi Buren

Things to Do

Assess your puppy's reaction to ignoring directions. If your puppy ignores you, put yourself in her paws. Check out her eyes, ears, and body language. Is she

- Anxious? You may be too far away, or the situation may be stressful or unfamiliar.

- Confusion has a similar look. Don't be too hard on her in either case. Simply reposition her and start from the top, simplifying your steps to build her success rate.

- Flippant? Is she blowing you off? Typical teenager stuff; stay cool. Either wait for her to correct herself (if she's on a tree or a long line), or give a quick-tug and say, NOPE! Return her to the position and reinforce your direction, even if she breaks three more times! Praise her cooperation.

Use a long lead to balance YES and NOPE. Ideally, you've been giving your puppy freedom on her long line for a while (see "Things to Do" in the section "5 Months," on page 171). Now it's time to balance the YES and the NOPE! Periodically give your puppy a direction: start with WAIT and her name. Each time you call out, stand near the long line. If she ignores you, pick up the line, give it a quick-tug as you say, NOPE. When she refocuses and gives a correct response, say YES to encourage her!

Gradually introduce other directions like the emergency down and the come. Use the instructions on developing your puppy's awareness described on page 183.

Games to Play

Four-footed fax (page 81) is a great game for this stage.

 **Check Yourself**

If she actually gets away from you, don't yell and chase her. Stay calm and follow her. Control your frustration because your puppy is still young and impulsive. A pack of playful dogs or a rodent can be rather irresistible. Once you're at your puppy's side, say, "NOPE," with a leash or a collar tug and start over. Do ask yourself—am I asking too much? If you don't already have one on her, attach a long line!

11 Months

Words of the Week

STAY: Now you're given unbridled liberty to use STAY everywhere, and use it often. The direction to STAY helps your puppy feel safe in all situations. Remember to stay close when the distraction is unfamiliar, mindfully extending your distance as you both grow confident. Here are everyday situations where STAY is vital (this is my short list—feel free to add your own situations to create a more customized list):

- Any time you want your puppy to sit calmly in the house
- Waiting for a light
- While talking or window shopping
- In the waiting room at your veterinarian's
- While you pay for items at the hardware store
- When someone wants to pet your puppy

STAY (out of sight): During Month 7, we practiced the disappearing act around an inside corner. Provided you've accomplished that, you're ready for the next step.

- Using the tree line or a sturdy object, place your puppy in a SIT or DOWN-STAY.
- Leave her physically; move out of sight. Don't look back (you'll look unsure); just remind her to "STAY," and go. If your puppy whines or fusses, it only means that you've got a little more work to do. Your pup already has or is developing separation anxiety (another word for overbonding).
- Return in thirty seconds, regardless of her behavior.
- If she's calm, approach, pause ten seconds, and then praise her.
- If she's wild, return to her side but don't look at or talk to her until she's quiet, even if it takes thirty minutes.
- Repeat this until your departures and arrivals are ho-hum. I use this one everyday at the local coffee shop: Whoopsie is a regular!

Things to Do

Create minefields. This one is fun to practice inside or out. See the sample chart below. First draw three columns on a page. List five temptations in each column, gradually increasing the intensity. Here's a list created for a client.

MINEFIELD TEMPTATIONS

A	B	C
Temptation 1		
Temptation 2		
Temptation 3		
Temptation 4		
Temptation 5		

Spread the five temptations randomly in an imaginary ten- by ten-foot area. Now go to it! Use your directions in a medley: walking your puppy by, calling her through, and reinforcing STAY directions right near each one. Balance NOPE with YES, remembering to redirect and reconnect after each direction. Once your puppy has gotten list A down, step it up!

Create a tree station. Secure a leash or a rope around a tree, leaving no more than four feet of slack from the base. You'll use this station to improve your puppy's acceptance of containment and separation. Follow the previous STAY and STAY (out of sight) exercises.

Games to Play

At this stage, choose games from chapter 5 that highlight your puppy's favorite hobbies.

12 MONTHS

Words of the Week

FETCH THE PAPER: Have you perfected the COME and BRING duo? Feel like getting fancy? Try the following to have your puppy fetch the paper.

- Start with a small section of the paper. Fold it lengthwise, and tape it closed.
  - Flip it around to heighten your puppy's interest.
  - When she reaches out, say, FETCH THE PAPER, and let her have it.
  - If she spits it out, fine. If she prances around with it, that's okay, too.
  - Does your paper come in a plastic bag? Put this section in the bag, tape it up, and repeat the previous step.
  - Play this game outside near the actual delivery location, gradually increasing the bulk until it's the full newspaper.
  - Teach the BRING by saying it as you run back to the door.
- Now you're ready for the send-off:
  - Have your puppy WAIT at the door.
  - Run out three-fourths of the way to the paper as you point toward it and say, FETCH THE PAPER, then turn and run back inside. Make a huge fuss!

- Run out halfway, then a quarter of the way, and then stand at the door, point, and say, FETCH THE PAPER.
- If your puppy drops it, try running back into the main part of the house, saying, BRING!

CARRY: Having a puppy who will help you carry things is neat. I promise you this: once your puppy has learned this, it can't be unlearned. She'll want to help carry everything from firewood to groceries, to paper towels as you're cleaning the house. For some people, it can be a double-edge sword; for others, it's a joy greater than chocolate.

- Start with your puppy's favorite object: a ball, for example.
- Bring her to your side, on- or off-lead: you be the judge.
- Bounce her toy around until she takes hold.
- Slap your leg and say, CARRY, as you walk briskly forward.
- Stop frequently in the beginning, praising her and making a fuss.
- Use GIVE as you stop (with or without food), teaching your puppy to place the object directly in your hand. (If she doesn't, place it back into her mouth and insist on a praiseworthy hand-to-mouth delivery.)
- Now graduate to other objects, starting with the identifiable shapes and textures.

Things to Do

Practice a few short-lead directional medleys. You've gone the distance, and the hard work is behind you. The next six months, however, can toss you a few curveballs. Don't be caught off guard. Continue your practice with a few short-lead directional medleys. Not only is it the last step before off-lead control, you can also use it to reinforce stationary directions, as well as HEEL and COME. If your puppy disregards you, pick up the lead calmly and give it a quick-tug. Also remember to

- Move smoothly from one direction to the next.
- Play music or be goofy to make it more interesting.
- Involve friends and family members.
- Teach others close to you how to give directions, too.
- Practice around increasingly greater distractions.

Pick your Magic Seven. You're going to have a handful of directions that you rely on most. Although you've spent time teaching each one, there will still be those that stand out, ones that your puppy will hear over and over, day after day. Make a clean list of seven of these directions, and pass the list around or hang it by the door or on the fridge. Everyone who comes into my home, from family member

---

🐾 Directional Medleys

- **Emphasize motion:** Practice in an open area. Start with HEEL, setting up distractions and obstacles to navigate. Vary the speed, the direction, and the reinforcement. Unscheduled rewards will keep your puppy on her toes. Blend in short STAY directions and one COME command.
- **Emphasize containment:** Secure a leash onto an immovable object. HEEL your puppy over and secure her, leaving her in a SIT or a DOWN. Now vary the time, the distance, and the distractions you introduce. Remember, if she's anxious as you return, walk in backward to reduce the excitement. Also blend in stationary directions, encouraging your puppy to move from one to the other: STAND-DOWN-SIT, SIT-STAND-SIT-DOWN, etc.
- **Mix it up:** Using all your words and routines, set up distractions, or work in a public environment.

---

to repair man, learns my two top favorites immediately: WAIT and BACK INTO THE HOUSE. These safety passwords help Whoopsie feel comfortable and calm with whoever is accepted into our home.

Proof your puppy. Although you should set up some proofs (check out examples of some proofs in the following list), life will provide you with a steady stream of distractions. Use the same techniques listed in the following paragraphs but adapt them to everyday distractions, and either ally a helper as your distracter or use irresistible temptations:

- HEEL: Work figure eights around your distractions. Walk up to, pass by, and navigate through them, reminding HEEL as you do and praising attentiveness. Quick-tug and say, NOPE, if your puppy gets distracted.
- COME: Have your distracter stand in the way. Ask him or her to hold a sandwich or pat another dog. Use NOPE if your pup is distracted, and YES when she stays the course.
- STAY: Have your distracter pull out all the stops. Remind your pup STAY. If you need to steady her, stand as near as you must, calmly repositioning her when necessary. Praise, praise, praise her containment. You've come so far!
- SIT, DOWN, or WAIT: Issue stationary directions as your distracter runs by or makes a racket: no excuses.

Sign up to take the Canine Good Citizen Test! The certificate is a sure sign of all your hard work! The Canine Good Citizen test—CGC for short—is a

noncompetitive test developed to recognize and certify dogs and their owners as responsible citizens. Although the test was developed and is promoted by the American Kennel Club, it is not limited to purebred dogs. Mixed breeds are encouraged to certify as well.

The CGC measures a dog's social skills and public manners and is not a competition. The goal of the CGC test is not to eliminate participants but to encourage pet owners to learn the skills necessary to train their dogs to be safe, well-mannered members of society.

> ### 🐾 Default Behavior
>
> At some point, your puppy should just start behaving without being asked. For example, she'll hop out of the car and come to your side. She'll walk at your heel without being instructed, she'll stop at stairs and doors automatically. You're graduating! Your lessons are so ingrained, they're an integral part of your relationship with her. It's awesome.

To pass the test, your dog must know the directions HEEL, SIT, DOWN, and STAY. The test is composed of ten evaluations:

1. Accepting a friendly stranger. To pass this test, the dog must allow a non-threatening person to approach and speak to the handler.

2. Sitting politely for petting. The dog must allow a friendly stranger to pet her while sitting at her handler's side.

3. Appearance and grooming. The dog must be clean and well-groomed and must allow a stranger (representing a veterinarian or a groomer) to handle and groom her without suspicion.

4. Out for a walk. The dog must walk attentively at the handler's side. To pass this evaluation, the dog does not have to heel perfectly or sit when the handler is instructed to stop.

5. Walking through a crowd. The dog must be attentive to her owner and in control as she is led through a crowd of people.

6. Sit and down on command/staying in place. The dog must respond to the handler's SIT, DOWN, and STAY directions.

7. Coming when called. A test to ensure your dog's reliably coming to you when you call.

8. Reaction to another dog. The dog must be in control and focused on the handler while passing another dog.

9. Reaction to distractions. The dog must remain calm and confident when faced with everyday distractions. The distractions at an evaluation might include a child running, a bicyclist, or a person on crutches or in a wheelchair.

10. Supervised isolation. For this test, the dog is held silently by a stranger and is expected to wait calmly when her handler disappears for three minutes.

🐾 Feeling Fancy?

No need to stop here! There are so many venues you can try, from competition obedience to athletic outlets for either or both of you. Visit my website, www.dogperfect.com, for dog-friendly activities and adventures!

If you think you and your dog are ready for the CGC test, contact the American Kennel Club at www.akc.org or the following address to find a program in your area.

Canine Good Citizen Program
c/o AKC
5580 Centerview Drive, Suite 200
Raleigh, NC 27606
919-233-9780

Games to Play

For games at this stage, contact others with your passion and check out my reference section or visit my website, www.dogperfect.com.

COMMON CONCERNS AND QUESTIONS

How do I handle my puppy's increasing aggression at the door? He gets really reactive when it's a man. I find I have to isolate him.

Call a professional now. Aggression is beyond the scope of this book. It will get much worse if you don't do something to make it better.

Is it possible my puppy is breaking her SIT-STAY for more than one reason? How do I determine one from the other?

Absolutely! The body language, the ear pitch, and her focus are dead giveaways. If she alerts to something else in her environment, her ears will pitch forward and she'll look away. If she's startled, her ears will go down, her body will jolt, and her eyes will dart from the sound to you. If she's defiant, she'll just up and go; maybe she'll flip around and stick her tongue out, but off she'll go.

Our puppy drops the ball just before he reaches us. How can I teach him to deliver it to our hands?

I had the exact same dilemma for a while. The problem is, if you or anyone else steps forward to pick it up, your puppy will test the protocol with everyone. Talk to everyone who plays ball with him, and ask them to teach him a new word: DELIVER. This means to your hand. Put Simba on a short lead, toss the ball in a small room, and as he approaches, take the lead and bring his mouth over your hand as you say,

Always end with success . . . YES!

"DELIVER." If you're coordinated, pop a treat in his mouth as he releases into your hand or shortly thereafter. Leave on the short lead during your regular routine, guiding your puppy's mouth to your hand as you say, "DELIVER." Now, ignore him when he drops it in front of you. Don't pick it up, look at him, or repeat yourself. If he wants to play, he'll know what to do.

My puppy darts to the side whenever I reach down to grab the short lead. I try to be sneaky, but he doesn't miss a trick.

Clever puppy. Try being smooth, not sneaky. If you reach and snatch, your puppy will interpret it as a game and will try to out maneuver you. Use a lead or a rope threaded through your short lead for a while. Avoid looking at him, too, when you reach for the lead; this cues confrontation. Smooth.

How do you know when you can trust your puppy (a) off-lead and (b) to roam freely in the home?

It's something you feel in your gut. A trust that generates a sense of kinship. I didn't feel it with my Whoopsie until she was 19 months old. I remember the day. You will, too.

Appendix

EXPECTING A PUPPY?

Are you reading this book before bringing your puppy home? My hat's off to you. Well-thought-out plans will help you avoid a host of mishaps and frustrations. I'm sure you have many questions. Here are some of the most frequent questions I get asked during my pre-puppy consultations.

What Kind of Puppy Is Right for Me?

When considering this question, write down how you'd like your life to look three years from now with your adult dog. Do you want him sitting on your lap or joining you for a jog? In our family, the number one priority was that our dog play Frisbee. Also important was a short-coated breed that would tolerate children. I wrote down every detail. I encourage you to do the same.

At the end of this Appendix is a chart with eight categories to consider. Circle your choice or put NI if it is not important to you.

Write down every detail. Think it through. Talk to your family. Something may matter tremendously, like size, sociability, or snout shape; others, like coat type or color, may not. Read breed books or visit online sites. You'll notice that the American Kennel Club divides puppies into seven categories, grouping them according to their genetic predispositions. Dogs in the Terrier Group, for example, have all got "game." Spunky and determined, they were bred to follow their instincts, not your direction. Although training can influence terrier breeds, their impulses often win out. If off-lead companionship is your goal, don't pick a terrier. You may be let down. For more information on the breeds, see the References at the end of this book.

What's Temperament Testing?

Believe it or not, you can tell a lot about your future dog when he's just a puppy. At seven weeks, many of the personality characteristics shine through. Before being swept off your feet by the first puppy you see, evaluate the personality traits that are best suited to your life's situation.

I've reconstructed a temperament test similar to the one that we used for Whoopsie. Decide on your ideal scores ahead of time (see the Puppy Assessment Form later in this section) and go for it. Be ready to walk away and wait. You've got the next twelve-plus years of your lives to enjoy together.

USING A PUPPY ASSESSMENT FORM

Rating system: Rate each puppy according to his reaction. Determine which adjective applies as you're testing individual puppies.

    A = Active   From bullying to energetic

    N = Neutral   From low-key to aloof

    P = Passive   From reserved to fearful

Exercise description: These eight exercises will give you insight into a puppy's personality. Read over the descriptions ahead of time.

1. **Observe:** If you're going to a breeder, ask ahead for the puppies' daily schedule and arrive at a time when they're normally active. Whether you're given a choice of puppies or it's been narrowed down to one or two, observe the pups as they interact. Note the active puppies who take charge and rough-house: are they bullying or fair (A)? Also watch for the puppies who hesitate or stay to themselves (P). Are there any puppies who seem happy playing quietly with or without company (N)? Think how this might apply to your life.

2. **Uplift:** After observing, take each puppy aside individually. Cradle his mid-body and suspend him four inches off the ground. If he squirms wildly and reaches out to mouth you, give him an A. If he squirms a bit but then relaxes, give him an N. If he shudders in fear or pins his ears back and tucks his tail, give him a P.

3. **Flip-Flop:** Next, lift the puppy up and cradle him upside-down like a baby. Does he squirm and try to grab at you with his mouth? That's an A. If he wiggles a bit and then settles happily, he gets an N. If he whimpers or pulls his mouth back in tension (a submissive grin), he gets a P.

4. **Gentle Caress:** Now sit next to the puppy and pet him. Gently stroke him at least five times to judge his willingness to be handled. If he immediately jumps toward your face or scampers away toward a more stimulating

Got Kids?

Bring your kids along if they can remain neutral; initial interactions can be informative. Young children can help out in this assessment with the Gentle Caress and the Crash Test. You will see how your future puppy may react to your children.

---

distraction, give him an A. If he relaxes and sits quietly or climbs into your lap, give him an N. If he belly-rolls, cowers, tucks his tail, pins his ears, or pulls his mouth back in tension, give him a P.

5. **Wacky Walk:** Stand up, shake your legs, clap your hands, and encourage the pup to follow you. Bend down like a monkey if you must; just do what you have to in order to get his attention. If he attacks your legs or gets distracted by a more interesting stimulant, give him an A. If he follows enthusiastically, looking up to your face for reinforcement, give him an N. If he sits and watches you quietly or withdraws in fear, give him a P.

6. **What's That?** You'll need keys or three pennies in a can for this exercise. When the puppy is distracted, make this noise above his head. If he jumps up or wrestles the objects, give him an A. If he ignores the sound or sniffs the objects calmly, give him an N. If he cowers in fear or runs away, give him a P.

7. **Crash Boom:** Walk at least six paces away from the puppy. Suddenly drop to the floor as if you've fallen and hurt your knee. Don't get carried away, but make it look fairly realistic. Does the puppy take this as an invitation to play? If so, give him an A. If he walks over and acts curious, give him an N. If he freezes fearfully or runs and cowers, give him a P.

8. **Umbrella Surprise:** Open an umbrella five feet from your puppy. Does he bark loudly and/or move toward it assertively (A)? Does he look up, puzzled, and then regroup (N)? Does he act confused or afraid (P)?

Assessment Form: After you've performed each exercise with a potential puppy, fill in his name or number and then rate each exercise with an A, N, or P (see previous descriptions). Then tally the score (see the explanation for tallying the score right after this form).

First Sight

Notice how the puppy greets you initially as well. Is he hyper? Cautious? Mellow? First impressions count.

PUPPY ASSESSMENT FORM

Name/Number of Pup	Observe	Uplift	Flip-Flop	Gentle Caress	Wacky Walk	What's That?	Crash Test	Umbrella Surprise

🐾 Other Priorities

Puppies, like children and people, are made up of a variety of traits and may be affected by the time of day or situational factors. Spend as much time as possible selecting your puppy. If you've got a hobby that you hope to share with your puppy, add a test for that, too. My husband wanted a puppy to play Frisbee with him. Our first test was to roll a disc by the puppy's nose. Whoopsie's 9-week-old reaction? She leaped out of my lap, raced over to pick up the disc, and raced back into my lap with unflagging enthusiasm.

TALLYING THE SCORE

Count up your As, Ns, and Ps and then take a look at the following:

- If you've got all As, you're dealing with a puppy who has a strong sense of self. Likely the leader of the puppy pack, he may try to maintain this position with you. Unless you have a strong sense of *your*self, experience raising a puppy, and time and patience, this pup is better suited to someone with a take-charge personality. This puppy is smart as a whip and will demand continual involvement.
* The all-N puppy is easygoing and relaxed. These pups are best suited for families on the go, as they tolerate chaos and can manage not being the center of attention.
- All Ps mean that, without appropriate socialization, this puppy may have confidence issues and timidity. This dear puppy needs a soft, loving hand; little to no discipline; and a person or people to help him develop poise, confidence, and a stronger sense of self.
- Ns and Ps mean this puppy is likely to be reserved and calm. In need of socialization and training to avert timidity with company, this puppy is easy to live with and does best in a structured home. Chaos feels unpredictable and unsafe.
- As and Ns combine to shape a puppy who is outgoing and playful but able to contain chaos and separation. This is often the best personality choice for active families. This is the personality type we tested for and found in Whoopsie Daisy.

RAISING KIDS AND PUPPIES

Mention the words *children* and *puppies* in the same sentence, and everyone envisions the ideal: constant companions, sleepy nights resting on the same pillow, and happy childhood memories spent sharing ice cream cones and rainy afternoons. Then come the preset requirements: that the kids will take care of their puppy and that the pup will be sweet and accepting, chew puppy toys only, play gently with minimal nipping, always come when called, and housetrain easily. Hello? Anyone who has attempted this knows that it's a fantasy. Puppies and kids are rowdy and full of energy, neither is focused and responsible 100 percent of the time, and raising them together requires a huge commitment of time. *Your* time. Puppies, like children, require constant consideration.

That said, I am the biggest fan of raising kids and puppies together. My childhood dog Shawbee can be found in all my favorite childhood memories. Whoopsie was, in fact, chosen to be my children's puppy. It is a viable dream!

The goal is creating the experience so that your kids will remember their puppy as a constant companion, not as a sibling rival. Here are some classic dos and don'ts:

- Do give your children attention first and foremost when greeting or playing with them. Let your children (especially the young ones) know that you still love them most of all.

- Do set a good example of how to interact with your puppy. Be calm and fair. Plan things out with the children: create a Needs Chart, decorate treat cups, make a Weekly Fun Chart, and stick to the plan. Take part in all the daily activities.

- Do play with them together. Kids and puppies love to play games and have fun; however, children use their hands, whereas puppies use their mouths. Neither of them may know how to interact well with the other species. Help your children discover which games work best (refer to the game list in chapter 5). Use props like the head collar if your puppy is too mouthy or a drag lead for interference. Have fun!

- Do let this project unite your family, not divide it. Use examples and metaphors in this book (and others you find helpful) to make it easier for everyone relate to the puppy's needs. (See the following Catch Phrase list.)

 ## Signs of Sibling Rivalry

Is your harmonious household turning hostile? Early signs of rivalry may be hard to notice, although your children will give you the first clues. If they're jealous of the attention you're giving your puppy or angry at the sudden disruption in everyday routines, this spells trouble. Whether your children are retaliating, complaining, or withdrawing, your puppy will have telltale signs, too:

- Excessive nipping, primarily with the children
- Mounting the kids, either to get your attention or when adults aren't around
- Competition for prized items like shoes and toys
- Hyperactivity when the children are home

- Do leave a drag lead on your puppy when the children are playing with him. If he's mouthy or confrontational, fit him with a head halter, which will drastically change the interactions from challenging to calm and cooperative.
- Do let your puppy sleep in the children's room in a crate or at a station to the side of the bed. If you have more than one child, the puppy can be rotated on a weekly basis: night to night is too confusing. The time spent together at night reinforces the children's seniority (they sleep a level above) and will strengthen the bond between child and puppy.

Kid-Friendly Charts and Phrases

Make a Weekly Fun Chart to encourage family participation (see the Weekly Fun Chart later in this section). Use whatever works. If your kids like cards, candy, or movies, bargain a reward for every ten initializations. Use catchy phrases to keep the situation light and fun. Here are some ideas of what to include:

Encourage after You Discourage: If someone tells the puppy not to do something, that person must encourage an alternative behavior and praise the puppy when he cooperates.

Kisses: Rub a frozen stick of butter or another spread on the children's hands. Extend the hand to your puppy and say the word KISSES as he licks it off.

Elevator Up and Elevator Down: Use this phrase and play this game whenever the kids are offering your puppy a reward. Hold the treat or the object above the puppy's head. If he jumps, say, ELEVATOR UP and lift your hand. If he sits still, say, ELEVATOR DOWN, and drop the hand below the puppy's chin. Open the hand and say, KISSES!

Close Shop: When your puppy's excitement rises or he's too jumpy, have your children stand tall and fold their arms in front of their faces. Since face-to-face interaction excites, this game teaches a puppy that jumping causes a withdrawal of interaction. Only calm puppies get face-to-face interaction.

Four-Paw Rule: All four paws must be on the floor to get attention or rewards. If your puppy jumps, *close shop* and review jumping in chapter 6 for other suggestions.

Three Strikes and You're Out: We're not talking baseball here, but if the analogy works, use it! Make two attempts to redirect a difficult situation (i.e., jumping); the third time, isolate your puppy until he settles down. Calmly isolate or lead your puppy away. Let everyone know the rule, and count each intervention so that the results are no surprise.

Stand Like a Statue: Puppies like to chase moving targets. The reverse also holds true. Help your kids pick a favorite statue, and call it out to head off a tumultuous situation, such as the Statue of Libery.

Peacock Position: This phrase helps your kids remember to stand straight when giving your puppy direction.

Word of the Week: Spotlight a new word each week. Write it on index cards, and post them around the house. Let the kids use treats and practice whenever they want. If you make too many rules, they won't help out. I left treat cups around, and each week Whoopsie had to do something new: sit, down, paw, roll over. The excitement became who could get her to do it the fastest.

Together, teach your puppy five words to help him understand you better. Emphasize sounds and signals, saying each direction like a short, quick bark.

SIT: A "say please" equivalent; a good instruction before offering your puppy anything cool, such as treats, toys, or attention.

WAIT: The freeze direction. Said clearly, it will teach your puppy to stop in his tracks.

MAT: Puppies, like kids, like having a special place. Choose a word that directs your puppy to his area.

BALL or **TOY** or **KISSES:** Key trigger words like these will help everyone engage or redirect your puppy's energy.

COME: The human phrase equivalent of this direction is the word HUD-DLE! Teach your puppy and your children together.

Other directions are important, too. For example, if your child is in charge of walking the puppy, learning HEEL will be an asset. And you shouldn't overlook tricks! Fun to learn, show off, and share, a snazzy BOW or a HIGH FIVE is icing on the cake.

 Whirling Dervishes

When things are getting out of hand, don't blame either party. Neither children nor puppies can control their impulses 100 percent of the time. Often, giving children a choice is most effective. For example, I might say, "I can see you're pumped up right now. It's obvious that Penny is out of control. You can help me calm her down, or she'll need to have some quiet time in her crate. What do you think?" And then, if things don't calm down, Penny would be escorted to her crate and given a bone or a toy. Secretly, she may be delighted.

Other Tidbits

Treat Cup Lessons: Let your kids use treats. To motivate your puppy's cooperation, even if you choose not to use them. Kids love sharing, treats guarantee quick responses, and the success rate will be addictive. (Note: If your puppy is assertive around food, use a toy or enthusiastic praise. If your puppy can overpower your child, chaperone their interactions.)

Transfer the Control: If your puppy is headstrong or is already overpowering your children, they may not be able to communicate leadership. Young kids can't assert themselves until they're old enough to stare you in the eye. Teach your puppy the basics, and then stand by and help transfer the power. Say your directions simultaneously, and help your child to position your puppy if the puppy ignores him or her.

WEEKLY FUN CHART

Time	Activity	M	T	W	TH	F	SA	SU
7 a.m.	Out							
7:15	Feed and water							
8:00–11:30	Lead, station or crate, supervised freedom							
11:30	Out and play							
Noon–Mid	Feed and water							
12:15 p.m.	Out and play							
12:30–3:30	Lead, station, crate, supervised play							
3:30	Out and play—explore							
4:00	Feed and water							
4:15	Outside							
4:30–7:00	Lead, station or crate, supervised freedom							
7:00–9:00	Family interaction							

Things to Avoid

Let go of expectations. Trying to control or boss your children will leave them feeling resentful and angry at the puppy and at you: Sibling Rivalry 101.

Shout or hit. If shouting at or hitting your puppy is your method, revise it—for two reasons. Shouting is perceived as barking, and it will make matters worse. Your puppy may get more assertive. Second, your kids will copy your tactics, and though your puppy may be subservient to you, he may challenge the children. Other corrections to avoid (for the same reason) are squeezing the muzzle, putting your fingers down your puppy's throat, and physical corrections like hitting or shoving.

Blame. Try not to point fingers—it unbalances the system. Although it may be true that your 7-year-old son is instigating rough play, talking about it will only highlight his role. Think of creative ways to refocus the energy, and work with your child privately to restrict privileges for errant behavior.

It's basic human psychology, I know. In fact, many of my theories come from reading child psychology books. Puppies and children share many similarities.

TWO PUPPIES: TWICE THE FUN OR DOUBLE TROUBLE?

The concept behind raising two puppies is truly admirable: they'll have each other to play with, they'll never be alone, and they're fun to watch together. I'll be the first to agree, but there is a flip side. Puppies speak their own language, and if they're raised together, you or your family may become secondary players in their world. The adolescent stage is a nightmare with just one puppy. Now try to persuade one pup not to chew on your shoe while the other prances around with your sock! Scolding a piddle accident when you're not sure who did it never feels right. Episodes like these diminish your clout. I'm not saying it can't be done; it's just more of a project if you're going to do it right. Here are some tips:

- Separate the puppies early on. Each pup should have his own crate, food dish, and blanket. The puppies are not identical. This fact needs to be respected.

- Give each puppy some special "me only" time. The puppies can be divided between family members, or you can leave one in the crate. Though one pup may stress more when separated initially, in time both will be more confident.

- Practice short five-minute lessons, both separately and together.

- Determine which puppy is dominant. Which one goes through thresholds first and reigns over bones and toys? Respect their chosen hierarchy: feed, greet, pamper, treat, and train this puppy more. The other puppy is a follower who doesn't want to be spotlighted and will gladly mimic the leader's behavior.

- With two puppies, you'll have a longer laundry list of losses. It's the way it goes. Before 5 months of age, avoid corrections at all costs. Making corrections casts you in an unfavorable light. The pups will roll their eyes and avoid you when you're upset. Follow all structuring suggestions and stay calm. It's a long year ahead, but you'll get through it.

- Teaching the concept of NOPE is possible at 5 months. Work them separately, initially using the exercise described on page 166.

TRANSITIONING A NEW PUPPY WITH OTHER PETS

Resident pets rarely share your enthusiasm for a new puppy. In fact, most are rather put out. Settled in their routines and averse to chaos, they'll notice the sudden shift in your attention. With some thought and understanding, you can make the transition easier, but be patient, as it may take some time.

Dogs

Can you imagine if your spouse (or your mom or dad) came in one night with another adult or child, declaring, "This is our new spouse (or child)! You're going to love her!" When you balked, you were dismissed quickly and reassured, "No, no, she's just great! She's so cute—just look at her. And she'll be here to play with you when I'm not around!"

Metaphor aside, practice these tips to ensure that your resident dog doesn't feel slighted:

- Don't change any routines. If the new puppy curtails the resident dog's house freedom, relocates the food dish, or terminates that dog's couch time with the kids, the intrusion will cause resentment. I guarantee it.

- Make the puppy a bonus houseguest. Suddenly start spoiling your resident dog—extra treats when the puppy's around, new games, an extra feeding at midday (a small sprinkling), and cuddle time. A light bulb may go off: "Hey, this puppy rocks! Let's get another!"

- All royalties go to the resident. Feed, greet, and treat her first. Deflect all attention to her when she needs it. Over-interact with your old-timer. The new puppy will value your dog's presence and will mimic her good manners. Make up a cool catch phrase like "Molly Most Important," or "You're Still Our Queen!" repeating it over and over whenever the two are together.

- Attach a drag lead to your puppy so that you can calmly refocus him when he's being a nudge. If your resident dog is acting bothered, she is. Help her out by removing the puppy. Also purchase Bitter Apple, a distasteful solution, which you can spray or rub on your dog's ears or coat to discourage the puppy's biting. If your puppy is just impossible, exercise him more and fit him for a head collar to calm and control him.

- Regarding toys, if your older one wants to hoard every toy on the floor, let her. It's her way of communicating rank; if you interfere, she may get rougher in her attempts convince you. If you want your puppy to have a toy, place it in his crate or tie several toys to pieces of furniture.

Cats

Cats rule. Your cat's reaction will depend on a lot of things: her age and prior association with puppies, how you manage the situation from the start, the intensity of your puppy's interest, and your overall patience with your cat's timetable. Acceptance may be a long road.

- Buy a playpen for your puppy. Allow your cat uninhibited freedom. The safe barrier empowers the cat's curiosity.

- Your new puppy will have a gigantic X on his head if his playroom coincides with the cat's feeding or bathroom station. If possible, relocate dishes and the litter box two weeks prior to your puppy's arrival. Otherwise, use a playpen as described previously.

- Until there's a co-species trust, keep your puppy confined either in a small room, in a crate, or on a lead when the cat is around.

- When your puppy's restful, take him into a small bathroom or a hallway on a leash. Next, bring the cat and place her on a high table or a ledge so that she can safely observe.

- If you're handling an older puppy who's already shown some excitement, fit him for a head collar or a Good Dog Collar (page 31) and attach a drag lead to enable calm management.

- Never scold the cat. It's humiliating. If your cat scratches the puppy, reassure your cat. If the cat's a bully, the puppy must learn avoidance early on. If you're truly concerned about your cat's aggression, speak to your veterinarian or a behaviorist.

Remember, cats are not lesser spirits than puppies. Dignify their existence, and most of them will learn tolerance.

Other Pets

The sooner you start, the better! Young puppies are easily confused and will mirror your reactions. For example, if suddenly there is a rabbit in the room, most young puppies will look to you for direction. Casual responses are best. Overprotective reactions are disquieting, and your puppy may get impulsive and predatory. If you're nervous, fit your puppy for a head collar or a muzzle and handle him on a leash, enabling control and ensuring your calmness.

If you've already had disastrous encounters, discover how close you can get the two animals to each other without an incident. Let's say your puppy's red zone is ten feet. Teach lessons at this distance using treats and toys, and gradually bring the two animals closer.

Temperament	Size	Activity Level	Sociability	Coat	Color	Ear Carriage	Snout
Outgoing	X-large	Sporty	Welcoming	Short	White	Ear up	Long
Strong	Large	Relaxed	Protective	Curly	Brown	Ear down	Boxed
Reserved	Medium	Enjoys walks	Cautious	Wavy	Black		Compensated
Relaxed	Small			Long	Patterned		
	Tiny			Hypoallergenic	Random		

Sarah's Doglish Glossary

attachment puppy parenting   A method of raising your puppy that encourages togetherness over isolation. Nights are shared. It accelerates emotional security; however, it can lead to overattachment if exaggerated.

attention-getting behaviors   Any behavior that gets your attention—even a glance! Sitting calmly and bringing a toy are good ones. Jumping, whining, pawing, barking . . . those are less endearing!

behavior memory   Once a specific routine or behavior is repeated ten to sixty times, it becomes part of your puppy's behavior memory. You can call it up by assigning a specific word to the action, e.g., SIT or PAW or INSIDE. Early traumatic events also make a lasting behavioral imprint. Bummer.

blaster   This macelike canister issues a startling effect, blasting a strong stream of citronella fluid. It can be used to short-circuit naughty behavior and to fend off approaching dogs or other animals during a walk.

bracing (brace)   Brace your puppy in a SIT-STAY position for all greetings. This helps to calm her and teach her the Four-Paw Rule! Nifty!

car stations   Give your puppy a special place in the car. Decorate it with a mat and a toy, and pre-secure a seat belt lead to ensure safe travels. Get in the habit of letting your puppy enter and exit the same door.

clicker-happy training   A gadget with a punctuating sound that accelerates behavioral memory.

close shop   A great way to extinguish jumping. Fold your arms over your face and ignore your puppy until she's on all four paws. Let her see that jumping eliminates interaction.

come front   An exercise-game combo that teaches COME as a command of closeness. It is also the third step in a three-part sequence.

confrontational play   Rough interaction that encourages nipping and jumping. Many puppies translate intended corrections as confrontational play.

containment aggression   Often when a puppy is tied outside or housed in a shelter pen or a pet store cage, the puppy develops a defensive reaction to perceived threats. When her adversaries withdraw or don't advance (which, of course, they can't), the puppy's ego inflates. When the barrier is removed, the puppy's aggression is often still pronounced.

containment anxiety   Again, the result of being tied outside or kept in shelter pens or pet store cages. A passive puppy who is traumatized by an aggressive neighbor may develop discomfort or fear in a pen or on a leash.

displacement activity   Anything that can be encouraged, from chewing a bone to sitting or fetching a toy.

drag lead   A light four-foot lead.

drag-lead freedom   Allowing supervised freedom with a light four-foot lead attached for easy interference.

finger lead   A short finger loop attached to your puppy's tag collar for quick control. Neat!

foundation directions   Five or six words that will be the bedrock of your life together. I suggest: LET'S GO, WAIT-OKAY, SIT, MAT-BONE, EXCUSE ME, NOPE, and your puppy's name.

frustrated territorial aggression (FTA)   Any puppy with the slightest trace of protective blood in her veins, who is confined in view of a roadway or a path, is doomed to FTA. It results from the perceived success of fending strangers off her territory. You may know your postman's route, strangers walk by often enough (sometimes with dogs in tow), and recreationalists cruise by unannounced, but each one reminds your puppy that her valor is what keeps your home and yard safe from intruders.

greeting station   A secured place in view of your entranceway. Ideally, your puppy should stand three to six feet behind you when you're opening the door. Luck won't help, a secured station will!

hand lead   An eight- to twelve-inch lead hanging from your dog's tag or head collar when you're supervising her. It allows corrections and/or guidance.

hip checking   This activity is popular with the adolescent crowd. It involves running at full tilt into a loved one and can be coupled with an above-the-hip nip. Rather unpleasant.

hyper isolation anxiety (HIA)   HIA results from too much confinement, in either a crate or a room, or from any form of outdoor isolation. Dogs are groupies by nature; long bouts of isolation create varying levels of anxiety, which results in hyper-manic behavior when they're reunited with their owners. This can quickly be come a vicious cycle.

lead (leading)   Leading is a form of passive control: you literally hold or wear your puppy's leash and lead her around with you. Inside and out, up and down . . . . a couple of twenty-minute leading sessions in the early days will have a tremendous impact. Your puppy quickly learns to focus on you for direction.

lead-abouts   Short five- to ten-minute leading sessions with a young puppy.

level training   Another passive lesson that is learned by simply keeping a young puppy on the floor while you sit on the couch or sleep on a bed. By staying one level above her for the first six months, you're teaching her to look up to you for direction.

line breeding   A term known in breeding circles for when related dogs are bred to produce a certain look. Unfortunately, brain power and temperament are often the cost. Look at all pedigrees before you buy your puppy: the pup's relatives should not be interbred for five generations back.

long line   A twenty-five- to fifty-foot outdoor drag lead that can be left on during supervised play. It allows your puppy to romp naturally while giving you the security of control or interference.

lure   A hands-free way to encode behavioral memory by using a toy or a treat to guide your puppy into a certain position, such as SIT or DOWN. It's also helpful with trick training and when encouraging your puppy toward a certain location.

mimicking   This exercise is ideal during the hot shot stage, although you can do it with a puppy of any age. Pretend that you're a dog, and mimic your puppy's behaviors: all the ones you love and want to see repeated. If she's calm and resting her head between her paws, do the same. If she's quietly chewing a bone, pretend you're doing it, too. Her ideas get reinforced, and she'll love you more for it.

mirroring   When mirroring your puppy, get into her head. Mirror her energy level. If she's sleeping, rest with her. If she wants to be zany, think of some creative games to play with her. If she wants to cuddle, you stay calm, too. Mirroring is ideal during the dependent (8 to 12 weeks) stage. You may try it with older puppies, too!

mischievous marker   Adolescent puppies who mark to get attention.

need confusion   Young puppies are unable to identify a specific need. Like children, they're aware of a discomforting physical sensation, but they are confused as to its origin. Poor dears. Nipping is often the result of their frustration, synonymous with a baby's cry.

need sensation   Prior to the discomfort of "need confusion," your puppy will have a "need sensation." If you learn to read her signs, you may be able to direct her at an early age, encouraging more direct communication.

Needs Chart   Puppies, like babies, have five basic needs: to eat, drink, play, go to the bathroom, and sleep. As a baby grows, she learns language in order to convey her needs. A Needs Chart helps you to establish words and routines so that your puppy can communicate with you as well.

overdistraction   When a puppy becomes too distracted by a food or a toy lure to learn or focus.

Peter Pan puppy   A dog who behaves like an incorrigible pup.

prize envy   If you interrupt your puppy as she's stealing or mouthing an object, she'll think you've got prize envy: that whatever she's found has value because you're willing to invest your time and energy to take it away. Needless to say, the item becomes more valuable; your puppy will go to greater lengths to steal and covet it. This goes for outdoor items, too—even poop. YUCK!

point training   Using the point of the index finger to direct your puppy. Subtle cues enhance the visual focus and the emotional connection: a puppy will feel involved in all situations where direction is offered, verbal or visual.

proofing   Using outside distractions to strengthen your puppy's focus on your directions.

reactionary biting   A reactionary biter is not always a vicious or even aggressive dog. These puppies bite as a knee-jerk reaction to pain, fear, or discomfort.

red flag   This marks a serious behavior or reaction. It warrants an immediate call to a behavior specialist or a professional trainer.

Red Zone   A term used for reactionary puppies. The Red Zone is the length of the distance in which your puppy is unable to focus while in the presence of a distraction. To practice "outside the Red Zone" is to move far enough away that your puppy no longer feels threatened.

reflecting   Take time out of your day to reflect your puppy. This is best started during the dependent stage (8 to 12 weeks), but it can also be a lifelong exercise to enhance understanding and closeness. During reflection time, do exactly what your puppy is doing. If she wants to chase butterflies, go with her. If she wants to investigate a bag, check it out, too. Stick to safe pastimes and those you'd like repeated.

reverse yo-yo   A technique to discourage jumping. Step on your puppy's leash so that she has just enough slack to jump up, but not enough to reach you. For maniac jumpers, it looks like a real cartoon. Up-Down-Up-Down-Up-Down-Up! When your puppy calms down, encourage, SIT, and pet her lovingly.

side swipe   This correction can be issued with a leash of any size (right down to a finger lead). Without touching your puppy, give the leash a sharp sideward tug, which should give your puppy the sensation of slipping on ice.

snack pack   A fanny pack or the like, which carries snacks and/or a clicker. Yes, your puppy may view you as her very own personalized Pez dispenser.

soothing effects of the mother's tongue   Back in the litter, your puppy's original Mom would clean her each day by forcefully licking her fur. This calming behavior brings with it a sense of security and love. You can simulate the same level of nurturing. With your hand, of course!

spray away correction   Using a spray bottle of distasteful solution—or, even better, a small canister—spray an invisible boundary around that which you want your puppy to avoid.

stage stuck   If a puppy's needs are not met during any given stage, she may become stage stuck, repeating behaviors while awaiting an appropriate reaction from her family. Many puppies get stuck in puberty when they're nearly grown, and they repeat behaviors (jumping, nipping, hip checking) in order to make one last attempt at top-dog status.

station (stationed, stationing)   Give your puppy her own special area in the rooms you share. Provide an identifiable area with bedding and toys, and pre-secure a leash if she fidgets.

station lead   A short two- to three-foot lead that is useful in teaching your puppy to STAY in her place.

tag collar   A beltlike flat or rolled collar that carries your puppy's tags.

target disc   A teaching device that uses a small disc to motivate your puppy's understanding of place.

teaching lead   My patented leash that transforms from a regular leash to a hands-free belt-lead combo, to a station lead—all with a change of the clip. Nifty!

team metaphor   A metaphor that's used to help you visualize your relationship. Every team needs a captain: the players look to him or her to organize their space and activities. That's it, in a nutshell. Are you the captain?

three strikes   Don't overwhelm yourself. If you've tried to direct, redirect, or correct your puppy's mischief three times, it's time for a time out. Isolating your puppy with a toy is not bad, as long as you don't get verbally or physically abusive. In fact, it may be just the thing she needs most: quiet time.

touch stick   A teaching device that's used to direct your puppy to targeted areas and help her learn behavior sequences.

treat dependent   Phasing off treats is important. An overreliance results in treat-dependency: your inability to get a reaction from your puppy without food in hand.

treat cup   Treats placed in a cup or a container. The shaking sound will be music to your puppy's ears.

trigger event   A traumatic event that happened during a puppy's impressionable period (8 to 12 weeks) that gets relived in the present, although the current situation is no longer life threatening. This often happens to young puppies who are isolated from their litters and feel overwhelmed during transport.

tush push   A walking technique that transfers the power of the leash to your backside, rather than to your arms. Essentially, the leash is held by both hands behind the back, and the tug is issued by pushing backward.

Weekly Fun Chart   A great way to involve the kids in the puppy's daily routine. Create the chart together. I encourage you to use whatever motivation will spark your child's enthusiasm, from toys to money to food.

yellow flag   This is a warning sign that the behavior could progressively get more serious. It's a good marker that there's work to be done!

References

There are so many books that do justice to strengthening the bond between you and your puppy. I've been a certified dog-book junkie since the age of 2. Like me, you may want to read everything you get your eyes on, and pick and choose what resonates with your situation. Here's a list of some of my top favorite authors, many of whom have several titles under their belt, in addition to some great websites that cross reference other great websites, and so on, and so on. . . . I've listed everything in alphabetical order.

AUTHOR LIST

NAME	ADDRESS/PHONE	WEBSITE/e-mail
Bsh Dibra	Paws Across America 3476 Bailey Ave. Bronx, NY 10463	bash@pawsacrossamerica. com
Bonnie Wilcox, DVM		bondvm@revealed.com
Bruce Fogle		www.barkingbuddies.com
Carol Lea Benjamin		www.carolleabenjamin.com
Cheryl Smith		winsmith@olypen.com
Chris Walkowicz		walkoway@revealed.net
Gail Burnham		Patricia.g.burnham@ usace.army.mil
Gary Wilkes	Click and Treat Publications 2344 E. Alpine Ave. Mesa, AZ 85204 480-649-9804	wilkesgm@aol.com

NAME	ADDRESS/PHONE	WEBSITE/e-mail
Ian Dunbar	James & Kenneth Publishers 2140 Shattuck Ave., #2406 Berkley, CA 94704	www.apdt.com/drablif@ aol.com
Jean Donaldson	The Academy for Dog Trainers 2500 16th St. San Francisco, CA 94103 415-554-3095	
Job Michael Evans		My mentor, who has passed away. His books can be found on Amazon and bookstores
Karen Pryor	Sunshine Books 17 Commonwealth Rd. Watertown, MA 02472 781-398-0754	karenpryor@rcn.com
Liz Palika		lizpalika@cox.net
Margaret Bonham		skywarrior@juno.com
Matin Goldstein, DVM	Smith Ridge Veterinary Center 230 Oakridge Commons Plaza South Salem, NY 10590 914-533-6066	(information packets available upon request)
Michael Tucker		
Mordecai Siegal		mordecai@mordecai.com
Peggy Tillman		
Sarah Hodgson	10 The Terrace Katonah, NY 10536	www.dogperfect.com
Stanley Coren		www.stanleycoren.com
Steve Applebaum		www.dawgbiz.com
Wendy Volhard		www.volhard.com

WEBSITE LIST

www.adpt.com
www.akc.org
www.all-about-puppies.com
www.aspca.com
www.canismajor.com

www.dogperfect.com (my site!)
www.dwaa.com
www.karenpryor.com
www.petfinders.com

Index